TRANSGRESSING BORDERS

TRANSGRESSING BORDERS

Critical Perspectives on Gender, Household, and Culture

Edited by
Suzan Ilcan and Lynne Phillips

BERGIN & GARVEY
Westport, Connecticut • London

Library of Congress Cataloging-in-Publication Data

Transgressing borders : critical perspectives on gender, household,
  and culture / edited by Suzan Ilcan and Lynne Phillips.
      p.   cm.
    Includes bibliographical references and index.
    ISBN 0–89789–518–5 (alk. paper)—ISBN 0–89789–659–9 (pbk.)
    1. Family. 2. Households. I. Ilcan, Suzan. II. Phillips,
  Lynne.
  HQ518.T67   1998
    306.85—dc21   98–9533

British Library Cataloguing in Publication Data is available.

Library of Congress Catalog Card Number: 98–9533
ISBN: 0–89789–518–5
     0–89789–659–9 (pbk.)

First published in 1998

Bergin & Garvey, 88 Post Road West, Westport, CT 06881
An imprint of Greenwood Publishing Group, Inc.

Printed in the United States of America

The paper used in this book complies with the
Permanent Paper Standard issued by the National
Information Standards Organization (Z39.48–1984).

10 9 8 7 6 5 4 3 2 1

Contents

Acknowledgments

We are very grateful to our contributors for their enthusiasm about this project and their interest in having it come to fruition. We would like to thank the Department of Sociology and Anthropology at the University of Windsor for its financial support and Jill Johns for her excellent technical assistance. The Social Sciences and Humanities Research Council of Canada (SSHRCC) and the Association of Universities and Colleges of Canada (AUCC) also financed our individual research, from which this project partially benefitted. We would also like to thank Dr. James Sabin and the copyediting staff at Greenwood Publishing Group for their encouragement and support. As always, we thank our "ties that bind," Dan, Alan, and Rachel, for their tolerance and perseverance.

Introduction

Borders isolate, classify, and segment people from one another. Through categories such as nation-states, public/private sectors, communities, occupations, households are often treated as discrete, independent entities. The chapters in this book redirect such common understandings by questioning the value or legitimacy of boundaries and offer alternative views that emphasize the multiple inter-linkages in people's lives.

Maintaining borders has taken on particular significance within the literature that has focused on familial and household relations. Prior to the late 1970s, the family was considered one of society's most important institutions because it tied the individual to society. Chief among its activities were the reproduction, maintenance, social placement, and socialization of the young (Davis 1948), meeting the needs of industrial organization (Goode 1963), and promoting the self-development of society's members (Lasch 1977). This focus on the functional operations of the family and household merely served to fortify the long standing convention that they had a "natural" role and structure that supported heterosexual marriage, procreation, and gender stratification and protected its members from all those things deemed "unnatural." Such idealized visions of these units were often grounded in a nostalgia for the Western "nuclear" family as it existed in the decade of the 1950s (see Stacey 1990; Cheal 1991; Coontz 1992) and in the universal appeal of "familism" as the last bastion of privacy. More significantly, however, these visions invented the borders of the West and nonWest, the natural and non-natural.

Since the late 1970s, social scientific accounts have emphasized the political positioning of the family and the household. Not only did researchers come to recognize their diversity (common-law couples, gay and lesbian families, single-parent families, co-resident households) in Western and nonwestern societies but they also revealed the androcentric, timeless, and individualistic biases of the more conventional views. Consequently, new questions and new problems were posed that uprooted "the" family and "the" household from their place in the unity of society (e.g., Donzelot 1979; Hartmann 1981; Barrett and McIntosh 1982; Medick and Sabean 1984). A focus on the location of families and households in class and gender struggles emerged as a way to confront the "unified interest" of these groupings (Hartmann 1981).

These and other similar challenges constituted an important turning point in family and household literature. Michele Barrett and Mary McIntosh took up such issues in their influential work, *The Anti-Social Family*. By deconstructing "familialism" and its popular Western appeal for issues such as emotional security and familiarity, having and raising children, and defending "natural" boundaries (e.g., the pursuit of "natural justice" in law or of "natural childbirth"), they argue that family values not only fail to realize their promise but also romanticize the anti-social relations in family, kinship, and household life (e.g., individualism, authoritarian and dependency relations, gender divisions of labor, domestic violence). Similarly, Olivia Harris' (1981) seminal article, "Households as Natural Units," opened the door for considering households as products of history and provided a caution to researchers who applied the western concept of household uncritically to other cultural contexts. Harris demonstrated how particular domestic boundaries are created and become naturalized through the process of commoditization. That is, as market relations develop and intensify, social relations that once were not considered distinct become differentiated as "domestic" or "waged," "private" or "public." Thus she concludes that households are more salient as market relations become more intrusive. These shifts in the literature were important for generating and reassessing forms of communality as well as for recognizing differences across and between cultures.

More recent studies emphasize family and household relations as the terrain of conflict, tension, and inequality. In fact, feminist researchers have been quick to point out that households are not homogeneous units and that gender and age relations underscore the forms that households take (e.g., Beneria and Roldan 1987). Since the early 1980s, much attention has been paid to the contested space of family and kinship (e.g., Medick and Sabean 1984; Diamond 1983; Fernea 1985; Loizos and Papataxiarchis 1991), the intervention of class, gender, and hierarchical relations in dwelling environments (e.g., Vernier 1984; Sacks 1984; Abdo 1985; Tilly and Scott 1987; Finch 1989; Fox 1993), and the regulatory influence of state and public policies on family and household members (e.g., Diamond 1983; Dickinson and Russell 1986; Deere and León 1987; Cherlin 1988).

One can also discern two different lines of investigation in the contemporary literature that problematizes the location of households in local and global settings. Some researchers argue that an understanding of households requires placing them, as units of production, within the dynamics of the global economy, and analyzing them as an institution of the world system (Smith, Wallerstein, and Evers 1984; Smith and Wallerstein 1992). Other researchers explore the cultural significance of household boundaries and domestic spaces (e.g., Moore 1996; Pellow 1996a, 1996b). The chapters in Pellow's collection, for example, indicate that "home" may mean something to people in ways that "household" (as an analytical category) do not. In her Introduction, Pellow notes that the boundaries of home are "a spiritual boundary that is ritually doctored in order to protect the household from outside influences that may have an impact on its life and livelihood" (1996b: 8). Both lines of investigation suggest new avenues for understanding the "ties that bind" people together globally and the variable meanings that mobilize these relations locally.

Attempting to explore some of this new terrain, the chapters in this volume test the limits of living together. By crossing boundaries and by problematizing gender and culture, we challenge the universality and fixity of codes that govern social relations. The chapters also illustrate the connections and disconnections, at the level of beliefs and customs, ideologies, or narratives, between agency and structure. In these ways, the volume presents the multidimensionality of people's histories, work activities, and lived spaces in relation to the making and unmaking of family and household dwellings. This brings us closer to an understanding of the importance of transgressing borders, of pushing against and going beyond conventional, popularized viewpoints, global histories, and national interests. Transgression is a way to confront and destabilize established forms, cultural norms, and the status quo (see also Weeks 1995; Barrett and Phillips 1992). Pushing against the limits exposes the weak points in those dominant social constructions and allows us to see what supports them. It also reveals the cracks in these governing codes and permits a glimpse at those "other" ways of living together that lie beyond.

However, the theme of crossing borders contains some important contradictions and tensions that also need to be explored. For example, Johannes Fabian (1993) has described how the practice of studying other cultures, wherein boundaries are crossed to understand the Other, only reinforces the key boundary between "us" and "them." This aspect of border crossing raises the question of whether we are "crossing" to perpetuate old ways of thinking or to create new ones. The issue is not a straightforward one for, as Janice Boddy (1993) suggests, the current interest in border crossings may be construed as evidence that the social sciences are once again the handmaidens of global power relations (today those of globalization, yesterday those of colonialism). Thus, while the theme of transgression contains positive possibilities as a lived, discursive, and analytical strategy, it can also involve risks. For crossing borders can embody exhilaration or fear, depending on the circumstances (Fabian 1993); in part, it depends on who or what is doing the crossing and whether or not invitations have been extended (Stephenson 1993).

The chapters in this volume share an interest in critical interpretations of "living together." This interest takes the authors in varied directions with different perspectives on the crossings of gender, household, and culture.

It is well known that the forms families take vary, both between and within societies that define themselves as culturally distinct. Yet, historically, particular notions of "the" family have dominated cultural landscapes. The chapters in Part I of this volume, " 'Health/Politics' and the Family," show how transgressing boundaries can be a political strategy for maintaining or regulating populations. In these first chapters we see how the state and capital redraw boundaries in ways that stretch their power and influence. Such transgressions can create new possibilities while at the same time signaling dangerous exclusions. The theme of "health/politics" reveals specifically the unity between the interests of those in power and forms of the family that favor structured social inequalities. A dynamic body politic employing the idiom of the family works to shape our "personal" choices in politics, sexuality, and reproduction.

In the first chapter, "From a Cancerous Body to a Reconciled Family: Legitimizing Neoliberalism in Chile," Ricardo Trumper and Patricia Tomic deconstruct the Chilean body politic to explain how the brutality of Pinochet's neoliberal regime has become normalized and hegemonic in the post-Pinochet era. Demonstrating that the authoritarian relations of the Pinochet regime both reflected and reinforced the image of the patriarchal family in Chile—including the values of *marianismo*, or self-sacrifice, for women—Trumper and Tomic argue that the acceptance of neoliberalism pivoted on a return to the discipline and authority represented in the traditional family form and *latifundia* relations. Akin to the other chapter in Part I, the authors reveal the efforts of the state to maintain a regressive status quo by traversing the borders between the private and the public. By drawing specifically from the work of Susan Sontag and Mary Douglas, Trumper and Tomic show how transforming Chile into a cancerous body justified radical, painful intervention in the population, a popular body "infected" by the politics of Salvador Allende's *Unidad Popular* in the early 1970s. Combined with the acceptance of a repressive family model, with Pinochet as the master patriarch, the metaphor of the cancerous body politic not only rationalized abuse within the family but also necessitated forgiving the abusers once the "healing" process had been completed. The image of the cleansed, reunited family without disagreements or quarrels has been central to the discourse of post-Pinochet Chile, while its underpinnings of discipline and terror have remained intact. Chile's reconciliation, the authors argue, has meant the creation of both a selective history, with partial memories and many silences, and a new neoliberal body/politic "with an instinct to kill," oriented around the narrow goal of individual profits.

Alan Sears and Barry D. Adam, in "HIV and the State of the Family," show how the "official" nuclear family form in North America is called upon to marginalize and blame people with the HIV infection. Citing the work of Stephanie Coontz and Mariana Valverde, among others, the authors review the recent history of state regulation of family forms in North America to highlight how the development of the "official" family had particular social and economic underpinnings that have been increasingly undermined by neoliberal policies today. Thus the authors place their argument within the context of both neoliberal restructuring, which has limited the viability of nuclear families since the 1970s, and the neoconservative call for a return to "the traditional family." They argue that AIDS has revealed the inadequacies of the neoliberal state model and the official version of what "the family" ought to look like, at the same time that it has been constructed as a threat to "the family" by the Right. Their chapter, based on a larger study in Michigan and Ontario, focuses on how people living with HIV deal with these contradictory tendencies. The authors show that, while people living with HIV transgress boundaries to create a range of support networks, these networks seldom fit the official family model. The non-recognition or non-support by the state of same-sex relationships, mother-headed families, and other familial forms can mean that people living with HIV, already struggling with very difficult situations, may be excluded from access to medical care, employment benefits, and social service programs. One of the strengths of this chapter is its emphasis on both the overwhelming power of particular familial borders in North America and the resiliency of people in their attempts to forge alternatives to them.

In studies of gender and household relations, conceptions of space and time have generally appeared peripheral to the more prevalent concerns of familial ideologies and the gendered character of household formation and organization. It has become increasingly clear, however, that the organization, management, and meaning of households in geographical settings have significant social, cultural, and political implications. The three chapters comprising Part II, "Gender-Geographies and the Changing Household," explore the interrelation of gender, household, and culture from feminist perspectives that focus on the politics of landscapes, the crossing of boundaries, and the remaking of space. In "Dissecting Globalization: Women's Space-Time in the Other America," Lynne Phillips examines how globalization efforts homogenize and typify rural women's lives in coastal Ecuador. She argues that globalization and its directive to transform the limits of time and geographical space place gender in a complex power dynamic. In particular, Phillips focuses on how emerging concepts of space and time potentially reshape women's options and responsibilities in household and work relations. By critically assessing key agricultural development processes and policies, the author outlines the conventional trends associated with women's roles under globalization, including the "feminization" of agriculture and the "proletarianization," "entrepreneurialization" and "domestication" of rural women. Phillips suggests that these four trends not only envision time from the developmental perspective of capitalism but preserve women's responsibility for domestic work, thus ignoring the unmapped spaces that women make and occupy. Drawing upon Elizabeth Grosz's theory on space and dwellings, Phillips explores other ways in which women think about and experience time and space. Through intensive research in coastal Ecuador, she highlights how rural women see their sense of place as central to the reproduction of a certain way of life. In their views of themselves as *casas* (houses) and in their ability to "make" time, women create and recreate a new geography that they can call "theirs." Like Suzan Ilcan's chapter, which situates women's spatial and temporal notions in a format of change and transformation, Phillips suggests that a revisioning of women's time and space opens the possibility for women to alter community spaces previously undervalued by globalization schemes. In this context, the author alerts us to those global categories and landscapes that tend to ignore the flow of people, places, and things.

Suzan Ilcan's chapter, "Challenging Settlement: Rural Women's Culture of Dis-placement," analyzes the ways in which women's social practices transform and dis-place the authoritarian household and its forms of settlement. The author begins by assessing the sedentary sites, the disciplinary spaces, that have long been known to individualize and direct groups of people according to regulated time and distinct labor divisions. She illustrates how disciplinary spaces, such as households, settle people into particular ways of living by dividing and combining their activities into organized totalities. Within these all-too-visible authoritarian spaces, women simply appear as victims of structures with fixed identities and trained habits. Building upon Rosi Braidotti's theories on transversality and Lila Abu-Lughod's notion of "writing against culture," Ilcan explores how nomadism is a useful methodological tool for challenging rigid institutional views of life and for understanding women's movements and their moments of sociality in northwestern Turkey. Like Sally Cole's perspective on reconstituting households as practiced by "retelling culture," Ilcan's approach draws our attention to the ways in which women create a space and time for themselves through their collective and recollective efforts. Through ethnographic and narrative accounts, the author highlights how women's politicized stories and mutual sharing of ideas confront local customs, compel nomadic alliances among women, and convey a critical awareness of the workings of power. According to the author, these practices force us to reconsider how disciplinary spaces are lived, how significant women's dis-placement activities are in the processes of social change, and how they counter the conventional (and often oriental) depiction of women's place in modern and colonial views of the "Middle East."

In "Reconstituting Households, Retelling Culture: Emigration and Portuguese Fisheries Workers," Sally Cole views gender and household relations as significant sites for theorizing relations of culture and economy. Through extensive fieldwork and the oral recording of life stories, the author examines the historical migration of men and women from the Portuguese fishing town of Nazaré to the Canadian towns located along the north shore of Lake Erie. In these towns, Cole describes the economic and cultural importance of men's work in the commercial Lake Erie Fishery and women's wage work in the fish processing industry. Through their everyday lives and work, nazarenos retell the story of Nazaré in their relations and ties to the household. Household images and recollections are, in fact, what nazarenos use to express and measure their closeness to the physical and symbolic space of Nazaré. In this transnational context, the author argues that households are storied spaces. These are spaces constituted and reconstituted in ways that embody both unity and difference, contradiction and tension. The nazarenos in Canada are shown to maintain the household ideology of the Nazaré fishery by constructing the household as a production unit whose members contribute their earnings to the household and whose resources are managed by women. In her use of Kathleen Stewart's notion of culture and history—especially the way in which this writer locates history in the images that people enact in the stories they tell—Cole analyzes the material and symbolic reconstitution of the nazareno household as an effort to mobilize household and gender relations through people's images of Nazaré and their practices of re-membering and retelling. This chapter reveals the way that transnational culture-building is linked to the poetics of place and time in emigrant community landscapes. The author's emphasis on history and memory resonates with Max Hedley's analysis of how First Nation peoples carry the mark of colonial history and reconstitute their lives in and through the cultural and political creation of household economies.

Colonization has been about the processes of exploration, conquest, or exploitation, depending on the location and the particular economic and political interests of colonialists. In its historical moments, it has marginalized people, places of habitation, and ways of living. These histories are, however, recounted and indelibly marked in memory. The three chapters that comprise Part III, "Colonialism, Community, and Kinship," explore the role of colonialism in circumscribing household and kin relations within community contexts. The authors discuss the effects of colonial encounters in reference to different geographical settings and from different beginning and ending points. In "Shadow of Domination: Colonialism, Household, and Community Relations," Max Hedley analyzes the sociohistorical issues surrounding the colonization and transformation of First Nation communities in Canada, with a particular focus on the reproduction of household, gender, and community relations on Walpole Island. Hedley documents the ways in which Aboriginal peoples reconstitute their control over their lives in spite of the history and effects of colonial domination. The author begins by delineating the federal government's late eighteenth-century policies toward the assimilation of Aboriginal peoples. In particular, he identifies policies that sought to destroy local patterns of leadership, religion, and language. The policy of assimilation, by fostering an interest in agricultural production, attempted to replace traditional systems of tenure and communal relations with a private property regime that established new forms of social inequality. Here, among other things, we witness the transformation of the communal economy of the early nineteenth century and the development of a household economy that "constrained people to focus on their own self-interest and therefore contained the imprint of the colonial project." In this household economy, work relations were tied to control over the reproduction of social and cultural life. In particular, women's position in the household economy gave them potential influence over everyday life, especially the manner in which young children were drawn into the lifestyles of older generations. Like Kathy M'Closkey's analysis of Aboriginal weaving as both ritual and work, Hedley argues that the organization of communal meals and celebrations (dancing, singing, games, storytelling) were important activities that not only affirmed cooperation and mutual reliance among household and community members but crossed the boundaries between work and pleasure. After the postwar years, however, this type of cooperation was slowly undermined by the mass entry of people into wage labor relations and by the proliferation of agencies and programs that sought to intervene in the affairs of individuals and families. This chapter brings to the forefront the profound, long-term effect of colonization and its creation of the institution of the household.

In "Weaving and Mothering: Reframing Navajo Weaving as Recursive Manifestations of *K'e*," Kathy M'Closkey analyzes the appropriation of the Aboriginal textile market by traders and manufacturers of trade blankets in the historical context of colonialism and in the currency of international capitalism. The author begins with a discussion of Navajo textiles and reveals their marginalization in the domains of western commerce, art, and religion and through their ties to gallery aesthetics and museum displays. Through extensive archival research on the business records of the Hubbells, the most powerful trading family that once controlled a significant portion of trade for the Navajo, M'Closkey refutes key assumptions dominating the scholarly literature on the Navajo, particularly those that ignore the economic significance of women's textile production. By reframing Navajo weaving, the author first informs us of the critical importance of weaving for Navajo women's economic survival and then illustrates how women lost control of the marketing of their textiles because of trader interference. At this critical moment in history, trade blanket manufacturers appropriated Navajo designs, and through traders, the Navajo wearing blanket became a new commodity, a "rug," around the turn of the century. Moving beyond viewing the rug as a mere commodity, M'Closkey delineates how weaving upholds *K'e* (kin relations as directed by the Navajo Creation Story) and replenishes Navajo cultural relations on many levels. Based on in-depth interviews with contemporary Navajo weavers, the author argues that, through weaving, women not only reflect Navajo community and kin values but also combine ritual and work as weaving is accompanied by songs, stories, and prayers.

Continuing the theme of colonialism, Judith M. Abwunza's chapter, "Gendered Kin and Conflict in Kenya," demonstrates how the basic premises of a precolonial way of life have been increasingly undermined for Logoli women and men in western Kenya. Abwunza outlines the importance of reciprocity and collectivity as concepts that formed the basis of the "traditional life" that Avalogoli still hold to be important. The relevance of these concepts today can be explained in part by the fact that they have been successfully incorporated into the capitalist relations that have been introduced through colonialism. Yet much of the colonial transformation of Kenya has involved processes that have created tension and conflict in the practices linked to the concepts of reciprocity and collectivity. By focusing on gendered kinship structures, and specifically on notions of "alliance," Abwunza highlights the difficulties women face in attempting to piece together "a proper way of life" in the context of land and food scarcity. Like the women in M'Closkey's chapter, Avalogoli women, though marginalized from resources, work daily to rekindle kin values and practices, attempting to minimize the effects of the ruptures caused by colonialism and neocolonialism. In doing so, they cross the boundaries of "women's place" (the yard) at the same time that they reinforce gender expectations to "provision" the family. Abwunza's study signals the centrality of gender in kin ideologies, relations, and practices and cautions us about the importance of close observation in cultural evaluations of kinship and work.

Part IV, "Work and (En)gendered Dwellings," deals with the way in which work informs the social processes involved in shaping households and their membership in particular ways. The organization and relations of work and the cultural meanings attributed to work and property are important dimensions in understanding gender and the material inequalities of women and men in household dwellings. The five chapters in this part are linked through the authors' interest in how households and their relations are shaped and reshaped by changing economies. In the first chapter, "Ties That Define and Bind: Exploring Custom and Culture in Nineteenth-Century Coastal Communities in Nova Scotia," Anthony Davis and Daniel MacInnes explore the cultural and economic histories of Canadian coastal fishing communities, with a particular focus on agency, marriage, and property inheritance practices in Nova Scotian households. The authors begin by situating the notions of custom and tradition within processes that feature systematic forms of power inequity. Drawing on the work of social anthropologist Gerald Sider, Davis and MacInnes view the social experience and organization of locality as shaped in the dominance of a class structure and a political economy and in socioeconomic relations of wealth appropriation and exploitation. In their historical research on coastal fishing communities, the authors draw our attention to the distinctive linguistic, ethnic, and religious attributes of communities. These attributes impart important qualities of community formation and identity. They argue that the household, especially the way in which it is linked through marriage and family ancestry to other households with similar backgrounds, is the site of cultural processes wherein identities and attachments are formed in relation to particular occupations. In their analysis of late nineteenth-century and early twentieth-century marriage records, Davis and MacInnes reveal that marriageable partners were increasingly found in association with fishing livelihoods, thus building solidarities between families with common work backgrounds. However, the family alliances formed through marriage do not translate into similar meanings and conditions for men and women: mid-nineteenth- and early twentieth-century registered wills and testaments clearly demonstrated the gendered inequality of property and inheritance relations. This chapter alerts us to the way in which agency, the capacity of people to engage in meaningful action, is actualized through culture and custom and expressed in the injustices of relations of structured inequality.

B. Lynne Milgram's chapter, "Craft Production and Household Practices in the Upland Philippines," explores how female artisans incorporate their culture of domestic weaving and wet-rice cultivation to further their own economic standing and those of their families. Like the historical focus of Davis and MacIness on the culture and customs of work and property, Milgram discusses the historical tradition of cloth production and its link to the work of female weavers in Banaue, Ifugao province, in the northern

Philippines. In line with much of the scholarship on Southeast Asian textiles, she documents how cloth production is tied to public celebrations and rooted in economic transactions. The author argues that women in Banaue's rapidly commoditizing economy, and in its framework of "equal opportunity," take advantage of their historical association to cloth production by using this association as a springboard to augment commercial weaving initiatives. Her in-depth case studies of artisan households reveal the divergent ways in which female artisans, with the aid of family members, move between craft and agricultural production and cross and recross such borders to negotiate their positions within and outside the household. Depending on the tourist market demand for commercial weavings, artisans divide their labor between craft production and cultivation to meet subsistence needs and to gain cultural capital. They also develop social support networks in their work efforts by participating in cooperative labor exchanges that blur the boundaries between production and reproduction. Paralleling M'Closkey's work on Navajo weaving, Milgram alerts us to the economic and cultural manifestations of craft production in the context of gender, household, and market economies. Rather than being marginalized by the forces of market capitalism, female artisans in the Filipino case are shown to work as "commodity-producing peasants" who negotiate their gender roles by accessing new opportunities to produce textiles for the region's growing tourist market.

In "Rural Women Face Capitalism: Women's Response as 'Guardians' of the Household," Parvin Ghorayshi is also concerned with how market capitalism has realigned rural women's access to resources. However, the Iranian case involves culturally different practices and ideologies that place greater limits on the abilities of rural women to participate in market relations. Ghorayshi first addresses the importance of placing rural women within a theoretical framework that both outlines the contours of capitalist and patriarchal control and recognizes women's agency and the complex choices they face within that context. This approach, begun by researchers such as Marie-Andrée Couillard, enables Ghorayshi to search beyond the one-dimensional image of rural Iranian women as bound by Islamic rules to understand their complex role as "guardians" of the household. To make this argument the author focuses on the village of Rostamkola in northern Iran. She notes that because of the cultural rules regarding women's place, it is men who have left the village to seek wage labor or engage in market activities. The resulting "feminization" of agriculture has left farming largely in the hands of women, offering women some space for negotiating a role as household guardians. Looking at specific households, Ghorayshi is able to show how women can become "the man for most of the year" in a village where men should be the main providers of the household. This situation is complicated by class relations, impoverishment, and the growing need for women to work at the same time that land remains legally in the hands of men. Yet women are resourceful in finding ways to gain access to money and other resources, even appealing, in one case, to the Islamic proclamation to help the weak and poor in order to obtain access to land. Ghorayshi's study highlights the importance of looking past ethnocentric or regional assumptions about "Islamic women" if we are to understand the complex relationships among gender, household, and culture.

Alan Hall's chapter, "Sustainable Agriculture: Implications for Gender and the Family Farm," considers these same relationships in the context of farming in Canada. Noting that the literature supports the view that women are increasingly excluded from the business of farming when conventional agricultural practices are undertaken, Hall poses the question: does sustainable agriculture, arguably an alternative to conventional agriculture, encourage the decision making and labor participation of women? To answer this question the author compares mixed organic farmers and conservation tillage farmers in southwestern Ontario. Describing the marked differences between the two types of "sustainable" practices, Hall points out that the separation of the farm (and men) from the household (and women) is not challenged by the conservation tillage model, while the ideal organic model—involving small-scale, low technology production to meet the needs of local markets—appears to permit greater gender equity in the labor and decision-making process. Yet Hall is cautious about predicting particular outcomes for organic farmers, not only because many aspects of gender ideology (e.g., who seeks out the required knowledge about organic production and who undertakes domestic labor) may not be altered but also because there is some evidence that organic farms can emulate agribusiness practices. Hall concludes that researchers need to clarify what they mean and what farmers mean by "sustainable agriculture," because agricultural families may adopt very different strategies, only some of which may lead to desegregated work and decision making in a way that integrates the boundaries of the farm and the household. This conclusion is significant for those researchers and activists involved in promoting more equitable environmental practices, especially those who assume a natural link between alternative farming, sustainability, and gender equity.

The final chapter, "Economic Restructuring and Unpaid Work," by Anne Forrest, analyzes the links between unpaid work on and off the job. Focusing on a variety of occupations in North America, the author shows how activities normally undertaken by men, both on and off the job, are more likely to be considered work and more likely to be paid, while the unpaid work that women face at home legitimates the undervaluing of their work inside and outside the home. Forrest reveals how this imbalance is further skewed through the restructuring of the economy, when much more energy is expended on the unpaid "work" of caretaking with the downsizing and privatization of the public sector. Expanded caretaking devolves on those who do the domestic work—that is, "women's work"—in our society, at the same time that restructuring often requires women to undertake paid work in order to make ends meet. The chapter highlights the extent to which lived-in and worked-in places are (en)gendered dwellings in North America. It stands as a grim reminder of the difficult challenges that people face in the structuring and restructuring of their lives.

REFERENCES

Abdo, N. (1985). *Women, Family and Social Change in the Middle East: The Palestinian Case.* Toronto: Canadian Scholarship Press.
Barrett, M., and A. Phillips. (1992). *Destabilizing Theory: Contemporary Feminist Debates.* Stanford: Stanford University Press.
Barrett, N., and M. McIntosh. (1982). *The Anti-Social Family.* London: Verso.
Beneria, L., and M. Roldan. (1987). *The Crossroads of Class and Gender: Industrial Homework, Subcontracting, and Household Dynamics in Mexico City.* Chicago: University of Chicago Press.
Boddy, J. (1993). "Other and Disoriented in No Man's Land." *Culture* 13 (1):63–67.
Cheal, D. (1991). *The Family and the State of Theory.* Toronto: University of Toronto Press.
Cherlin, A., ed. (1988). *The Changing American Family and Public Policy.* Washington, D.C.: Urban Institute Press.
Coontz, S. (1992). *The Way We Never Were: American Families and the Nostalgia Trap.* New York: Basic Books.
Davis, K. (1948). *Human Society.* New York: Macmillan.
Deere, C., and M. León. (1987). *Rural Women and State Policy.* Boulder, Colo.: Westview Press.
Diamond, I. (1983). *Families, Politics, and Public Policy.* New York: Longman.
Dickinson, J., and B. Russell, eds. (1986). *Family, Economy and State.* New York: St. Martin's Press.
Donzelot, J. (1979). *The Policing of Families.* New York: Pantheon.
Fabian, J. (1993). "Crossing and Patrolling: Thoughts on Anthropology and Boundaries." *Culture* 13 (1):49–53.
Fernea, E. (1985). *Women and the Family in the Middle East.* Austin: University of Texas Press.
Finch, J. (1989). *Family Obligations and Social Change.* Cambridge: Polity Press.
Fox, B., ed. (1993). *Family Patterns, Gender Relations.* Toronto: Oxford University Press.
Goode, W. (1963). *World Revolution and Family Patterns.* New York: Free Press.
Harris, O. (1981). "Households as Natural Units." In *Of Marriage and the Market,* ed. Kate Young, Carol Wolkowitz, and R. McCullagh. London: CSE Books: 49–68.
Hartmann, H. (1981). "The Family as the Locus of Gender, Class, and Political Struggle." *Signs* 6 (3):366–94.
Lasch, C. (1977). *Haven in a Heartless World.* New York: Basic Books.
Loizos, P., and E. Papataxiarchis, eds. (1991). *Contested Identities: Gender and Kinship in Modern Greece.* Princeton, N.J.: Princeton University Press.

Medick, H., and D. Sabean, eds. (1984). *Interest and Emotion: Essays on the Study of Family and Kinship*. Cambridge: Cambridge University Press.

Moore, H. (1996). *Space, Text, and Gender: An Anthropological Study of the Marakwet of Kenya*. New York: Guilford Press.

Pellow, D., ed. (1996a). *Setting Boundaries: The Anthropology of Spatial and Social Organization*. Westport, Conn.: Bergin & Garvey.

Pellow, D. (1996b). "Introduction." In *Setting Boundaries*, ed. D. Pellow. Westport, Conn.: Bergin & Garvey.

Sacks, K. (1984). "Kinship and Class Consciousness: Family Values and Work Experience among Hospital Workers in an American Southern Town." In *Interest and Emotion: Essays on the Study of Family and Kinship*, ed. H. Medick and D. Sabean, 279–99. Cambridge: Cambridge University Press.

Smith, J., and I. Wallerstein, eds. (1992). *Creating and Transforming Households: The Constraints of the World-Economy*. Cambridge: Cambridge University Press.

Smith, J., I. Wallerstein, and H. D. Evers, eds. (1984). *Households and the World Economy*. Beverly Hills, Calif.: Sage.

Stacey, J. (1990). *Brave New Families: Stories of Domestic Upheaval in Late Twentieth Century America*. New York: Basic Books.

Stephenson, P. (1993). "On Crossing Borders and Boundaries: A Parallax View of the Postmodern Experience." *Culture* 13 (1):59–62.

Tilly, L., and J. Scott. (1987). *Women, Work and Family*. New York: Routledge.

Vernier, B. (1984). "Putting Kin and Kinship to Good Use: The Circulation of Goods, Labour, and Names on Karpathos (Greece)." In *Interest and Emotion: Essays on the Study of Family and Kinship*, ed. H. Medick and D. Sabean. Cambridge: Cambridge University Press.

Weeks, J. (1995). *Invented Moralities: Sexual Values in an Age of Uncertainty*. New York: Columbia University Press.

PART I

"Health/Politics" and the Family

From a Cancerous Body to a Reconciled Family: Legitimizing Neoliberalism in Chile

Ricardo Trumper and Patricia Tomic

> "El perdón es la expresión
> MAXIMA DEL AMOR"
>
> Forgiveness is the
> ULTIMATE EXPRESSION OF LOVE
>
> —Graffiti in Cartagena, Chile

Historically in Chile, family, church, and state have interlocked to conform to a system of class, gender, and race domination, a regime of power. While patriarchal relations in the family have remained relatively uncontested, the state has been the subject of struggles to reformulate it during much of the Chilean republic. These conflicts with the state, culminating with the military coup in September 1973, were aimed at both the refoundation of Chilean capitalism and the strengthening of the traditional Chilean family.

During the military regime, from 1973 to 1989, the Chilean state was known worldwide as *the* archetype of brutality, "an international pariah, known mainly for the murderousness of its military rulers" (Friedland 1995). Chile was seen as a country occupied by its own army and its inhabitants subjected to terror. Many analyses explained the military coup as a result of the combined interests of American imperial policies and Chilean dominant classes to impose the first neoliberal experiment (Temple 1995:2), "the longest running structural adjustment program in the world" (Bello with Cunningham and Rau 1994:42). Today Chilean neoliberalism is hegemonic and the military dictator, General Augusto Pinochet (1974–90), is no longer portrayed as a monster. Immediately after the military handed over the government to a civilian one in 1990, the military regime began to be called "the past regime" (Cassen 1995) as if there had been a case of collective amnesia about the dictatorship. More so, since 1994, when Eduardo Frei Ruiz-Tagle was elected president, there has been an effort to flaunt the continuity of neoliberalism, making no distinctions between dictatorship and democracy, while portraying Pinochet as a statesman. The terror that lasted so long for so many, which prompted a mass exodus, killed, tortured, and maimed, and stole, deceived, and militarized, seems to have been buried deep in the recesses of the Chilean mind, but is certainly not forgotten. Meanwhile, neoliberalism rules sovereign in Chile today. In this chapter our questions are simple: how has a system based on such brutality been normalized, legitimized, and glorified? How did it become hegemonic after the dictatorial phase ended? More so, how has Chilean neoliberalism become "the" prototype to follow in many parts of the world, given the history of its inception? Following Antonio Gramsci's idea that the economy only sets the framework for social relations but does not determine them, we argue that a set of ideas/representations has been created by the military and the elites that has been essential for the consolidation of neoliberalism. Indeed, metaphors of family and reconciliation, body and disease, and sports and competitiveness have played a critical role in the establishment and permanence of such a ruthless system.

Neoliberalism would not have been possible in Chile without a value system connected to brutal discipline. For a long stretch in Chilean history, an authoritarian classist, racist, and sexist system of *latifundia* relations has permeated all activities of everyday life based on *patrón-inquilino* (landowner-tenant) relations of extreme subservience. Indeed, while capitalist relations have been a feature of urban Chile since the nineteenth century, until the 1960s the *hacienda* dominated the Chilean countryside and established the basis of the everyday interaction between classes. Its model served as the paradigm for social relations and for a system of vigilance, control, and discipline that has been accepted as the norm at all levels of life, in military barracks, hospitals, schools, and indeed the patriarchal family. In fact, a central goal of the military coup in 1973 was the restoration of discipline and conservative values, in other words, the redisciplining of the population into "*latifundia* relations."[1]

Pinochet (1979:57) voiced the quest for *latifundia* discipline behind the military coup: he argued that even before the Unidad Popular there had been a breakdown in authority and that even the discipline imposed by politeness and urbanity had been eroded, resulting in aggressive behavior and bad manners. He concluded, to justify the military dictatorship, that Chileans had "lost their respect for authority." Indeed, lack of discipline was a recurrent theme in the official discourse in the period following the coup. For example, in its Communiqué 36, the military junta that overthrew the Allende government ruled that "the principle and practice of work discipline must be reestablished." Lucía Hiriart, Pinochet's wife, stated, "[w]hat we need the most now is discipline . . . which had completely disappeared" (*El Mercurio*, 30 Sept. 1973:34). Also, *El Mercurio* (4 Oct. 1973:17) displayed a picture of adolescents in school uniforms and stated that there was a "[b]road acceptance by high school women students of the new disciplinarian measures . . . proper norms for women's dress had been reiterated, such as the prohibition of wearing clogs . . . and the uniform dress more than ten centimeters above the knee." They were all interpreting the historical view of discipline and authority held by the Chilean dominant classes, who constantly seek out signals of deference from the powerless. The breakdown of this norm was explained by the military and the upper classes as partly due to a collapse of the patriarchal family.

Chilean patriarchy and military ideology share a value system based on authoritarian principles and hierarchies, which promotes a distribution of functions according to "traditional sexual stereotypes" in the family as well as in the larger society (Valenzuela 1987:11). The military explicitly understood the patriarchal family as an essential disciplinarian unit in society. For example, the Declaration of Principles of the military junta stated that the family "is the fundamental basis of society . . . a school of moral formation." Closely linked to the junta's idea of the family was its view of womanhood; they saw the family as the institution through which women achieve their natural mission, motherhood. The ideal of womanhood in Chile is defined by the concept of *marianismo*. The ideal woman is epitomized by the Virgin Mary, the pure mother who is willing to control her body urges, to sacrifice her life to procreation and child rearing, and who naturally places herself and her children under the control of a husband (Lehmann 1990, 1991; Montecino 1993; Valdés 1991). This vertically integrated *familia mariana* became one of the main metaphors of the junta's view of Chile.

Boyer (1992) has shown the historically reciprocal connections between models of family and state. In the Chilean military regime, not only was the *familia mariana* a commonsense representation of the organization of everyday life, but this image of the family matched the barrack representation the military had of society (Valenzuela 1987:11). The view of family as motherland and motherland as family led the regime to speak of "a national family": "We want a motherland of brothers, united by the common soil that Providence has offered us." Indeed, the military used the family metaphor to portray the image of a Chilean people united by invisible bonds of love, a kind of comradeship that existed deep down in people's souls, that had been unnaturally broken during the Allende government, and that the majority wanted reinstated. For this, the restoration of discipline, the fatherly authority of the military, was needed. From the beginning, Pinochet took pains to present himself as the patriarchal father of the country, a stern authoritarian head of the family of Chileans. During his dictatorship he presented himself as a rough, simple, and firm but fair man, who resembled the majority of other Chilean male "heads" of families.

The image of the family of Chileans permitted the military regime to ignore class and power divisions and to decree that class struggle was an invention of elements foreign to the Chilean kin. Thus the family representation of the country linked Chilean racism and chauvinism with the coup. The presence of thousands of Latin American refugees who had arrived in Chile in the 1960s and early 1970s was used as a metaphor for a foreign invasion by nonmembers of the national family. Against them the military unleashed their fury as a hunt for foreigners was set loose and thousands were imprisoned, tortured, expelled, or murdered.

In fact, the hunt against foreigners allowed them to juxtapose the image of Chile as cohesive and patriarchal with the image of a body threatened by a foreign invasion. This served to justify brutality, the cruelty of the coup, terror, and the methods employed to impose fear that otherwise do not have an easy explanation. The Allende government could have been toppled without resorting to heavy artillery, rockets, air bombardment, and other military tactics. Thus there was the need to create the image of Chile as a sick body to excuse the regime's unwarranted cruelty. This in turn helps to explain the population's acceptance of brutality and in many cases their complicity with it.

Douglas (1978:122) has pointed out that "the body is a model that can stand for any bounded symbol" and that "its boundaries represent any boundaries which are threatened or precarious." The connections between the images of the body and the state, "the body politic," are common (Scheper-Hughes and Lock 1987). In Western thought, the use of the body as a metaphor in politics is historically widespread. Most probably, neither Pinochet nor the other military officers who toppled the Unidad Popular in the 1973 coup had read Hobbes, Spencer, Durkheim, or any other theorist or social scientist who has made these connections. However, the military used the body as a metaphoric construct; they looked at the long, thin sliver that represents Chile on the map and imagined it as a body over which they could act. The mother country, the body of the female *patria*, needed male intervention, male discipline to defend it.

The body offered as a metaphor for Chile was then presented as threatened by the supporters of the Unidad Popular. The image that, at least in part, drove the military's rage and helped to legitimize the coup and its brutality was the sketch of a sick body struck by cancer. The use of cancer, "the malady of Chile" (Pinochet 1979) as a metaphor for the Unidad Popular was most appropriate for their genocidal fury, xenophobia, classist and male chauvinistic views, and anticommunist ideologies. They juxtaposed the geographical image of the country as an elongated sick body with those of a family threatened by foreign elements and an unruly body needing healing by (military) experts who, as in all aspects of Chilean medicine, mix healing and discipline for the powerless patient.

Accordingly, the xenophobia that swept Chile in its search for foreigners—when speaking with an accent was cause for imprisonment in a concentration camp or denunciation as a dangerous extremist—was also justified and driven by cancer metaphors. Racism is almost official discourse in Chile, and the cancer metaphor heightened it. Cancer is often spoken of as an infection (Weiss 1995). Thus the metaphor of Chile as a body invaded by these infectious "germs" conveniently explained the foreignness of the ideology of the Unidad Popular, the doctrine of national security, and the need for war or surgery to eradicate the alien infection or tumor.

Certainly, the discourse of the body played a role in the brutality of the military regime. Sontag (1990) has explained that the use of the image of cancer in politics infers the existence of "malign" cells that extend like a demonic presence and that the use of the disease metaphor serves as justification for violent punishment to eradicate evil. She argues that to suggest political cancer is to recommend "radical" treatment, brutal surgery, the crematoria. Indeed, this was the case for the Chilean coup. We remember vividly how the references to cancer and surgery amplified our fear. We did not need a theoretical interpretation of what the military meant when they offered radical surgery: we knew that the equation was cancer/surgery/death/pain. These generals, who had ordered the presidential palace bombed—and the subsequent murder of many of the defenders who had surrendered—were not just killing in the heat of combat (if such a thing really exists). Their choice of arms represented their hatred of and paranoia about communism as well as lack of discipline and cancerous growths. Although we know that many of the justifications they offered were mere excuses, we believe the image of the cancerous body was implanted in their minds and also drove them. These familiar images shaped their discourse and prompted their actions.

These men in fatigues, unsmiling behind dark glasses, acted as the "medical experts" called to cure the sick body of Chile. Gustavo Leigh, the commander of the air force and a member of the military junta, mentioned in a public intervention on the day of the coup that "after three years of enduring the Marxist cancer the Chilean people are willing to excise it to the final consequences" (*El Mercurio*, 13 Sept. 1973:5). In turn, Pinochet declared that freedoms would be reinstated "when we get rid of the Marxist cancer" (*El Mercurio*, 20 Sept. 1973:1).

The model of cancer is particularly frightening because of the images it brings to the mind: in the medical model, everything can be used in order to save a patient's life, from coarse surgery to the burning of radiation,

from murder to the use of the electric prod. In Chile, this image was articulated within the context of what medicine has historically been for the
powerless, a harsh process of disciplining individuals into health in the
common wards where the "patients" do not have a say and where often
the idea is that pain has to be endured (Trumper and Phillips 1996). Thus
cancer was a crude code for surgery without anesthesia. The body of *Chile
popular*, to use Touraine's (1974) term, was to be subjected to painful
surgery by male doctors in boots and uniforms with electric prods and
guns. In this surgery to be performed on *La Patria*, no nurses (mostly female in Chile) were to be allowed to comfort or take care of the patient.
Indeed, the military acted out its fantasies. "Surgery" was practiced to in-
flict pain, to discipline, and for the good of business in the operating rooms
of the torture chambers. However, surgery was not performed only with
the *picana eléctrica* (electric prod), but also on the "economic body," which
was subjected to the "discipline of the market."

The metaphor of disease and the body ties in well with neoliberal economics. The idea of macroeconomic indicators is influenced by mechanical
laboratory views of the body. Economists take the "pulse and pressure" of
the economic body, looking for symptoms that only their particular expertise can measure. As cancer is an ambiguous disease, the economic body
may also be likened to a sick body. A country may be represented as attacked by malignant political cells and sickened by economic cancer. Economic cancer also justifies an "economic" medicine where everything can
be used, including the shock treatment prescribed for Chile. For the economic body, the "experts" or economic "doctors" eventually evoked electroshock—a brutal form of treatment to deal with economic sickness—to
subject the body of Chile to the discipline of capital. Thus the metaphor
of cancer also served as a justification for the complicity of other members
of Pinochet's team, the civilian accomplices, the surgeons in gray suits who
operated on the economic patient, such as Jorge Cauas, a Christian Democratic minister of finance when the *tratamiento de shock* was launched;
Sergio de Castro, the most powerful neoliberal minister of Pinochet and a
university professor, who served as the *maestro* of Chilean neoliberal economists; American professor Arnold Harberger, the *maestro* of de Castro
and many Chilean economists at the University of Chicago, who regularly
visited Chile to prescribe economic violence; and Milton Friedman, the
"great professor" who explicitly used the term "shock treatment" while
counseling Pinochet not to worry about his poor external image.[2] Cancer
images then legitimized not just (male) torturers, working full-time to
"heal" the "body of Chile" with their prescriptions of pain and disciplining,
but also the role of the economists and businesspeople.

This brutal "treatment" of electroshock was explicitly tied to repression.
The economists were linked in practice to repression to a much larger ex-

tent than they would like to recognize publicly. Not only did they know that terror was widespread but they used it for their "prescriptions." There is a striking testimony by one of the "doctors": to apply the shock treatment "it was necessary to keep the patient tied to the bed" (quoted in Osorio and Cabezas 1995:15). In other words, for economic repression/shock, the electric prod was needed. Yet the body metaphor not only prompted the involvement of the economists and other civilians but also helped to exonerate them of their obvious complicity with torture, dictatorship, and capital.

Briefly, the interconnected Western view of the individual body and the political body not only see the body as a machine but also as divided into different systems that function more or less independently of one another. Each system requires its own specialists. Thus, in a state imagined in this way, a ministry of finance may be imagined as working independently of one responsible for repression. This has allowed Mónica Madariaga, a minister of justice for Pinochet, to claim to have worked on the same "body politic" (a "body in pain") with General Manuel Contreras, the head of the DINA, the dreaded secret police, but independently, with no responsibility for "disappearances." This disjunctive element may help explain why no one has questioned why Pinochet's early director of the budget, Juan Villarzú, or the military junta's first minister of finance, Fernando Léniz, or the already mentioned Sergio de Castro among many others, have retained positions of great power and have not been held accountable for their complicity with the dictatorship. Today Léniz is a successful businessman. Villarzú is a powerful minister in the "democratic" government of Eduardo Frei, and de Castro is the wealthy chair of the board of the largest company that emerged from the privatization of pensions, a respected operator in the privatized taxation and welfare system he helped create for the benefit of national and international capital. This suggests that, with different imagery, situations like these may not have been possible. Indeed, if the view of the body were holistic, these people, and many others, would not have eluded their responsibility.

By 1978, as the military and the dominant classes felt confident that the neoliberal regime was consolidating, the discursive images of Chile used by the regime began to change. Metaphors of pure pain gave way to those of legitimation. The figure of the nation as a diseased body began to be replaced by the juxtaposition of two images: the nation as a body in recovery and the already discussed idea of the nation as a family that needed to recover its former harmony. In the key speech for the fifth anniversary of the coup, Pinochet (1978) explained the "Law of Amnesty" that granted impunity to those who had conducted the physical repression as an attempt of the regime to seek "reconciliation" ("the will to an authentic national reconciliation that prompts the government"). At the same time, he attacked those who denounced it as elements seeking to "reopen new wounds in a national community." The image of a diseased body was being transformed; however, its full transformation had to wait for almost a decade.

The debt crisis of the early 1980s resulted in one of the worst depressions in Chilean history. The first challenge to the military regime—more or less spontaneous and widespread—took the form of massive popular protests, in particular in *poblaciones*. As Bengoa (1990:9) admits, "[f]ew times were we closer to what in political literature is called 'popular mass insurrection.'" The revolt was so popular and spontaneous that the elite-dominated political parties "were placed in a secondary position." The regime and the Chilean elites reacted with panic.

The Chilean elites have traditionally feared and despised the rest of society. In our interpretation, a split in the Chilean elites had facilitated a process of democratization and working class and peasant advances that had culminated in the Revolución en Libertad, the government of Frei Montalva of the Christian Democratic party, and the Chilean road to socialism, the Unidad Popular government of President Allende. Yet, except for their affiliation to Christian and Left political parties and for adopting a rhetoric of progressiveness in matters of public politics, it is now clear that the differences between groups in the Chilean dominant classes have remained relatively minor. Independent of their political affiliation, the elites share a *latifundia* ideology, similar everyday life experiences, and fear of and contempt for the rest of the population, mixed with different amounts of paternalism. The explosion of popular discontent in the early 1980s brought the elites back together through the recreation of the imagery of reconciliation. A process of reconciliation was prompted by both the fear of the "other" and also the opportunity to consolidate and deepen the process of total capitalism within *latifundia* relations that the neoliberal/military regime was imposing. As usual, the elites were to interpret their own reconciliation as that of all Chileans. Here the church played a central role.

Faced with the protests of the early 1980s, the military regime moved thousands of soldiers to quell the insurrection, killing, torturing, vanishing, and occupying the streets. More important, conditions were ripe for beginning a process of legitimation of neoliberalism. The elites in the military regime, in the opposition, and in the church maneuvered toward an agreement to control popular unrest and to move slowly toward a civilian government that would retain the neoliberal economic, social, and ethical framework of the military dictatorship. The regime subsidized a giant operation to keep Chilean corporate capital afloat, decisively propelled the sale of companies and resources to national and transnational capital at bargain prices, and sluggishly reorganized its political cadres. The military version of neoliberalism tried to cling to the control of the state in the voting booths, while the opposition that eventually formed the Concertación, an alliance of Christian Democratic and Socialist parties, accepted the 1980 Constitution dictated by Pinochet and participated in the voting contests set by the military framework. Yet, unsure of the reaction of the population they had helped demobilize, the Concertación program promised to reform the Constitution and seek means to redress the brutality of years of dictatorship. In turn, by 1986, the Christian Democratic and Left parties managed to put an end to the protest, and in 1988 they dismantled the Comando Unitario de Pobladores, a committee of *población* leaders who represented an independent nonelite political movement. However, for those who had borne the brunt of repression, had lost the limited powers they had gained in the past forty years, and had lived in poverty for sixteen years, the idea of returning only to an electoral version of the military regime was still problematic. In this context, the Catholic church, which has historically been and still is a powerful institution that has served the dominant classes, also intervened in the process of moving toward neoliberalism with a new face. Thus Pope John Paul II made a trip to Chile to promote a negotiated solution to a change in government that would keep the tenets of neoliberalism and *latifundia* relations untouched. To do this he rekindled the metaphor of reconciliation already put forward by Pinochet in 1978.

Indeed, the metaphor of the country as the patriarchal family was once again an apt one. It invoked an accepted and uncontested institution in Chilean society. The Chilean family is assumed to be indissoluble. Although in practice annulment is possible through a legal loophole for the wealthier middle and upper classes, divorce is illegal. Thus evoking reconciliation is to conjure a familiar notion of inescapable customary power that many have accepted as the norm. Moreover, in addition to being forever, the institution of the family is potentially abusive, where males often brutalize women and adults abuse children. Thousands of women and children who are or have been abused are expected to continue their lives with those who have power to mistreat them (Lehmann 1990:32–34). What better then, for those in political, economic, social, and repressive power, than to invoke once again the *familia mariana* as a metaphor? Reconciliation was summoned because it signified what Rockhill (1993) considers the basics of abusive family relationships: to keep the power structure intact the powerless must have selective memories, keep silent, show love and manners, "forgive and forget." Rockhill's reflections about herself are also applicable to Chile as a metaphorical family in its connections with the neoliberal/ military dictatorship:

We are constantly faced with constraints upon what can be remembered, in the presence of whom. These constraints sediment the public/private divide. When I transgress that divide, I run into the regulation of the speakable, which I experience breathlessly, as a knot in my gut, the cold grip of fear around my heart. I trace the words that haunt me—traitor, hypocrite, cruel—to break their regulatory chains, to track the materiality of my fears. I struggle with the emotional and material investments that make me vulnerable to regulation, and sometimes choose to follow a politics of silence (Rockhill 1993).

The pope's visit was to sell forgiveness; it had an enormous impact. He demanded that the church "persevere in its efforts for unity and reconciliation" (*Revista APSI*, 6–19 April 1987:1; see also *Revista APSI*, 20–26 April 1987:1). This message was quickly embraced by the elites in the opposition and the press. For instance, "left-wing" politician José Antonio Viera-Gallo wrote: "The content of the John Paul II's speeches . . . is structured around the concept of reconciliation. The central idea is that the country must close its wounds . . . reconciliation is based on the democratic ₍aditions of the Chilean people" (Viera-Gallo 1987:5). Soon after the pope's visit, the plebiscite of 1988 was called by the military regime to decide if Pinochet would remain in power. A year after the regime's defeat, there were elections to replace Pinochet. The images of body and family became central in both campaigns.

As they had done in the years that followed the coup, the dictatorship played with the images of Chile as a body. However, now they represented the nation as a body in recovery. Instead of a cancerous body in need of harsh medicine and brutal surgery, they argued that Chile now required the gentle touch of the nurse. The medical image of the surgeons in gray was replaced by the image of a woman in white. Cancer was being replaced by precariously closed wounds. For example, in 1989, when asked for the location of corpses of the disappeared, Pinochet, the main (public) "surgeon/torturer" of the past sixteen years, answered: "What could be gained? Nothing. Only to open the wounds" (Correa and Subercaseaux 1989:126). Although the nature of these "wounds" was left undefined, patience and understanding were prescribed for healing them.

In turn, although accepting the image of a patient in recovery, the Concertación campaigned mainly under a discursive framework that reclaimed the pope's message of reconciliation. At the time of the plebiscite, the NO campaign (the opposition to the continuation of Pinochet as "president") called for reconciliation and peace: "without hatred or violence, vote NO." The image was one of reencounter, a nation of "brothers," putting an end to disagreements and quarrels, restoring accord, harmony, and happiness.

For its part, the church also reemphasized the metaphor of reconciliation. In 1988, the Permanent Committee of the Episcopate reclaimed Chile as a family, explicitly pointing out that "political adversaries . . . are not enemies, they continue to have and to love the same motherland, and to be part of the same family. We will never tire of calling this to mind" (*Revista Hoy*, 10–16 Oct. 1988:8). Thus, despite a seemingly agitated confrontation to end a brutal military dictatorship, a vacillating process of translating the rebonding of the elites into a widespread consensus developed throughout this period.

Indeed, the employment of the metaphor of family in the process of reconciliation facilitated the handling of the immediate past while dismissing a history of exploitation and class struggle, power, and the peculiar Chilean apartheid system resulting from the mixture of capitalism and *latifundia* relations. The election of Concertación candidate Patricio Aylwin furthered the implementation of neoliberalism and the reinterpretation of the dictatorship.

Hesitantly the elites maneuvered toward implementing the accords of a negotiated transition. This was a period of uncertainty and vacillation over how to resolve the legacy of the military period while accepting neoliberalism as the economic, social, and ethical matrix. As democratic gestures, political prisoners were very slowly freed and exile was terminated. On the other hand, Pinochet's constitution of 1980 remained unchanged to serve as a framework of civilian neoliberalism. Against popular demands of justice, a discursive framework emerged to seek widespread consent. The Aylwin government moved eagerly to cleanse the past by reaffirming the notion of the possibility of reconciliation in the Chilean family.

It was difficult to legitimate the continuous presence of members of the former regime in all sectors of power and their consorting with the elites of the Concertación in politics, private schools, neighborhoods, and resorts. Above all, it was hard to justify the strengthening of many of the institutions of the dictatorship, such as the independence of military institutions from civilian control, the power and independence of military courts, and the tenure of Pinochet as commander in chief of the armed forces. The differences between sectors of the elite were forgotten. The "prodigal sons of the established order" (Marín 1997:E22) had returned to the open defense of their class and power interests. In this way the Concertación became a partner of the past system, while the differences between the civilian and military phases of neoliberalism began to fade away. However, during this period the anger and frustration of sixteen years of dictatorship lingered. A small number of human rights organizations and the will to justice of the population still remained active.

Thus the Concertación had to address what was euphemistically called *el tema de los derechos humanos* ("the topic of human rights"). In April 1990 it established a commission to examine human rights violations: La Comisión Nacional de Verdad y Reconciliación (The National Commission of Truth and Reconciliation). This commission had a limited mandate to compile existing information on human rights violations concerning only those who had died. As similar commissions, it was a "symbolic ritual" that was intended to legitimate both the military and civil faces of neoliberalism, a reunified elite, and to allow the government to present itself as a defender of the "common good."[3] The commission pretended that knowledge about the crimes of the military was restricted to the direct perpetrators, thus exonerating the many other accomplices from judges to economists, from politicians to the indifferent. For this it employed the now familiar metaphors of a wounded body in recovery—"to close an open wound in the national soul"—and of reconciliation—"reconciliation on the basis of truth and justice" (*Informe de la Comisión Nacional de Verdad y Reconciliación* n.d.). The result of the inquiry created a very brief commotion and some outrage but had ambivalent consequences. Its mandate was to seek the truth, as if this had not been known by everyone. Thus it offered the opportunity for many to pretend that terror had been unknown, that murder, torture, robbery, and all the repression that began on the day of the coup in 1973 had been restricted to a few perpetrators and occasional victims. In the end, not even those who were directly responsible were punished, much less the vast number of accomplices.

The period of hesitation gave way to one of triumphalism wherein the military and civilian phases of neoliberalism have been presented as a legitimate continuous process of which to be proud. Eduardo Frei Ruiz-Tagle, a Christian Democratic and Concertación member, replaced Patricio Aylwin in 1994. His election marks the consolidation of neoliberalism as a legitimate form of government. By then the "topic of human rights" had almost disappeared. For example, on one occasion when it flared up, Frei argued that "the country has moved forward on the road toward national reconciliation and it must continue to do so," adding that "the country rejects . . . any form of probing in the wounds of the past. . . . [I] will seek to promote a climate that facilitates understanding in matters of such importance for the national soul."

However, in the mid-1990s, one crisis remained to be solved to legitimate neoliberalism, the murder of Orlando Letelier, a former minister of the Allende government, who was killed in Washington, D.C., in 1976 by an assassination team sent by the military regime. When in 1978 the military and its allies dictated an amnesty law to exonerate the military from its crimes, the U.S. government forced the Pinochet regime to leave Letelier's murder outside the purview of that law. For years the case was stalled in the courts. However, the power of the U.S. government made it possible finally to indict a few members of the Chilean repressive system, including the head of the DINA, the powerful General Contreras and his lieutenant, Brigadier Espinoza. In 1995, almost two decades after the assassination, a light sentence was imposed on Contreras and Espinoza by the Chilean courts.

Not surprisingly, at this point the images of a reconciled family were again invoked. For example, Sergio Onofre Jarpa—a very powerful politician of the Chilean Right, who was heavily implicated in the coup and, as one of the ministers of the interior of Pinochet in the 1980s, directly responsible for part of the dictatorship's violence—was quite clear in mak-

ing this connection. As Contreras was refusing to go to jail, the newspaper *La Segunda* (9 Aug. 1995:18) asked Jarpa, "What do you think will happen if the problem of human rights is not solved?" He answered: "we will carry on in the same manner we have been doing until now: like a marriage that does not get along." However, Contreras' imprisonment provided the elites with the opportunity to eliminate the last obstacles to the legitimation of the neoliberal/*latifundia* system.

Contreras went to a specially built jail, where, under the control of the army, he and the smattering of military men who might be condemned for violations to human rights were to spend their sentences, in comfort, away from the frightful conditions of common prisons or of the maximum security jail, where left-wing political prisoners have to spend their much longer and harsher sentences. As the Contreras incident permitted the government to reaffirm the legitimacy of both the courts (whose members were heavily implicated with the military repression and remain in office) and the self-amnesty law of 1978, and simultaneously to consider the violation of human rights resolved, the metaphor of family and reconciliation became much less used. By 1995 the imagery of Chile was one of a group of friends—"a deep, horizontal comradeship" to use Anderson's (1991) often-quoted expression—or, better still, of a family that had quarreled but had remained united. More important, reconciliation suggests that the present democracy intends to go back to the traditional harmony of the Chilean family: a mythical past when Chileans were at peace and had no social or political contradictions.

Thus the politics of reconciliation have been basic for neoliberalism because it has extended silence over the sharp historical class struggles of Chilean society, the painfully slow pace and unfinished nature of democratization even before it was reversed in 1973, and over the brutality of Chilean capitalism, historically premised on savage exploitation. Finally, reconciliation has implied the possibility of accepting the repression, murders, and tortures of the military dictatorship without attempting to transform the system that fostered that terror and without punishing the many culprits and accomplices. The result has been to deny the existence of class differences and the apartheid that pervades every aspect of social relations, that is, to legitimate neoliberalism. However, as neoliberalism has become hegemonic and the elites have become one, a new image, again centered on the body, has become prevalent in two forms: the image of a little jaguar and that of a competitive sportsperson.

Today the country is portrayed as a ferocious animal, a brutal predator, a jaguar capable of winning in the competition with other countries. However, the image of a sportsperson is being superimposed over that of the jaguar, an image carefully designed by politicians, the press, economists, and businessmen (there are no businesswomen in Chile *mariano*). Indeed, in order to inculcate this picture, a massive press campaign portrays a world in which ranking is paramount and to be part of a mythical "top ten" is the goal of peoples and nations, from tennis competitions to world trade. The sportsperson fits well with another image resurrected from the dictatorship, that of modernization, loosely understood as a mix of North Americanization and total capitalism.

A few sportspeople are presented as the embodiment of Chilean success. In fact, newspapers headline the position of Chileans in international competitions, in soccer and recently in tennis. Using the ranking of the Professional Tennis Association, a concept of "top tenness" decorates the newspaper stands almost daily. These images project an impressive Chilean presence in an Americanized modern world. The new body of Chile is presented as a modern one, sharing in a global culture of consumerism and competition, capable of achieving a modernity that import substitution is shown as having been unable to achieve in the 1950s and 1960s. This is a neoliberal body, with neoliberal ethics, a muscular and fierce body with an instinct to kill, that would stop at nothing to achieve individual profits. Unlike the body of the past, sick with cancer, this body is imagined without wounds, healthy and cleansed.

Yet neoliberalism has not transformed the conservative nature of Chilean society. On the contrary, as the notions of reconciliation and family were at the center of the hegemonization of neoliberalism, the *familia mariana* became more legitimate. It received legal cosmetic changes in 1989 as the Chilean government was forced to abide by the United Nations Human Rights Charter. For example, today women do not have to ask permission from their husbands to work outside the home, nor must a wife follow her husband to the residence he chooses. Nevertheless, ideologically, legally and in everyday life the *familia mariana* continues to be predominant. Indeed, the path of the Chilean bourgeois revolution to capitalism and liberalism has at the same time been the path to conservative *latifundia* relations including the strengthening of the *familia mariana*.

ACKNOWLEDGMENTS

Camilo Trumper's comments and critical thinking were invaluable. We would also like to thank the warm welcome of the Programa Interdisciplinario de Estudios de Género of the University of Chile, where we spent several months of a sabbatical leave working on this article. This work was made possible by the financial assistance received from the Social Sciences and Humanities Research Council of Canada and the Okanagan University College.

NOTES

1. For an interpretation of "*latifundia* relations," see Trumper and Phillips (1995) and Ibáñez (1993). A good glimpse of *latifundia* relations of power—and

how they translate into everyday life—can be found in an article written by Pinochet Lebrún (1970) in the first part of this century.

2. For Harberger's and Friedman's advice to the military junta, see, for example, Monckeberg and Correa (1975).

3. The Comisión Nacional de Verdad y Reconciliación resembles commissions of inquiry used by other governments. For an analysis of the objectives of commissions of inquiry, see Ashworth (1990) and Richardson, Sherman, and Gismondi (1993).

REFERENCES

Anderson, B. (1991). *Imagined Communities*. London and New York: Verso.

Ashforth, A. (1990). "Reckoning Schemes of Legitimation: On Commissions of Enquiry as Power/Knowledge Forms." *Journal of Historical Sociology* 3 (1): 1–22.

Bello, W., with S. Cunningham, and B. Rau. (1994). *Dark Victory: The United States, Structural Adjustment, and Global Poverty*. London: Pluto Press.

Bengoa, J. (1990). "El tiempo que viene." *Proposiciones* 18:7–14.

Boyer, R. (1992). "Women, *La Mala Vida*, and the Politics of Marriage." In *Sexuality and Marriage in Colonial Latin America*, ed. A. Lavrin, 252–86. University of Nebraska Press.

Cassen, B. (1995). "Au Chili, les sirènes de l'oubli et les dividendes du libéralisme." *Le Monde Diplomatique* 491 (Feb.):8–9.

Correa, R., and E. Subercaseaux. (1989). *Ergo Sum, Pinochet*. Santiago: Zig Zag.

Douglas, M. (1978). *Purity and Danger: An Analysis of Concepts of Pollution and Taboo*. London: Routledge and Kegan Paul.

Friedland, J. (1995). "Pinochet's Comments on General's Sentence Cast Cloud over Chile." *Globe and Mail*, (20 June): A9.

Ibáñez, F. (1993). "It Is Not WHAT You Do, but HOW You Do It: Cultural Risks and HIV/AIDS in Chile." *Border/Lines* 27:19–25.

Informe de la Comisión Nacional de Verdad y Reconciliación. (n.d.). La Nación, 3 fascículos.

Lehmann, C. (1990). "Bread and Roses: Women Living Poverty and Popular Feminist Education in Santiago, Chile." Unpublished M.A. thesis, University of Toronto, Department of Education.

———. (1991). "Bread and Roses: Women Who Live Poverty." In *Popular Culture in Chile*, ed. K. Aman and J. C. Parker, 113–23. Boulder, Colo.: Westview Press.

Marín, G. (1997). "Enrique Lihn: líneas para un prólogo." *El Mercurio* (27 April): E22–23.

Monckeberg, M. O., and M. Correa. (1975). "Los consejos del profesor." *Ercilla* (2 April): 19–22.

Montecino, S. (1993). *Madres y huachos: alegorías del mestizaje chileno*. Santiago: Editorial Cuarto Propio.

Osorio, V., and I. Cabezas. (1995). *Los hijos de Pinochet*. Santiago: Planeta.

Pinochet, A. (1978). "1973–1978: Cinco años de orden, progreso y libertad," Mensaje del 11 de septiembre de 1978.

———. (1979). *El día decisivo, 11 de septiembre.* Santiago: Andrés Bello.

Pinochet Lebrún, T. (1970). "Inquilinos en la hacienda de su excelencia." In *Antología Chilena de la Tierra*, ed. A. Corvalán, 81–112. Santiago: ICIRA.

Richardson, M., J. Sherman, and M. Gismondi. (1993). *Winning Back the Words: Confronting Experts in an Environmental Public Hearing.* Toronto: Garamond.

Rockhill, K. (1993). "Home Cries." *Tessera* 14 (summer):36–44.

Scheper-Hughes, N., and M. M. Lock. (1987). "The Mindful Body: A Prolegomenon to Future Work in Medical Anthropology." *Medical Anthropology Quarterly* 2 (1):6–41.

Sontag, S. (1990). *Illness as Metaphor and AIDS and Its Metaphors.* New York: Anchor.

Temple, G. (1995). *Globalization and the Decline of Social Reform.* Toronto: Garamond Press.

Touraine, A. (1974). *Vida y muerte de Chile popular.* Mexico: Siglo Veintiuno Editores.

Trumper, R., and L. Phillips. (1995). "Cholera in the Time of Neoliberalism: The Cases of Chile and Ecuador." *Alternatives* 20 (2):165–94.

———. (1996). "Give me Discipline and Give Me Death: Neoliberalism and Health in Chile." *Race and Class* 37 (3):19–34.

Valdés, T. (1991). "Being Female and Poor: A Double Oppression." In *Popular Culture in Chile*, ed. K. Aman and J. C. Parker, 67–112. Boulder, Colo.: Westview Press.

Valenzuela, M. E. (1987). *La mujer en el Chile militar: todas íbamos a ser reinas.* Santiago: Ediciones Chile América, CESOC ACHIP.

Viera-Gallo, J. A. (1987). "El Papa, la reconciliación y la democracia." *Revista APSI* (20–26 April): 5.

Weiss, M. (1995). "Cancer and Imputed Infections." *The Sociological Review* 43 (1):1–35.

2

HIV and the State of the Family

Alan Sears and Barry D. Adam

Most people in North America no longer live in the orthodox "family" defined as the heterosexual marital union of a man and a woman along with their offspring in a single household. The groups in North America that have been hardest hit by HIV infection (gay men, impoverished urban residents, particularly people of color, and intravenous drug users) are even less likely to live in this "official" family that inhabits national imaginations and is institutionalized in law and social policy.[1] This chapter draws on the experiences of people living with HIV or AIDS to examine two major themes. First, we look at the individuals and relationships that seropositive people rely on most for emotional, financial, and practical support in order to identify the family forms that are actual and meaningful to them. Second, we examine the pressures faced by these families in an era of declining social services, cutbacks, and retrenchment. We focus here on personal relationships outside of sexual or couple relationships, which have their own dynamics and raise particular issues with regard to HIV infection (see Adam and Sears 1996: ch. 4).

This chapter draws on a larger research project examining the processes through which people deal with the effects of HIV infection on their personal, family, and work relationships (Adam and Sears 1996). The project involved open-ended interviews with 60 people with HIV disease or AIDS and 40 of their friends, family, and lovers. Of the 60 HIV-positive respondents, 13 lived in southwestern Ontario in Canada and 47 in southeastern Michigan in the United States. We talked to a diverse range of people: 38 described themselves as coming from European backgrounds, 20 stated they were black or African-American, and two were aboriginal.[2] The sexual orientation of the respondents was 37 gay or homosexual, 7 bisexual, and 16 heterosexual. We spoke to 48 men and 12 women. Most of the respondents had low incomes; 35 were living on less than $10,000 per year.

THE MAKING OF FAMILIES IN THE POSTWAR PERIOD

It is a shared premise of the chapters in this book that there is no single, eternal, and natural way of organizing households, primary intimate relationships, and biological and social reproduction (Barrett and McIntosh 1982:34–40). Rather, family forms have changed over time and vary within societies. In contemporary capitalist societies, the state has played an important role in regulating families (Ursel 1992:55). State regulation typically followed a model set by late nineteenth-century and early twentieth-century social reform movements rooted in Judeo-Christian precepts of the family as an exclusive site of sexual expression and a central place in networks of intimacy and social support. "The family," in this sense, marginalized other forms of sexual expression and intimacy including at various times homosexuality, heterosexual relations outside marriage, single parenting, and the sex trades.

Family forms have also been shaped by economic changes. Indeed, state and religious initiatives to shape "the family" have at times attempted to "defend" families against the corrosive effects of commodification and the exploitation of labor but also, somewhat contradictorily, have pressed them to accommodate to the needs of capital. Moral reformers, employers, and state policy makers have attempted to institute and police an official family form, at least since the late nineteenth century. In doing so, traditionalists have tended to call for the policing of emigrants from family orthodoxy rather than for control over social conditions that both undermine traditional families and create opportunities for innovative intimate relations. Traditionalists, then, tend to associate the "decline" of the orthodox family with the rise of feminism, lesbian and gay rights, social welfare programs, and multiculturalism (Gairdner 1990; Murray 1984).

Stephanie Coontz (1992:23) argues that an idealization of the 1950s family is a crucial reference point in these discussions. This historical moment tends to define the image of the family for the political right wing as a self-reliant unit based on the heterosexual couple and their children. This "family," so the story goes, reached its pinnacle in the 1950s and has since been eroded because of a variety of pernicious changes. Coontz (1992:25–32) challenges the myth of "the family" by pointing out that the 1950s family was a new development rather than a traditional form. A number of historical developments came together to create it. The rapid spread of industrial unions through the 1940s, combined with the overall conditions of economic growth, created conditions of rising working-class living standards. This provided increased space for domestic life and new possibilities for the single-income working-class family. The widespread eviction of women from paid employment after World War II forced them into domestic roles. As Ruth Milkman (1987:103) argues, "the ideology of domesticity was revived with a vengeance after the war." The increased incomes of working-class families also provided new access to commodities, ranging from refrigerators to cars, from homes to television sets. These new commodities both defined a new purpose for the household (as a unit of consumption) and increased tendencies toward atomization by privatizing the community life of the urban neighborhood into the enclosed households of the suburb.

At the same time, the expansion of social programs during the 1940s added a new dimension to the state regulation of family forms. It had been a central project of social policy since the early twentieth century to promote a particular form of family. Social policy before World War II had centered largely on moral forms of regulation, ranging from visits of public health nurses to teach women how to mother, to purity campaigns against sexually transmitted diseases (Sears 1995; Valverde 1991). New social programs introduced during and after World War II, such as unemployment insurance and family allowances, added new economic forms of family policy to complement the moral ones.[3]

But the moment of the 1950s family was short-lived. Important changes began in the 1960s that undercut some of the basis for the model family of the 1950s. Economic changes (both the economic boom and the growth of service sector employment) created a huge demand for women's paid labor and drew larger numbers of women into the labor market. The rise of the contemporary women's movement challenged the sexual division of labor that grounded the 1950s family. Postwar changes accelerated longer-term historical trends that gave workers greater opportunity to follow personal preferences in forming both heterosexual and homosexual relationships (Adam 1995).

The process of capitalist restructuring that began in the early 1970s and gained momentum through the 1980s and 1990s has continued to undermine the basis for the 1950s family.[4] Cutbacks in social programs have led to the intensification of women's domestic labor at the same time as women's participation in paid employment has remained high (Leach 1993; Bakker 1996; Connelly and MacDonald 1996). Working-class living standards have eroded, and those people who need social assistance have been attacked. The process of commodification has extended more deeply into daily life, whether in the form of McDonalds birthday parties for children or the development of new businesses to fill the gaps in the declining welfare state. David Harvey (1989:284–88) discusses the ways in which the pace of commodity consumption has been increased as its realm has broadened. All of these factors contribute to a situation in which domestic life is under stress.

"The family" has become a right-wing rallying call at a time when the capitalist system itself undermines the social and material base for the 1950s lifestyle that the Right sees as a model. The 1950s family, embodied in Republican party commercials featuring a "house with a white picket fence," remains a powerful icon with widespread emotional resonance.

AIDS, then, has pointed to the inadequacies of conventional and official discourses around "the family." AIDS came about at a time when "the family" was in decline as an actual lived reality yet in full bloom as an ideological battle call of the Right (Adam 1992b). Moral policing became transformed with the disciplinary agenda of the neoliberal state (Kinsman 1996:3–5). AIDS appeared at a historical moment when government austerity measures were reducing social services available to families that fit the officially recognized form. Caregiving to the young, the old, and the sick, which had increasingly become the responsibility of the welfare state, were being divested in the 1980s and 1990s. Neoliberal rhetoric, propounded widely by conservative politicians and the corporate media, now demanded tax reduction (especially for the corporate sector) and, in response to the growing deficits that resulted from falling tax payments, downsizing of government services. The neotraditional family ideology that accompanied these changes conveniently called on families (usually meaning "women") to take up the slack as caregiving was "privatized" into the home. Since the 1980s, households have been pressed to intensify wage and domestic labor to provide the material resources required to make domestic life. This is particularly true of people living in poverty and mother-led families.[5] In U.S. cities, AIDS is part of a broader crisis confronting people living in poverty who are primarily African-American and Hispanic. A full understanding of this crisis must take into account the economic and social conditions deriving from poverty, racism, and gender inequality (see Baca Zinn 1990; Jarrett 1994).

For families that did *not* fit the officially recognized form, which included many African-American families and virtually all gay and lesbian relationships, a wide range of support services was denied through disqualification. Virtually from its inception, AIDS has been constructed as a threat to "the family" and a warning to those who do not live by its strictures (Watney 1987). Yet perhaps paradoxically, AIDS has forced homosexual relationships into public discussion in unprecedented ways as the actually existing ways in which many people are forming personal, intimate relationships and support networks have become increasingly visible (Adam 1992a). In Canada there has been piecemeal recognition of same-sex relationships, particularly through gaining partner benefits in collective agreements. The first comprehensive legislation that would have recognized same-sex relationships was defeated in the province of Ontario in 1994 (Adam 1995: 136–38; Kinsman 1996:313–16); a similar bill was introduced in British Columbia in 1997. This has brought about debate within lesbian and gay communities over the contrasting costs and benefits of state regulation of same-sex relationships.

People living with HIV, then, find themselves navigating a complex terrain. They may find some room for acceptance of diverse ways of living (lesbian and gay, single parents, common law), yet familial ideology is still a powerful force. They may make places for themselves inside families or other personal relationships, yet remain outside "the family" as officially defined.

FAMILIES OF ORIGIN AND FAMILIES OF CHOICE

Mass media portraits of AIDS and families have tended to rely on a dominant narrative of exclusion from the warm hearth of family support, punctuated by heartwarming stories of acceptance and overcoming. The experiences of seropositive people are, in fact, much more variable and complex. One of the challenges faced by people with HIV is in the area of personal relationships. The disclosure of an HIV-positive diagnosis can have a powerful impact on all sorts of relationships. Individuals must assess quite carefully whom they can and should tell. Life with HIV disease may also create new needs for emotional or financial support that need to be addressed through friends, families, or lovers. Finally, an HIV-positive diagnosis may lead people to reassess priorities and make decisions about the value of different kinds of relationships. Michael Bury (1982:169–70) argues that diagnosis with a chronic illness creates a "biographical disruption" for individuals. People actively call upon various resources to reorganize their lives in different ways. This may include the decision to continue life as if nothing had changed, though even that represents a choice with new meanings (Adam and Sears 1996:xii–xiii). People living with HIV may find they have new needs to be filled through personal relationships. HIV infection can create a range of social, economic, and health problems that must be faced through drawing on different resources. Personal relationships of varying types can provide important resources in these circumstances.

Many of the people we spoke with stressed the importance of their relations with family members. Marcia, a single parent, relies on her mother "for everything": "That is my bank vault. I can always go to mom when you can't go anywhere else. I have been like that all my life with my mother" (heterosexual black woman). A number of people feel closer to their families of origin as a result of working through issues related to HIV infection. Daniel put it clearly: "I think the whole family is closer because of it. You know, we've had to deal with a major issue together and now we've all pulled through it, so it's brought us closer together. It's made life a little bit more serious, you know. Maybe it makes you forget about your other problems, other piddly little things that are going on within the family" (gay white man).

Whether or not their families of origin are accepting, people describe a range of relationships that they draw on for support. These relationships often meet needs that the official ideology of "the family" would consider to be familial. Indeed, in some cases people used family-related vocabulary to describe these relations. Crystal, for example, gestured to the two other HIV-positive women participating in the interview with her who were not blood relatives to tell us whom she relied on: "I think these people here, my sisters. . . . The only people that care are people who really understand, just like you. And my family, they don't care because they don't understand" (heterosexual black woman).[6] Jodi used similar terms to describe her household: "We are like the sisterhood. There are four of us who went through recovery together [and] live in the same apartment" (heterosexual white woman).

Dino, a caregiver for his HIV-positive friend Simon, also used kinship terminology to describe their relationship: "I've known him for two years. He has no family here. I'm like a surrogate big brother" (gay white man). It was not only physical distance that separated Simon from his family of origin. He had not told his parents he was gay. Dino went on to describe a caregiving network that included a lesbian friend and a former lover of Simon's.

A few gay men had important supportive friendships with people who had been lovers. Jack described his caregiving relationship with Roland: "We always remained friends. . . . I think it is better than it used to be because he understands now that I do care. . . . I will be here for him, which is important for him. He doesn't have a boyfriend now" (gay white man).

Some used the vocabulary of friendship to describe their intimate networks. Indeed, some people contrasted friendship relations to those with their families of origin in order to demonstrate their importance. Sheila turned to friends in times of real need as she did not believe her mother could deal with the situation: "But if I get real emotional and upset, and bummed out, I will talk to a couple of my girlfriends. So I don't really depend on my parents. My mother really can't handle it" (heterosexual white woman). Jessie used similar terms to explain her caregiver relationship with an HIV-positive woman. "I was there because I would want someone to be in my corner if I was like that. 'Cause a lot of times, family members, you can't talk to them. I know from my own experience. I can talk to friends more then I can my own family. I put my trust more in them then I do my family" (heterosexual black woman).

Dan had been forced by financial considerations to move back close to his parents. He wanted to move back to his friends. Clarence had both good and bad experiences with both his family and his lover's. Some of his friendships were more important to him. One of the important qualities of friendship for him was simply their presence: "Quite often friends become true supporters. They want to be with you. They want to hold your hand, just be here. 'Let's watch Jeopardy' " (Clarence, gay Aboriginal man).

Of course, not all relations with friends turned out to be supportive. Peter felt that his friends pulled away when they found out he was HIV-positive: "Friends, especially gay friends, I was immediately distanced. . . . It was because they didn't know how to be a friend to somebody with AIDS" (gay white man).

A few people turned to support groups rather than their previously existing personal relationships to deal with HIV-related issues. Carl found it easier to ask for help from a support group than from friends: "Emotionally, who I rely on most would have to be my support group here. I rely on my friends and I share things with them. But I have a hard time reaching out for support. . . . I find that with support groups I can get the support more, not to where I'm embarrassed or feel like I'm asking for favors" (gay white man).

In contrast to Carl who found it hard to reach out for help, Andrea sought out support groups to avoid imposing. Andrea did not want to be a burden on her family and sought out a women's support group: "I just don't want to put that burden on them, for them to worry about it. So that is where the support group comes in. That is why I had to find me a support group, and I had to go to one where I could express exactly how I feel. . . . That is why it is so important for me to catch up with the ladies" (heterosexual black woman).

A number of people turned specifically to lesbian and gay relatives to deal with issues of HIV infection because they were presumed to be more grounded in AIDS issues and to be more understanding. Emma, a lesbian, moved to Windsor to take care of her gay uncle Daniel who is HIV-positive: "I'm Daniel's person in life to tell him that everything's going to be OK. I always tell him that. . . . I support him in everything he does. . . . I knew full well that by coming to Windsor and living with him, . . . I would be taking responsibility on my behalf" (lesbian white woman). Heterosexuals may also turn to lesbian and gay relatives after being diagnosed as HIV-positive. Ninia gets little support from any family members aside from her gay brother. Kevin counts on the support and expertise of his brother, who is both gay and a hospital worker: "My brother in Chicago, he knows that I am infected. He works in a hospital, so he knows different things about the disease, plus he is gay so he should know a lot about it. He accepts it" (heterosexual black man) (Adam and Sears 1996:99).

People draw on a variety of personal and familial relationships as they make a life with HIV. People with HIV who are parents face particular challenges. Widespread beliefs about HIV infection tend to lead heterosexual women (and their doctors) to believe that they are not at risk (Patton 1994:99–102). It is possible for women to be diagnosed with HIV infection either during pregnancy or as the result of a child's illness. Further, many HIV-positive women have limited access to resources such as testing and information as a result of poverty and other factors (Hunter 1995:36–37).

Rhonda was one of the women who told us she was diagnosed while she was pregnant. She went to her doctor as a result of pain she described as "female problems" during pregnancy. "Usually when you have female problems, they ask that you be tested. And so I thought, OK, no problem, because I am not going to have HIV. And so she ran a test on me, and she called me at home, left a message on my recorder that I contact her right away. . . . That is how I found out. I was pregnant and . . . I had no idea whatsoever that this is what it could be" (heterosexual black woman). Luelle found out her HIV status after her infant son was diagnosed. She could not face the diagnosis at that time: "I had my son, and they tested him. . . . I went home first, and they kept him three days. . . . When they told me to come and pick him up, that's when they told me. It was like a denial thing, I blocked it out. I blocked it out for so long I started forgetting it" (heterosexual black woman).

There are particular problems that parents who are HIV-positive may face. Gordon explained that he did not have the stamina to keep up with his daughter: "We have a . . . daughter, and her energy level, as you know, is extremely high. . . . 'Daddy, let's go play some baseball. Let's go to the park and play some baseball, for 3 hours or whatever.' And that became a real problem with me, because of guilt. . . . But I explained to her that I just don't have the energy to do that now. 'Daddy has an illness, I am not very sick today but I have something' " (heterosexual white man). Robbie, a gay man, feared his ex-wife's reaction if she found out he was HIV-positive: "And, uh, if I told them that I was positive then their mother, my ex-wife, would make sure I would not see them" (gay white man).

Parents face the difficult challenge of discussing their HIV status with their children. Gordon and his wife are both HIV-positive. He found he had to reassure his daughter when both of them were sick at the same time: "She was terrified on a couple of occasions when I wasn't feeling well, and [my wife] wasn't feeling well with other things, that this was AIDS and you were going to die. And it took a lot of time to explain to her that, where she felt comfortable" (heterosexual white man). Paula disclosed her HIV status to her teenage son when he got in trouble with the law and had to make a court hearing: "I told him when we was walking back. We talked about it all the way till we walked to the bus stop. I tried to straighten him up, maybe he'll do better in school" (heterosexual black woman).

Some of the other issues HIV-positive parents face are discussed later, in the section on social programs and assistance to families. People with HIV face different challenges in dealing with family and other personal relations.

There is a very good chance that someone who is HIV-positive is at odds with "the family," the official ideology reinforced by the state and other institutions. This may pose real barriers in their relations with their own families, who may or may not meet officially sanctioned standards. Many families rise to the challenge of surmounting the ideology of "the family" to include HIV-positive relatives. Others do not.

FAMILY TENSIONS

Many families find ways to be supportive of people living with HIV. Other families communicate rejection to their HIV-positive relations, whether intentionally or not. AIDSphobia, the irrational fear of the spread of HIV through casual contact, is one of the strongest ways that families express rejection. Gregory's family put him in a kind of quarantine (Adam and Sears 1996:103). They insisted on practices that had nothing to do with the actual spread of HIV infection: "They told me they wanted me to use separate dishes, separate bar of soap, separate toothpaste; everything, always separate. I said well forget this, and I just moved out on my own" (gay white man). Research shows that AIDSphobia is strongly related to heterosexism and homophobia, prejudicial attitudes and practices against lesbians and gay men. Individuals with antigay attitudes are far more likely than others to have irrational fears about HIV transmission (Pleck, O'Donnell, and O'Donnell 1988:49). But it is not only gay men who face AIDSphobic behavior from family members. Crystal's mother also insisted on measures that resembled quarantine: "I couldn't go in the refrigerator, she would get it for me. I couldn't use her bathroom. I had my own glass, plates. If anything of mine was washed, she washed it. . . . It was real hard, because I didn't know what was happening with me" (heterosexual black woman). Camillo's family took him out to restaurants but would not let him visit their house.

The impulse in some families to quarantine people living with HIV infection can take a particularly severe form where children are involved. Heterosexist myths of homosexual predatory behavior toward children (whether as molesters or recruiters) may be reflected within a family as a threat of infection. Dan was made to feel unwelcome at his nephew's birthday party: "I went to a birthday party for my little nephew, and my sister's father-in-law was sitting there making all these negative comments. I didn't realize they were referring to me, at first. Something to the effect of, 'Oh, what is he doing here?' . . . I was really shocked, because I always thought he was a nicer man than that. He was upset that I was at the birthday party, and there were several people . . . making jokes about infection and stuff" (gay white man).

The contradictions of AIDS and families are played out clearly here. AIDSphobia, one of the most hurtful family responses to HIV infection, is strongly related to heterosexist attitudes and practices. These attitudes and practices are promoted as part of the ideological construction of "the family" as the single legitimate expression of sexuality and intimacy. The official ideology of "the family" creates impediments to caring in actual families with HIV-positive members, whether or not the individuals themselves are gay or lesbian.

AIDSphobia thrives in the moral atmosphere of condemnation and distance that surrounds HIV infection. AIDS has been constructed as a moral condition resulting from transgression, particularly the disruption of family norms (homosexuality, "promiscuity," and so on). This construction implies that people living with HIV are to blame for their own infection with the exception of a minority of "innocent victims" who do not transgress (Schellenberg, Keil, and Bem 1995; Treichler 1988; Watney 1987). The attribution of blame can insinuate itself into families. Marcia's sisters blamed her for her daughter's HIV-positive status: "They said this, 'How could you do that to that little baby, to my little girl? How could you do that to her?' I didn't feel any different, they were just judging me" (heterosexual black woman).

Many of the apparently personal problems associated with living with HIV have roots in larger societal arrangements and practices. For many people, the social organization of medical services, religious and family ideologies, and the actions of employers imposed burdens that far exceeded the difficulties caused by the symptoms of the HIV disease itself. These problems could be traced not simply to the attitudes of other people, which might have been relieved through adequate information, but to the institutions of the larger society.

FAMILY AND STATE

AIDS has occurred in a period of contracting welfare state programs of all kinds. Indeed, it is possible to argue that the conditions of impoverishment and diminished resources have provided the conditions for the spread of AIDS and other epidemics. Merrill Singer (1994:933) argues that HIV infection in American cities must be understood as part of a broader health crisis facing the urban poor that results from such factors as unemployment, poverty, homelessness, violence, and inadequate health care resources. AIDS is linked to poverty in two ways. First, HIV infection has disproportionately affected people living in poverty in American cities, particularly members of African-American or Latino communities (Schneider 1992:20–21). Second, many people living with HIV infection are forced into poverty in the course of their illness, particularly in the United States where the absence of a universal health care system impoverishes people through medical debt, dismissal from jobs (so that employers can avoid premium hikes), and "spend down" to qualify for Medicaid health care coverage.

The experiences of people living with HIV in two nations—one with a single-payer universal health care system (Canada) and one with an uneven patchwork of private, corporate health care providers (United States)—point starkly to the impact of state services on quality of life (Adam and Sears 1996: ch. 7). Canadian study participants had little to say and few complaints about access to medical services, while many U.S. participants experienced lengthy and difficult struggles to gain even basic medical care. Just at a time when people are experiencing considerable stress and illness due to HIV disease, they often find they must cope with a corporate bureaucracy intent on finding ways to throw them off their health care plan. When illness becomes severe enough to require leaving work, access to medical services may become especially problematic. Medical services, which are dependent on employment status, may be withdrawn in the U.S. system, leaving people with AIDS to deal with both rapid impoverishment and diminished health care just at the moment of greatest medical need.

The "pro-family" right wing has argued that the welfare state weakens the family system and cutbacks foster self-reliance. The experiences of people living with HIV provide important examples of the ways in which social program cuts make life much more difficult for actual, existing families (as opposed to the mythical model family of the 1950s). Poverty and lack of services create serious problems for people living with HIV.

HIV infection in a situation of inadequate social programs can create new forms of economic dependence. Dan lost a job and then moved between states. As a result he was ineligible for social assistance for a period and required financial assistance from his parents: "For me it feels like I am in high school or something, it is just too, too dependent" (gay white man). Roger's social assistance check did not cover his expenses: "I was getting $420 a month and my rent was $405, so my sister was helping me at the time. She was paying my electric bill" (gay white man). Brad had to get rid of his assets to qualify for assistance. He turned to his family for support when the assistance was not adequate: "They forced me to get rid of the house and car before they would give me any assistance. But then the assistance I was going to get wasn't going to be very good. And that is when my family came and got me" (gay white man).

These relations of economic dependence could emerge in friendships as well as family relationships. Jeff depended on a friendship network for financial support when living on a disability pension. "I'm living on disability pension now and I have had to adjust my world financially and socially to live within my means. . . . And fortunately enough, I have a lot of gay friends . . . who have the physical comforts that they can share with me, such as a home, extra appliances, extra furniture that they're not going to miss" (gay white man).

The American health care system also contributed to a sense of dependency. Jim had to maintain coverage through his mother's workplace benefits. "All the while my mother has kept me insured. . . . I do need this

medical coverage and so I have been able to help my mother from time to time. . . . They take out a deductible from her every month, for continuing me on as a carrier. So I have been able to assist her with that expense" (heterosexual black man).

Others were not in the position of having a family member with good medical coverage. Tony amassed a large medical debt because of health care expenses and lost pay from time off work: "I needed the time to recover, but man you have got to pay the bills. Well, I decided I am not going to worry about it. My hospital bill is up to about $60,000 and if I worried about it everyday. . . . I know I don't have that kind of money, there is no way they are getting it from me" (gay white man). Carl had to leave work in order to qualify for medical coverage. He had still not received coverage when we spoke with him. His last line of defense was to be his family: "I ended up having to legally not work, to get the medical attention I needed, because I'm not insured. . . . I could get sick tomorrow, and not have anything, I'm lucky I have family" (gay white man).

It was largely downwardly mobile individuals who complained about the inadequacies of social assistance benefits in these interviews. In contrast, some of the most impoverished people we spoke with found they had access to new resources after being diagnosed with HIV infection. Donna felt she had access to resources for her son that she would not have had otherwise: "[My son] has everything, things that if I wasn't HIV-positive, I couldn't afford to buy. . . . Baby bed, playpen, walker, everything that he needs. It has changed my life for the better. It is a bad thing to say, but it has" (heterosexual black woman).

This statement certainly shows the absolute lack of resources Donna had before she was diagnosed. It would seem likely that discussion of welfare-related problems would be more prominent if these interviews were conducted today. Social assistance has been cut seriously in both Michigan and Ontario since these interviews were conducted in the early 1990s. The difficulties people faced in trying to deal with life on social assistance are even greater now.

Some of the most impoverished people we interviewed were women who were single parents. They often raised issues about problems with services. There are serious gaps in the services available to single parents, particularly revolving around the provision of adequate child care. Ninia wanted to look for a job, but "for one thing, finding a baby sitter or daycare for the child would be a problem. Because, even though I did find a place that takes HIV children, they will not dispense medication" (heterosexual white woman).

Single mothers, especially those with histories of intravenous drug use, were often fearful of availing themselves of social services because of the power of social service professionals. Shadonna was worried about what might happen to her children in the event she was hospitalized. "But if they [single mothers] get sick they won't come in, they won't see about them-selves, because of the fear of their baby being taken away. They don't have anyone to take care of the child, it has to go into a foster home. They have to go back through all that red tape to get their kids back" (heterosexual black woman). The lack of resources (such as twenty-four-hour child care within hospitals) means inadequate health care for mothers and pressure toward the dissolution of actual families that do not conform with the model of "the family." Shadonna described some of the services she felt single mothers living with HIV required. "We need more drug treatment centers for women with HIV, because the two play hand in hand now. We nccd more shelters, where they will take moms with sick kids, with HIV. Which they don't do, if the child is sick they can't go in the shelter. We need housing, clean housing, for the mom and kids . . . who is infected" (heterosexual black woman).

The pressure toward the dissolution of actual families is reinforced by the legal system, which recognizes only the official family form. There have been some gains in the struggle for same-sex relationships, but those have been largely at the level of workplace benefits in a handful of union con-tracts. In fact, none of the participants in our study was able to avail him- or her-self of a medical plan held by a same-sex partner. As discussed above, legislation that would have recognized same-sex relationships was defeated in Ontario in 1994. Other jurisdictions, such as Michigan, retain sodomy laws. Far from providing legal protection for gay relationships, these laws subject them to criminal prosecution and leave all lesbian and gay people vulnerable to discrimination without recourse to legal remedies. This lack of legal recognition can create emotional and economic hardships for HIV-positive people in gay couples. The family of David's partner took over his estate after he died. He lost his job at the same time when the death of his partner "outed" him to a homophobic employer.

CONCLUSION

The experiences of people living with HIV show that they very often do have supportive networks of friends, lovers, fiancés, and relatives, but that these familial networks often vary from the narrow model of "the family" institutionalized by the law and state programs. The social organization of medicine, employment benefits, and social service programs show class and family bias that withhold support from the existing support networks of people most affected by HIV disease. The erosion of social programs in the neoliberal era of the last twenty-five years has further jeopardized the well-being of people with life-threatening illness. Policies that draw distinctions between the "deserving" and "undeserving," and, in the case of the United States, profit-making health management organizations, conspire to remove support from those in greatest need. The recognition and support of same-sex relationships, and the provision of day care to mother-headed families would take important steps toward building on the strengths and capabilities of those already struggling against adverse conditions.

NOTES

1. We are using "the family," in quotes, to describe the official family system backed by the state and institutions such as the church and the schools.

2. Some people mentioned other ancestries in addition to the one they mentioned first. Two people also mentioned Aboriginal ancestry and one, black ancestry.

3. The introduction of these new policies is discussed in Guest (1980:106, 132–33) and Ursel (1992:190–223). The shift from moral to economic regulation is covered in Tomlinson (1981:67–72).

4. The board outlines of this process of restructuring are sketched in Harvey (1989:141–89).

5. Of course, as Linda Gordon (1994) points out, the financial support of single mothers was inadequate even at the height of the welfare state.

6. Jarrett (1994:41–42) found that women-centered extended kin networks were important to the African-American single mothers she interviewed.

REFERENCES

Adam, B. D. (1992a). "Sex and Caring among Men." In *Modern Homosexualities*, ed. K. Plummer, 175–83. London: Routledge.

———. (1992b). "The State, Public Policy, and AIDS Discourse." In *Fluid Exchanges*, ed. J. Miller, 305–20. Toronto: University of Toronto Press.

———. (1995). *The Rise of a Lesbian and Gay Movement*. New York: Twayne.

Adam, B. D., and A. Sears. (1996). *Experiencing HIV: Personal, Family and Work Relationships*. New York: Columbia.

Baca Zinn, M. (1990). "Minority Families in Crisis: The Public Discussion." In *Women, Class and the Feminist Imagination*, ed. K. V. Hansen and I. J. Philipson, 363–79. Philadelphia: Temple University Press.

Bakker, I. (1996). *Rethinking Restructuring: Gender and Change in Canada*. Toronto: University of Toronto Press.

Barrett, M., and M. McIntosh. (1982). *The Anti-Social Family*. London: Verso.

Bury, M. (1982). "Chronic Illness as Biographical Disruption." *Sociology of Health and Illness* 8 (2):137–69.

Connelly, M. P., and M. MacDonald. (1996). "The Labor Market, the State and the Reorganization of Work: Policy Impacts." In *Rethinking Restructuring: Gender and Change in Canada*, ed. I. Bakker, 82–91. Toronto: University of Toronto Press.

Coontz, S. (1992). *The Way We Never Were: American Families and the Nostalgia Trap*. New York: Basic Books.

Gairdner, W. (1990). *The Trouble with Canada*. Toronto: Stoddart.

Gordon, L. (1994). *Pitied but Not Entitled*. New York: Macmillan.

Guest, D. (1980). *The Emergence of Social Security in Canada*. Vancouver: University of British Columbia Press.

Harvey, D. (1989). *The Condition of Post-Modernity*. Oxford: Blackwell.

Hunter, N. D. (1995). "Complications of Gender: Women, AIDS and the Law." In *Women Resisting AIDS*, ed. B. E. Schneider and N. E. Stoller, 32–56. Philadelphia: Temple University Press.

Jarrett, R. L. (1994). "Living Poor: Family Life among Single-Parent, African-American Women." *Social Problems* 41 (1):30–49.

Kinsman, G. (1996). *The Regulation of Desire*. Montreal: Black Rose.

Leach, B. (1993). "Flexible Work, Precarious Future: Some Lessons from the Canadian Clothing Industry." *Canadian Review of Sociology and Anthropology* 30 (1):64–82.

Milkman, R. (1987). *Gender at Work*. Urbana: University of Illinois Press.

Murray, C. (1984). *Losing Ground: American Social Policy 1950–1980*. New York: Basic Books.

Patton, C. (1994). *Last Served? Gendering the HIV Pandemic*. London: Taylor and Francis.

Pleck, J. H., L. O'Donnell, and C. O'Donnell. (1988). "AIDSphobia, Contact with AIDS and AIDS-Related Job Stress in Hospital Workers." *Journal of Homosexuality* 15 (3–4):41–54.

Schellenberg, E. G., J. Keil, and S. Bem. (1995). " 'Innocent Victims' of AIDS: Identifying the Subtext." *Journal of Applied Social Psychology* 25 (20):1790–1800.

Schneider, B. (1992). "AIDS and Class, Gender, and Race Relations." In *The Social Context of AIDS*, ed. J. Huber and B. Schneider. Newbury Park, Calif.: Sage.

Sears, A. (1995). "Before the Welfare State: Public Health and Social Policy." *Canadian Review of Sociology and Anthropology* 32 (3):169–88.

Singer, M. (1994). "AIDS and the Health Crisis of the U.S. Urban Poor." *Social Science and Medicine* 39 (7):931–48.

Tomlinson, J. (1981). *Problems of British Economic Policy*. London: Methuen.

Treichler, P. (1988). "AIDS, Homophobia and Bio-Medical Discourse: An Epidemic of Signification." In *AIDS: Cultural Analysis, Cultural Activism*, ed. D. Crimp, 31–70. Cambridge: MIT Press.

Ursel, J. (1992). *Private Lives, Public Policy: 100 Years of State Intervention in the Family*. Toronto: Women's Press.

Valverde, M. (1991). *The Age of Light, Soap and Water*. Toronto: McClelland and Stewart.

Watney, S. (1987). *Policing Desire: Pornography, AIDS and the Media*. Minneapolis: University of Minnesota Press.

PART II

Gender-Geographies and the Changing Household

3

Dissecting Globalization: Women's Space-Time in the Other America

Lynne Phillips

"Woman can change better'n a man," Ma said soothingly.
"Woman got all her life in her arms. Man got it all in his head."
—*Grapes of Wrath*, 1939

In this chapter I consider the potential consequences of globalization for women in the Other America[1] by focusing specifically on how emerging concepts of time and space may reshape rural women's options and responsibilities, keeping a critical eye on how their reading of space-time may challenge "global" expectations. Any assessment of the impact of globalization ultimately depends on particular notions of change, duration, and place, since what appears to be changing globally may not be so understood locally, just as what appears to be unchanging in some localities may not be constituted as such for those who live there. What constitutes change and for whom? The question becomes more tricky when we look at it from the point of view of women. Many versions of Western history compel us to see women's endless connection to "the domestic"—wherein a woman has "got all her life in her arms"—where the more women's lives change, the more they apparently stay the same. Does a woman's constant "place" always permit her, as the Steinbeck quotation implies, a certain flexibility not afforded to men—*can* she "change better'n a man?" Or does globalization, with its intent to transform the limits of time and geographical space, so radically disturb women's place that this "flexibility" no longer exists? And, if the latter, would this constitute liberation for women or a kind of annihilation?

These are some of the questions that have been shaping my thinking about globalization, though a striking feature of the globalization literature on time and space is its relative absence of discussion about women. Concepts of hyperspace, spatial flows, deterritorialization, and localization imply that globalization holds a potential for the dispersion of power, but without an investigation of whether and how power remains gendered, we must consider such arguments suspect. That there is also (so far) little evidence that globalization *un*genders domestic responsibilities (and indeed seems to extend them for women) indicates that a kind of "flexible sexism" (Massey 1991) may be applied to new production systems as well as to academic discussions about them.

My general argument here follows the suggestion by anthropologist Robert Paine (1995) that, while we may be tempted (by television and electronic media) to think that globalization can be understood primarily from "our" vantage point, the economic, political, and cultural differences that continue to be produced throughout the world make this highly unlikely. Analyzing globalization from the point of view of "others" brings to the foreground the wide variations in resources to which people have access— variations that shape how people interpret and contest "global" time and space—and helps to shatter the myth that the processes and outcomes of globalization are universal.[2] Specific consideration needs to be given to how gender, class, and ethnic distinctions may permit the construction of alternate space and time within particular localities.

Through an assessment of recent literature on rural women in the Other America and my own fieldwork experiences, I argue here that dissecting globalization from the point of view of rural women's space-time offers us an opportunity to rethink the landscapes of globalization that are currently being drawn. The "invisibility" of rural women throughout the Americas is well known, despite decades of feminist research oriented toward making them "visible." Escobar (1995) argues that an "economy of visibility" is a central aspect of capitalist accumulation and modernity wherein spaces to colonize are constantly being created and recreated. While this is an argument that goes some way to explain the persistence of rural women's invisibility, I am proposing that such invisibility may also indicate a particular use of space and time by rural women that sidesteps their vulnerability to the discipline of capitalism, a possibility that requires a focus on the micropolitics involved in rural women's occupation of named and unnamed spaces. From this perspective, if rural women attain a certain visibility (or invisibility) through globalization, we should be prepared to understand this process to be a product of both women's agency and the effectiveness of current policies to make "the rural" profitable.

Thus, while I am making the argument that there may be great variations in the way in which people engage with globalization, it should also be clear that I am not advocating a particularist or relativist approach. Because there are commonalities in the kinds of transformations that are being promoted in people's lives (e.g., reduced state support, self-discipline, consumption of new technologies, and being "plugged in" to the global market[3]), there are some important patterns regarding the potential imposition of global time and space. Capital's recent search for new markets and higher profits has involved the intensification of the process that both names new spaces to colonize and "downloads" activities deemed unprofitable. Because of the gendered character of social services (e.g., women's responsibilities for social welfare), the family (e.g., women's obligations to undertake child and household care), and the labor market (e.g., women as cheaper, docile labor), this process has had specific effects on women's lives. Women are faced daily with new parameters for organizing their households: not only are the concepts and practices of work being transformed, but the "rules" concerning access to food, water, housing, health services, and education are constantly reworked by policies that emphasize a less government assisted, self-disciplined future. This process extends the spaces for which women are seen to be responsible, in a context where resources are already scarce after more than a decade of structural adjustment and neoliberal policies.

To begin to explore the question of what spaces these processes might be creating, recreating, or denying for rural women, I identify four main trends, using examples primarily from northern Argentina and highland coastal Ecuador. I suggest that while these trends provide important information regarding the pressures being brought to bear on rural women's lives, their full implications cannot be elaborated without unpacking the largely hidden assumption of "domestic" labor. A consideration of rural women's domestic space-time in coastal Ecuador hints at the varied meanings women might bring to their engagement with these processes, but also raises an issue of the vulnerability of women's space in current conditions.

THE FEMINIZATION OF AGRICULTURE, THE MASCULINIZATION OF WOMEN

The intention to eliminate trade barriers to capital accumulation in rural contexts has meant the dismantling of agricultural subsidies, credit sources, and marketing boards on the one hand and higher prices for agricultural inputs and household necessities on the other. In both Argentina and Ecuador, agriculture for small farmers has become a precarious occupation, making sources of income other than agriculture necessary for family survival. In highland Ecuador, where indigenous women are working small plots of land while their spouses have jobs in construction or plantations elsewhere, a process usually termed the "feminization" of agriculture has been taking place since the implementation of neoliberal policies in the 1980s. While this term implies that somehow agriculture has changed with men's withdrawal from it, what we are witnessing is simply the persistence of subsistence agriculture, a persistence related not so much to women's fuller participation but to the continued lack of appropriate, accessible technology for pursuing "modern" agriculture combined with the need to maintain low-cost ways to feed the family. Yet gender has been central to how this process has been interpreted. For example, some researchers claim that development workers in Ecuador now go to the farms only on the weekend to get information because otherwise one finds "only women" in the countryside (a comment on the dismissal of rural women's knowledge). Questions are also being raised in the media about how a nation can progress when its agriculture is being undertaken by women who are becoming "masculinized" (Radcliffe and Westwood 1996:152).

But the "feminization" of agriculture does not always take place within the context of subsistence agriculture. I recently visited a tobacco-growing colony in northern Argentina (province of Misiones)[4] to find that far from "helping" men out on the farms, as they have in the past, women are undertaking virtually all of the farming while their spouses work elsewhere. In this case, farmers do not have secure ownership of the 20 hectares of *tierra fiscales* on which they work, and once again production is more labor-intensive than technologically driven; but agricultural production is entirely controlled by multinational companies that buy (and only pay for) the final product, and farmers plant and care for tobacco according to company instructions. While men still apply the required pesticides (the overuse of which is recently being questioned by regional medical doctors and local nongovernmental organizations), women are now knowledgeable about production and the market in a way that seems to surprise even them.

With women's greater control over agriculture within this context, it may be tempting to argue that a hidden consequence of globalization is the increased empowerment of rural women. But such an argument rests on the assumption that empowerment derives primarily from control over production, and the issue of the "masculinization" of women clearly complicates such an argument. The question that needs to be raised is what is "control" in this case and how do we assess who "has" it, a question that, as we see later, can be more fully explored when we consider it from the perspective of time and space.

PROLETARIANIZATION OF RURAL WOMEN

A second trend we can identify is the opportunity for increased paid employment for rural women through globalization. There are numerous studies now of the employment of women by transnational corporations, and the debate continues about whether this is a source of empowerment for women (Levidow 1996; Ward 1990). Ong's (1987) research on Malaysia is unique in its consideration of the radical transformations in concepts of time in such work, and how young rural women struggle with the extended patriarchal constraints placed on them. However, the fragility of such employment is often missed in this debate, a point that makes one question why so much discussion has centered on potential empowerment, since rural women's employment is often quite fleeting. A good example can be seen in the flower plantation industry in highland Ecuador. The flower industry is a perfect symbol of globalization, with its just-in-time production system in other parts of the world so that "we" can have fresh-cut flowers on our dining-room tables. The flower industry emerged in Ecuador with the promotion of "nontraditional exports" in the 1980s; plantations hired primarily rural women who were seen to be better at undertaking repetitive, detailed tasks (Noel n.d.).[5] Yet today the flower industry, faced with maternity leaves and loss of work time, seems to have lost its interest in women employees and is now hiring the "more reliable" men. In the meantime, the employment of both rural women and men in the highlands, combined with the drastic increase in land prices since the entry of the flower industry, has raised concerns about the abandonment of agriculture altogether (Martinez and Barril 1995; Noel n.d.).

This situation leaves young rural women with their one previous option for paid employment, becoming *empleadas* (maids).[6] An unfortunate irony (not lost on employed middle-class feminists in either Ecuador or Argentina) is the extent to which the time of *empleadas*, who are most commonly young rural women, is being squeezed to an even greater extent by the changing working conditions of middle-class women whose paid work time is being expanded by demands for "gringo" *almuerzos* (sandwich lunches, with no *siesta* or *descanso*) and extended hours. In this case, middle-class women's "flexibility" to work longer hours rests on the backs of rural women who—not having *empleadas* to absorb the time necessary for family concerns—are not seen as "reliable" by flower plantation companies.

ENTREPRENEURIALIZATION OF RURAL WOMEN

Becoming entrepreneurial has been stated rather unequivocally as the new goal of development in the post–cold war era. In the globalized world, not only *can* everyone be an entrepreneur, but they *ought* to be, for this would reflect the world as it should be—everyone in perfect competition with each other in a free (of government) world market. There is a tremendous effort afoot to apply this policy specifically to women, who have suddenly been recognized as being entrepreneurial all along, especially in what used to be called the informal sector. This discovery seemed to have helped the World Bank to come to the conclusion in 1993 that investing in women's issues has "consistently high rates of return." The over-

whelming emphasis today on "microenterprises," as opposed to cooperatives or other forms of collective organization, indicates the shift in
orientation, and it is curious the extent to which such policies focus on
women (see Babb 1998; Blumberg 1995; Buechler et al. 1998). The concept
of microenterprises stresses autonomy (minimized dependence on credit and
government), self-initiative, and market "smarts"; development has come
to mean giving women the "tools" to get there.

In rural areas, the focus is on helping women to start their own businesses, so that "they won't be left behind," as one Argentine development
worker put it. This includes programs to give women business skills and
appropriate knowledge regarding the market. One official in the ministry
of agriculture in Ecuador told me that they see such projects as the opportunity "to give women experience in accounting, managing money, figuring
out how to balance expenses and income in order to make a little profit,
to give them experience with this sort of thing so that ultimately they can
operate through private banks." However, in case after case, the assumption that such "tools" are being applied to a level playing field is shown
to be a major problem: the different relations among women and between
women and men consistently undermine the success of new enterprises and
often have negative effects on well-established women's organizations in
the long run (Phillips 1995a).

In globalization's search to make the rural profitable, the above three
trends reveal the potential emergence of class distinctions among rural
women. Perhaps this then should be considered the impact of globalization:
the "seasoning" (Silverblatt 1987a) of rural women for class relations.
However, while this conclusion might tempt a prediction of major transformation in rural women's lives, it is only part of the story—for another
characteristic that we see in these three trends is the precariousness of the
new spaces apparently being offered to rural women. Not only is the feminization of agriculture frowned upon at the national level, and the alternative paid employment opportunities for rural women ultimately limited,
but the promotion of rural women as entrepreneurs seems to be far from
a success story. In order to explain this aspect of the current situation, we
must consider a fourth trend.

DOMESTICATION OF RURAL WOMEN

Theoretically at least, while the feminization of agriculture involves the
stretching of women's time and space in a way that makes their presence
(or absence) in the community or household more open to discussion and
criticism, "domestication" involves situations where a variety of women's
activities, interests, and expectations becomes more circumscribed by the
household and family, and less "relevant" for discussion by the nation,
community, and (curiously) most analysts.

What we might think of as a classic case of women's domestication can be found in K. A. Stølen's book, *The Decency of Inequality* (1996), on rural women in northern Argentina (Santa Fe province). Stølen historically documents the case of Italian immigrants who came to Argentina's northern colonies more than a hundred years ago. They brought with them a "code" whereby women's sexuality is highly guarded and money and land are tightly controlled by men, a situation that women view as "decent" as long as men uphold their responsibility to provide for the family. Stølen argues that women's time and space are strictly curtailed because of their close association with the domestic. This association is so powerful that even when changes in the division of labor do take place—in historical periods when women's labor is needed in the cotton fields or their time is freed up through lower fertility rates—the "complementary hierarchical" plan which places women in the household, dependent on men who have control over money and the market, remains intact. Thus, in the current context, modern technology is introduced into farm production in such a way as to ensure the maintenance of women's domestication through the continuity of gender ideals and practices.

This is a picture of gender relations that does not hold any surprises for us; indeed, it may well fit with our stereotypes of rural women and men's lives anywhere: the women are the mothers/wives, while the men are the farmers. We see women's "flexibility" to move in and out of particular productive and reproductive relations without fragmenting their seemingly constant occupation of domestic space, a case where apparently the more things change, the more they stay the same.

Yet Stølen seems to provide a useful counterpoint to the above example from the nearby province of Misiones. If modern technology moved into tobacco production, would men move back into agriculture or would agriculture in this region be abandoned by small farmers altogether? In either case, would women end up "domesticated"? Or, are there limitations to Stølen's model that complicate ready answers to these questions? To explore this issue further, we need to consider some alternative conceptions of time, space, and power.

TIME, SPACE, AND POWER

If we were to summarize the overall implications of the above four trends, we could argue that capitalism continues to have an uneasy relationship with agriculture (a point that still needs research support in the current context of globalization) and that the maintenance of this difficult relationship depends to a great extent on the flexibility of rural women. But what does "flexibility" mean in this context? Let us reconsider the domestication argument by noting the possibility that the concept of flexibility might have various meanings and implications. Is the domestication of women a portrayal of gender relations that we reproduce because of the limitations of our vision, "seeing" space and time only from the well-entrenched perspective of capitalist discipline? Perhaps in our temptation to map the world as either family or work, we are missing unmappings, the unspoken spaces that women might occupy and shape. Perhaps we are trained only to see how women "spend" time and not how they might *make* time. If they make time to tell stories about their domestic space, is that not a way of naming it as theirs? And if they name it as theirs, is this an indication that their notion of flexibility speaks of a different space-time than that of globalization?

A crucial theme that runs through all the trends suggested above is the assumed importance of maintaining women's responsibility for domestic work. On the one hand, it has been argued that, the concept of flexibility as a central component of "good domesticity" has been emphasized as part of the development of the global food system (Goodman and Redclift 1991). In the current context of globalization, not only does this argument highlight how capital can gain considerable advantage from women's heretofore comparatively *disadvantaged* position of marginality in the labor force (a point that Arizpe and Aranda (1986) noted for women's work in the Mexican strawberry business), but it hints that globalization may be looking to "feminize" the global labor force, not so much in the sense of employing women but in the sense of using the model of women's flexible, jack-of-all-trades-master-of-none labor to transform the characteristics of a good worker. In part this is what Mies, Bennholdt-Thomsen, and Werlhof (1988) mean when they speak of "housewifization" (see also Acosta-Belén and Bose 1995).

On the other hand, however, this point brings us to the difficult place of figuring out whether or not the hegemony of "our" concepts of space and time makes the goal of understanding alternative notions of flexibility impossible, a place that raises the issue of power and how it is *spatialized* within the process of naming, renaming, and not-naming. This is where an analysis of how women might think about and experience time and space[7] offers a different way to conceptualize the "domestication" of rural women and ultimately to address the issues of change, duration, and place in the context of globalization. Specifically, can rural women name space as "theirs" and to what extent and in what way do they do so?

The concept of "women-as-houses" identified by peasant women in coastal Ecuador (Phillips 1990) is useful for this discussion. Viewed from the perspective of time and space, this concept encapsulates women's sense of place: *casas* (houses) are essential for life, a center point around which all other activity must be understood. Though women consider themselves "housewives" here, they distinguish this term from the Western usage by saying that they *are* houses not only in the sense that houses are the places through which women experience and interpret the world but also in the sense that women are the key to the reproduction of a particular way of life. The spatialization of power relations is indicated in the precarious connections men have to *casas* despite the fact that they are generally the household's main source of income. It is expected by women that men will *andar* (wander), but this is part of why women understand their space and time to be so crucial to the maintenance of life. They see themselves as stable and dependable (unlike men); to them the *casa* is seen to be a valuable domain of knowledge to which men are marginal. Moreover, it is women's elaboration as houses that permits them to *andar* well beyond the physical dwellings within which they cook, eat, and sleep. In a sense, they bring their place with them.[8]

This sense of space has particular implications for women's time, for it means that life is not experienced as disjuncture, something to be categorized as distinct intervals, as it is by peasant men. Not surprisingly, I have found it infinitely easier to do life histories with men than with women because women simply do not use the markers that researchers are accustomed to expect. I suggest that it is their different notion of time that explains the difficulties I have had talking to women about change. It was only when we began to discuss their *sueños* (dreams) that I could begin to get glimpses of how women view their world (Phillips 1996). When one does not chart one's life, when life instead is something that one inhabits and reproduces, time is both endless and more elusive. Women's constant visiting with others, and their insistence that others visit them despite the "work" they might have to do, indicates not only that they are able to "make" time, but that they do it for social purposes, to create and recreate an alternative geography, a place in which to live together.

It is because of Steinbeck's concern to grasp the gendered differences of time and space that his book on poor rural families in the 1930s strikes a chord for me. On the page following the quotation opening this chapter, Ma says: "An' that's one more thing a woman knows. I noticed that. Man, he lives in jerks—baby born an' a man dies, an' that's a jerk—gets his farm and loses his farm, an' that's a jerk. Woman, it's all one flow, like a stream, little eddies, little waterfalls, but the river, it goes right on. Woman looks at it like that" (p. 440). We can imagine that capital might have quite an interest in investing in people who think about time as flow rather than as "jerks," since more production can be squeezed into situations where time is not accounted for, as the case of homework suggests. But let us consider here the possibility that because peasant women's time in this case is extended for different purposes than individualist capitalism and is intricately connected to their sense of place—a place which is, I would argue, very different from the sense of space as something to be "conquered" through better planning or new technology—there is a potential for women to maintain a different notion of flexibility over which they can assert a kind of ownership.

Peasant women's notion of space-time is daily negotiated among themselves through gift exchanges and interhousehold visiting. It is something
that older women clarify to younger women as an important place to claim
and maintain. It is used as an explanation for the failure of development
projects seeking to make them profitable. And there are hints that a move
to less familiar contexts, to cities and towns for example, puts this space-
time, and thus women, at risk. In such contexts the work schedules and
demands of male partners, the greater intrusion of television, and the de-
creased connections with other women to share this space leave women
vulnerable. A marked shift from the idea of mothers-as-houses to women-
in-men's-houses takes place. I suggest that this shift marks a colonization
of women's space and time and creates what we might call "homeless"
women.[9] Consider the words of Carmen, a young woman who lives with
Mario (her partner) in a coastal Ecuadorean town, while her mother and
most of her sisters live in the countryside: "Mario used to complain all the
time before I had the baby that I was always out and about and never at
home. He likes me at home. Now with the baby I'm home all the time. He
comes home for *almuerzo* (midday meal) at 1:00 p.m., then leaves again
for work. Then he doesn't come home until about 7:00—and sometimes
he doesn't come home until very late. There are times when I never see
him." That this is Mario's home is made very clear: "He has a bad temper
and *por gusto* comes in and starts complaining about everything in the
house, and makes everyone's lives miserable. I don't say anything. I just
wait for it to blow over." Mario does not want Carmen to work outside
the home, but he gives her money only sparingly, for food "which is usually
gone before the week is up." She tries to make a little extra money for
herself through a lottery that some people on her street have organized.
The television (which is always turned on) occupies a central place in Carmen's home, both for the children (who in this way are kept "out of the
way" when she is cooking, cleaning, and feeding the animals) and for herself (to watch *novelas*, or soap operas). As if to highlight the invasion of
the male world into what would be considered "her" home if Carmen lived
in the countryside, one ad (for a credit card company) that played constantly while I was at her house had a voice-over that said: "Money, money,
money, money—makes the world go around!"

Taken together these examples clarify the disservice we may be doing by
assuming the nature of the domestic unit or by lumping together rural
women who might identify themselves as housewives as the product of
"domestication." We have seen that there are at least two very different
possibilities within this category. One possibility is exemplified by Carmen's
case and Stølen's ethnography cited above, where women appear to have
become disenfranchised from their knowledge and their place, and the
household has become a male, ordered space over which women have little
control. But we have a glimpse in the peasant Ecuadorean case of another

version of spatialized power relations, where women "are" knowledge and place and from which men are marginalized.

The point here is that cultural interpretations of how life may be differently spatialized and temporalized are essential for us to understand in order to make a nuanced assessment of the impact of globalization on rural women. So, for example, let us take our first trend, the feminization of agriculture. Here, once we consider the situation through the lens of space-time, the division of labor "transformations" in the Ecuadorean and Argentine cases cannot be interpreted in the same way. On the other hand, Stølen shows that for immigrant farmers in northern Argentina, the "field" is male space, with inheritance of land going to the eldest male in the family. Women apologize for being visible in this space. On the other hand, for peasant farmers who define themselves as *indigena* in the highland Ecuadorean case, the relationship of gender to agriculture involves a different reading of the spatialization of power relations since historical (and pre-historical) indigenous representations emphasize the complementarity of the division of labor in the agricultural process, with both women and men being required to maintain the fertility of the earth (Silverblatt 1987b). In Andean knowledge systems, conceptions of the "field"—a colonial concept, anyway—did not represent male space but a place where both genders "helped" the land find its strength; and the "home" was not something separate, but viewed as absolutely integral to this process (Gudeman and Rivera 1990). Furthermore, the use in highland Ecuador of indigenous (Quechua) terms such as *ayllu* ("community"), conceptions that cannot really be done justice in English translations, indicates the continued importance of elaborating space-time from indigenous points of view.[10] It is clear that indigenous women's activities are vitally linked to the reproduction of community as a people-in-place, as Weismantel (1988) has ably shown. By persistently knitting together their specific ties with others, rural women create the community spaces undervalued by globalization—both in highland Ecuador, through their responsibilities for maintaining the diet, clothing, and ritual practices of indigenous identity, and in northern Argentina, symbolized by women's faithful serving of *mate* tea to all who visit. As one woman put it to me, "with so many things separating us, at least with *mate* we stay a little more *unidos*."

Such activities are eclipsed by globalization (and indeed by the general policy of the state and international agencies to promote the independent farmer) in the name of modernity. If we think of naming as modernity's attempt to regulate space within this context, some of the labels employed in the four trends outlined above, such as "masculinized" or "domesticated" women, become a little suspect. Who is naming what spaces and for what purposes? To consider Stølen's case again, once we consider *why* domestication is considered to be a "decent" situation by the women involved, other analytical spaces begin to open up. Stølen only hints at the importance of class and modernity in her case, but the existence of a land-less laboring class (*criollos*) seems to be the key to men's control and women's self-regulation of women's sexuality and domestic activities within the landowning community. A central goal of the immigrant landowners is to ensure that land is tightly controlled by them. Thus, domestic value is being named in this case by "modern" farming families as a marker of their superiority within a classist system that benefits both males and fe-males. It is because Stølen does not pursue this line of inquiry that we are left with the characterization of women's work as "timeless" rather than as a response to specific historical conditions.

If we take naming to be an aspect of modernity's power, it is also im-portant to consider that one of the basic assumptions of Western feminism is that naming is a form of empowerment. Consider the phrase "the fem-inization of agriculture," a phrase that emerged primarily from feminist research on rural development to dispel the myth that "the" peasant farmer was always male in the current context and to give greater visibility to rural women's work. However, not only is it unclear whether peasant women themselves view the process in the same way, but it is questionable that such labeling empowered peasant women (indeed, one could argue that it left them vulnerable to national criticism). We should note also within this context that the cases we have considered suggest a difference between Western women's desire for individual space, to have "a room of one's own," and the desire of peasant women, in coastal Ecuador at least, to maintain their place as houses and maintain their linkages with others.[11] Achieving autonomous space permits a spatialization of power relations that does not favor these women; it is considered a dangerous move, easily becoming a space subject to control by others, as we saw in the case of Carmen. It is not surprising then that the evils of living in towns and cities is something about which peasant women in this region constantly lecture their children.

The lesson here is that if rural women are not overtly naming spaces as "theirs," this does not necessarily mean they are not creating them. Peasant women's space-time in coastal Ecuador may be less accessible to research categories that are steeped in the language of exploration, surveying, and measuring but it is nonetheless a place created for and by them. On the other hand, in a society not only dominated by the goals of modernity but also widely recognized (by Ecuadoreans themselves) to be *machista* and "que no quiere dar espacio a la mujer" ("that does not want to give women any space"),[12] such a place must be recognized to be extremely vulnerable. Visibility puts it at risk, a caution to Western feminist researchers who specialize in "explorations" of the Other. Elizabeth Grosz warns men that until they can rethink their appropriative relationship to space and "respect spaces and places which are not theirs, entering only when invited, and accepting this as a gift" (1995:57), women's contributions to alternative ways of conceiving space and place should not be made available to them. Perhaps this stands as an appropriate warning for all researchers as well.

A thorny issue that has long perplexed modern philosophers is how does one theorize the untheorizable? In this case, the question that ultimately has been raised is *should* one? Do we protect these spaces by denying their existence (a practice that does nothing to destabilize our dominant ways of knowing) or do we refine science to detect and monitor such spaces more ably? As social scientists concerned about globalization, perhaps the best way through this conundrum is to ensure that we carefully listen to, experience, and observe the world so that, like good artists,[13] we are able to paint "dense and fibrous, granular and fecund" landscapes that would include maps and charts, of course (for they are indeed a large part of current experience) but that would also include "feints," "whispers," and "rabbit holes" that hint at space-time experiences other than those readily available to us, and at places we can enter "only when invited." Whatever form they take, our landscapes must be able to encourage alternative readings of space and time at the same time that they discourage the desire to occupy and annihilate such knowledge.

CONCLUSION

> Is it possible to kill time
> Without wounding eternity?
>
> —sidewalk graffiti, Quito, 1996

The argument here has been that in order to understand the implications of globalization for rural women, we need to know much more about how the different emerging and merging spaces for women, such as the four trends discussed above, are being locally understood and acted upon and how they link up with alternative notions of time and its allocation. Viewed from this perspective, we have seen that while globalization processes work to fragment rural women's space-time through the development of class relations—a process that constitutes a kind of annihilation for rural women who may understand "all their life to be in their arms"—one of the constraints on such development is the unquestioned linkage of women to the domestic. The latter term has been shown to hold some potential for creating alternative spaces that encompass different notions of flexibility, such as making time for recreating hidden community spaces, that challenge the intentions of the current capitalist assault to tie the individual ever closer to a domestic-defined notion of "work" and a market-defined view of "life."

Joanna Kerr (1995:2) has argued that globalization "has made the international women's movement develop new strategies of multinational resistance. Feminist activities are now pursuing women's equality beyond the parameters of national governments, challenging the de facto policy makers of international financial institutions, transnational corporations and regional trading organizations." While it is important to recognize the potential for developing new alliances to globalize women's concerns within this new context, the other point that I have tried to make in this chapter is that feminist researchers working on globalization issues need to be especially cautious about our assumptions and analytical categories, for they often feed all too well into the (often empty) promises of modernity and globalization. From a truly international feminist perspective, it is important for us to take a step back and think, "is this a world in which women have a *place*?" Or has our notion of space become so masculinized, we would not know a woman's place if we were offered one?

ACKNOWLEDGMENTS

I would like to thank Sally Cole and Suzan Ilcan for their comments. I would also like to thank the rural women in coastal Ecuador who generously offered their space and time to permit the writing of this study. A version of this chapter was presented at the Annual Meetings of the Canadian Sociology and Anthropology Association, St. John's, Newfoundland, 9 June 1997.

NOTES

1. As part of this chapter is about modernity and the power of naming, I am hesitant to use terms such as Latin America and South America which are often used to hide the signification of a less-developed Other. I prefer the term the Other America because it hints at the arbitrariness of such distinctions.

2. I view "global" time as capitalist time and its associated notions of discipline writ large. There are evident cultural variations within global time itself (see Biernacki 1994), though this too is seldom recognized by the armchair globalization theorists.

3. A poster for a recent "virtual" conference on "Power and Integration in the Americas" (FOCAL, April 1997) visualizes the Americas as being integrated via a large electric plug that is inserted into each continent.

4. This observation was made possible through the generosity of Gabriela Schiavoni, who has been working in the region for a number of years (see Schiavoni 1995).

5. This information on the flower industry in Ecuador, and what follows, is based on personal communications with Nicole Noel, who undertook research there in 1997 for her forthcoming M.A. thesis titled "Gender and the Flower Industry in Cayambe, Ecuador."

6. Within the context of globalization, another possible option for women is homework, but this employment opportunity, with its contradictory impact on gen-

der relations, as evidenced in Beneria and Roldan's 1987 study, is much more likely to be available for urban than for rural women.

7. Without an understanding of rural women's perceptions of time and space, we are encouraged to assume that the dominant classes and corporations are completely successful in imposing their vision of the world. This assumption is a limitation of Radcliffe and Westwood's (1996) arguments about time and space in Ecuador.

8. In her analysis of women and architecture, Elizabeth Grosz makes the distinction between *space* "as territorialized, as mappable or explorable," something to be penetrated and colonized, while *place* is "occupation, dwelling and being lived in" (1995:57).

9. Here again I am borrowing from Grosz's analysis: "The containment of women within a dwelling which they did not build, which indeed was not even built for them, can only amount to a homelessness within the very home itself" (1995:56).

10. In considering the case of Ecuador, it is unfortunate that Radcliffe and Westwood (1996) tend to naturalize the concept of cyclical (indigenous) local time, contrasting it with linear (capitalist) national time (1996:83), because the distinction between cyclical and linear time is a fairly recent construction (nineteenth century; see J. Smith in Bender and Wellbery 1991). Moreover, there is much more hybridity to Ecuadorean "capitalist" time than they indicate. One need only note the nationwide hullabaloo about Ecuador switching to daylight savings time in 1992, when it was widely argued through the media that such a change would threaten the country's sense of "natural" time (rising with the sun).

11. To clarify the point about individual autonomy being made here, a self-reflexive note is in order: my own concern about the colonization of women's space struck me as I reconsidered an experience I had as I headed off to do my research last fall. I was in my airplane seat on my way to Buenos Aires, feeling somewhat guilty about leaving my six-year-old who was starting first grade, but at the same time relishing the thought of having "time to myself." So my mind was in "autonomous time" mode when the flight's movie, *Multiplicity*, popped on the screen. This is a movie about a man who uses the latest (secret) technology to multiply himself so that he can maintain his status as a good employee and also become all the other things he really wants to be—a good father, a good cook, and a good husband—and at the same time have some free time for himself (to, of course, play golf). All this is necessary in part because he insists that his wife not work outside the home, despite her preference to do so. This film was so far removed from my own experience that I wanted to scream, and yet all I did was sit there and stare in disbelief at the screen (throwing down my headphones in disgust every five minutes). Rather than thinking about this experience simply as an invasion of patriarchal reality into "my" space, it is perhaps more interesting to think about it as an indication of the extreme vulnerability of women's autonomous space, a space that easily collapses without some collectivity to name it otherwise. Note too that this patriarchal version of reality has a specific message—that technology is a kind of male desire, a desire for another ("freer," even more disembodied) life that does not threaten *existing* privileges. I raise these points because it has been said that Western time has served, and continues to serve, colonial interests. If the time that is currently being globalized can be shown to be a kind of "male-technology time,"

then we need to consider not only the subtle ways in which gender relations in the globe are being prepared to service the needs of such interests but what collective alternatives women might be able to make available for consideration.

12. This quotation is from an article in *Hoy* (7 Nov. 1996:15, insert), one of Ecuador's national newspapers, on the sexual assault of a young woman by fifty-seven male high school students.

13. This connection was made for me through the work of painter Landon Mackenzie, whose York University exhibition was reviewed by Gary Michael Dault, "A Crisscross Journey through Canada's Psyche," *Globe and Mail*, 17 May 1997:E10. The following quotations are from phrases used in the review. I use the metaphor of landscape in a different context in Phillips (1995b).

REFERENCES

Acosta-Belén, E., and C. Bose (1995). *Women in the Latin American Development Process*, eds. Temple University Press.

Arizpe, L., and J. Aranda. (1986). "Women Workers in the Strawberry Agribusiness in Mexico." In *Women's Work*. eds. E. Leacock and H. Safa. South Hadley, Mass.: Bergin & Garvey. pp. 174–193.

Babb, F. (1998). "From Cooperatives to Microenterprises: The Neoliberal Turn in Post-Revolutionary Nicaragua." In *The Third Wave of Modernization in Latin America: Cultural Perspectives on Neoliberalism*, ed. L. Phillips. Wilmington, Del.: Scholarly Resources Press.

Bender, J., and D. Wellbery. (1991). *Chronotypes: The Construction of Time*. Stanford, Calif.: Stanford University Press.

Beneria, L., and M. Roldan. (1987). *The Crossroads of Class and Gender*. Chicago: University of Chicago Press.

Biernacki, R. (1994). "Time Cents: The Monetization of the Workday in Comparative Perspective." In *NowHere: Space, Time and Modernity*, ed. R. Friedland and D. Boden. Berkeley and Los Angeles: University of California Press.

Blumberg, R. L. (1995). "Gender, Microenterprises, Performance, and Power: Case Studies from the Dominican Republic, Ecuador, Guatemala and Swaziland." In *Women in the Latin American Development Process*, ed. C. Bose and E. Acosta-Belén, 194–226. Philadelphia: Temple University Press.

Buechler, H., J. M. Buechler, S. Buechler, and S. Buechler. (1998). "Financing Small-Scale Enterprises in Bolivia." In *The Third Wave of Modernization in Latin America*, ed. L. Phillips. Wilmington, Del.: Scholarly Resources Press.

Escobar, A. (1995). *Encountering Development: The Making and Unmaking of the Third World*. Princeton, N.J.: Princeton University Press.

Goodman, D., and M. Redclift. (1991). *Refashioning Nature: Food Ecology and Culture*. London and New York: Routledge.

Grosz, E. (1995). "Women, *Chora*, Dwelling." In *Postmodern Cities and Spaces*, ed. S. Watson and K. Gibson, 47–58. Oxford: Blackwell.

Gudeman, S., and A. Rivera. (1990). *Conversations in Colombia: The Domestic Economy in Life and Text*. Cambridge: Cambridge University Press.

Kerr, J. (1995). "Globalization Will Set Beijing Apart." *Progressions* (North-South Institute) 2 (1):2.

Levidow, L. (1996). "Women Who Make the Chips." In *Women, Work, and Gender Relations in Developing Countries: A Global Perspective*, ed. P. Ghorayshi and C. Bélanger. Westport, Conn.: Greenwood Press.

Martinez, L., and G. Barril. (1995). *Desafíos del desarrollo rural frente a la modernización económica*. Quito: IICA.

Massey, D. (1991). "Flexible Sexism." *Environment and Planning* 9:31–57.

Mies, M., V. Bennholdt-Thomsen, and C. Werlhof. (1988). *Women: The Last Colony*. London: Zed.

Noel, N. (n.d.). *Gender Relations and the Flower Industry in Cayambe, Ecuador*. M.A. thesis in progress, University of Windsor.

Ong, A. (1987). *Spirits of Resistance and Capitalist Discipline: Factory Women in Malaysia*. Albany: SUNY Press.

Paine, R. (1995). "Our Event-full World . . . the Challenge to an Anthropologist." *Culture* 15 (2):105–16.

Phillips, L. (1990). "The Power of Representation." *Dialectical Anthropology* 15: 271–83.

———. (1995a). "Contested Identities: Rural Women in a Neoliberalizing Ecuador." Paper presented at the CALACS Annual Meetings, Toronto, November.

———. (1995b). "Difference, Indifference and Making a Difference." In *Ethnographic Feminisms*, ed. S. Cole and L. Phillips. Ottawa: Carleton University Press.

———. (1996). "Toward Postcolonial Methodologies." In *Women, Work and Gender Relations in Developing Countries*, ed. P. Ghorayshi and C. Belanger. Westport, Conn.: Greenwood Press.

Radcliffe, S., and S. Westwood. (1996). *Remaking the Nation: Place, Identity and Politics in Latin America*. London: Routledge.

Schiavoni, G. (1995). *Colonos y ocupantes: parentesco, reciprocidad y diferenciación social en la frontera agraria de Misiones*. Posadas: Universidad Nacional de Misiones.

Silverblatt, I. (1987a). "Imperial Dilemmas, the Politics of Kinship and Inca Reconstructions of History." *Comparative Studies in Society and History* 30 (1):83–102.

———. (1987b). *Moon, Sun and Witches*. Princeton, N.J.: Princeton University Press.

Stølen, K. A. (1996). *The Decency of Inequality: Gender, Power and Social Change on the Argentine Prairie*. Oslo: Scandinavian University Press.

Ward, K., ed. (1990). *Women Workers and Global Restructuring*. Ithaca, N.Y.: ILR Press.

Weismantel, M. (1988). *Food, Gender and Poverty in the Ecuadorian Press*. Philadelphia: University of Pennsylvania Press.

4

Challenging Settlement: Rural Women's Culture of Dis-placement

Suzan Ilcan

> Not all nomads are world travelers; some of the greatest trips can take place without physically moving from one's habitat. It is the subversion of set conventions that defines the nomadic state, not the literal act of traveling.
>
> —Rosi Braidotti, *Nomadic Subjects*

In this chapter I focus on the ways in which women challenge the disciplinary space of the household. Specifically, what I am interested in are the social practices that transform and dis-place these most authoritarian and controlling spaces. The conventional understanding of women's place in the "developing" world views the household as a site of gender politics where relations of hierarchy, authority, and power are brought to bear on women and shape them into "subjects" of this social environment. At the same time, however, there has been little research on how women reappropriate these social spaces. What I argue here is that they are not simply subjects of the household space, its timetables, and its routines, but they create, through their collective and recollective strategies, a space and time for themselves. Through these processes women reconstitute their lives outside of institutional arrangements.

In light of these issues, I explore how rural women, through their provisioning of space and time, devise alternative ways of living and thinking that are both political and communal. I begin by setting out the shifting, theoretical boundaries that have encouraged me to think not only about the movement of our ideas but the attractions of movement for women. Primarily through ethnographic illustrations from northwestern Turkey, I examine the conditions under which women live in the settled space of households: the site of duty that often regulates women's time because the caring, feeding, and reproduction of household members (as well as the production and consumption of household goods) presuppose a place for such activities. From here, I show how women shift away from regulated activities and authoritarian relations and create a liminal space from which they are able to speak the unspoken, tell stories, and invoke change. I suggest that this shift calls for the invention of particular relations, where other geographies and forms of agency and empowerment can be engendered. In this transgressive context, women's *nomadic* encounters are shown to produce new perceptions of and possibilities for material life, especially for those who enter into communities and households from the "outside" and establish bonds and mobile coalitions with one another. This nomadic theme is depicted through women's everyday practices and their diverse narratives of dis-placement.

SHIFTING GROUNDS

Most research on women and space in the rural "Middle East" conceives the "private" sphere of the household as a site of women's seclusion and oppression, a place that controls women's identity, mobility, and sexuality. There is no doubt that the spatial and temporal organization of these rural household economies positions particular women in marginal ways. This is due, in part, to endogamous marriage practices, virilocal residence and property inheritance patterns, and the moral codes of behavior that circumscribe stringent gender divisions of labor.[1] However, and in line with new feminist insights against conventional or Oriental depictions of women (e.g., Melman 1996; Khouri 1996; Blunt and Rose 1994; Abu-Lughod 1993; Göle 1991; Mohanty 1991, 1992), it is important to bear in mind that women are capable of changing the disciplinary regime of the household and its settled ways. I think here of Lila Abu-Lughod's *Writing Women's Worlds* (1993) and her concern with the generalizations that have been made about Middle Eastern women and how these have produced a homogeneous, coherent, and timeless portrayal of women's experiences and of "culture." By working against generalizations, by "writing against culture," Abu-Lughod undoes the "typicality" of women's lives so often produced in social scientific accounts. She accomplishes this by illustrating how Awlad 'Ali women contest and challenge common interpretations of "Bedouin culture" through the textual technique of storytelling. In her words, "telling stories . . . could be a powerful tool for unsettling the culture concept and subverting the process of 'othering' it entailed" (1993:13). Similar to this critical ethnographic style, and following some of the feminist reflections of poststructuralism and postcolonialism, I explore how the concept of nomadism is a useful methodological tool for challenging the rigid, institutional views of life and for understanding rural women's movements and their moments of sociality that disturb their practices of settlement.[2]

The concept of nomadism is a metaphorical style and tool of thinking that cultivates alternative accounts and elaborates "new frameworks, new images, new modes of thought." As analysts, it allows us to think through and migrate across established boundaries without burning bridges. It is a move against conventionally bound frameworks (Braidotti 1994) and "outsider" perspectives that are often associated with the sedentary presumptions of modern[3] and colonial constructions of culture. Unlike imperial and colonial discourses, especially their spatial and temporal delineations of power and dependence upon fixed views of "other" people and places, nomadism is a useful theoretical and methodological mode for thinking about the movement of our thoughts, for setting into motion universalized ideas, peoples, and places, and for considering the specific "circuits of travel" (Ong 1995:351). This mode of thinking permits one to question what is taken for granted, what is already in "place," and to disturb "one's own thinking habits" (Minh-ha 1991: 21). It encourages a change in our habits of thinking and a revitalization of the way in which we analyze social relations, such as women's space and time relations. In this way, it involves moving away from always targeting women as victims of hierarchical and disciplinary spaces to a focus on recognizing women's ability to dis-place relatively binding structures and their affiliated practices. This notion of dis-placing routine ideas or activities, what I call a *nomadic disposition*, relinquishes the nostalgia for permanence: it strives to cross boundaries and denaturalize fixed identities, habits, and practices. This concept parallels Minh-ha's discussion of the way in which "strategies of displacement" confront the world of compartmentalization and the systems of ties it generates (1991:23). It resonates with Probyn's "outside belonging," a term used to instill the movement associated with the wishing to belong, particularly the manner in which one's productive desire to belong "places us on the outside" and provides immense political possibilities (1996:9). And it reverberates with Abu-Lughod's (1993) "writing against culture," a powerful concept and tool for refusing to generalize typical particularities and for subverting uniform and eternal accounts of culture.

Perhaps more important, nomadism is a kind of critical awareness that resists *settling* into socially coded modes of thought and behavior (Braidotti 1994:5). People's unsettling endeavors, such as women's activities of movement and contest, signal a minority group's critical awareness about being active and bringing about change, as opposed to living in the past and merely accepting the rigidity of hierarchical relations and chronologically regulated time. In this regard, nomadism coincides with bell hooks' (1990) "politics of location." This "politics of location" involves interrupting "one's place" and creating a space of "radical openness," a new location from which to articulate a critical response to domination and a new sense of the world. Both of these concepts propel and set into motion different possibilities for thinking about one's position and relationships with others. In counterdistinction to inhabitation, nomadism is a way of understanding the process of transformation. It is ultimately about *changing places*: the capacity to dis-place one's habitat and routine habits.

SETTLING IN: DISCIPLINARY SPACES AND SOCIALLY DIRECTED TIME

It is well acknowledged that disciplinary spaces (such as the social institutions of correction and training, schools, workshops, households, and so forth) prescribe gestures and command bodies; they are spaces that confine people to act, behave, or work in particular ways according to chronologically regulated time and labor divisions. As common sites for individualizing and directing groups of people according to a homogeneous orderliness, people here are not born into their places: they need to be trained, socialized, and controlled in specific ways.[4] In patrilocally extended households, for example, senior elders have considerable authority over other household members, and this means that young adults, especially daughters and in-marrying or virilocal women, are, and have been, subject to distinct forms of corporeal inscription and social regulation (Moghadam 1993; Starr 1989; Kandiyoti 1988). Thus these spaces are marked with a certain mode of detailed political investment of the body, where the art of discipline proceeds from the distribution of individuals in an "enclosure," a place different from all others and relatively closed in upon itself (Foucault 1979:139–48). It is in these relative enclosures, which are designed and organized for specific duties and practices, where we also witness the settling of individual habits, lifestyles, and movements.

Disciplinary spaces settle people into particular ways of living. They divide and combine activities into unified motion. Settling into a particular place accommodates socially coded modes of thought and behavior, permitting likely encounters and sources of interaction, experience, and knowledge. For example, in some rural Middle Eastern household dwellings, such as extended households, women are placed in hierarchical positions based largely on age, kin, and authority relations (Moghadam 1993; Sirman 1995:201; Kocturk 1992). This settling potentially situates them in positions of unpaid, domestic, and farm workers and envelops them to spaces of duty, of perpetual and endlessly repeatable tasks that have increasingly little recognition[5] in comparison to paid work positions (see Erman 1997: 264). Especially relevant in this context are the numerous narratives that describe how former peasant women in the community of Arzu in northwestern Turkey[6] have become *confined to the home* ("evlerine kapandi kaldilar") since the development of mechanized farming in the 1950s. One older, male farmer clarifies the changing role of women during this process of modernization:

I bought my first tractor in 1952 and my first harvesting machine in 1953. With the introduction of these machines in the area, there was not even enough work left to be done for men, let alone women. With the use of harvesting machines, the need for sickles was reduced dramatically. . . . After mechanization, women had less to do and their life became more comfortable. They used to bake their own bread and do the laundry manually. Now they have stoves and washing machines. Now they have fridges. Before that, they didn't have them. They now have vacuum cleaners. In the early days, they didn't have carpets. Also, these pull-out beds are new; they weren't available in the old days. They didn't have heaters either; instead, they had ovens in which they would burn coal or wood to provide heat. Today, women's work is easy. They now have water heaters: you press a button and it provides hot water. Now they have drinking water at home; whereas in the old days you had to transport buckets of water from the community fountain.

The modernization of farming in this region, especially the introduction of labor-saving farm technologies, the importation of Western, commercial seeds and fertilizers, and the increasing market demand for agricultural products, has not only produced new divisions based on social class but has restructured lifestyles and social arrangements and reordered the movements of people. Within this format of change, new spatial conceptions of gender and work relations have also emerged. For example, most *modern* men in Arzu are now considered to have acquired the necessary knowledge, technology, and outlook to meet the demands associated with agricultural production, market economies, and commercial exchange relations. They rarely engage in subsistence farming activities, nor do they spend much of their time at home during the planting and harvesting seasons, as they did in the past. Rather, their time has been increasingly geared toward the market through their engagement in an elaborate social network: a network of buying and selling relations in the case of the trade of agricultural commodities, of labor exchanges in the case of the local labor market, of banks and less formal financial "houses" in the case of the circulation of capital. With the increased production of exchangeable goods (along with their transport, delivery, and sale), the extension of town markets, and the expansion of capitalism, the spaces for men now extend far beyond community boundaries and local work sites. Not surprisingly, men leave their marks in places where women do not. They leave their impressions with town bankers, coffee shop owners, and itinerant merchants. They leave their signatures on property deeds, bank notes, and transport licenses. The territories, architectures, and sites that they occupy, and the routine activities they engage in, vary from those of women.

Since the mechanization of farming and the increasing absorption of men in formal market relations, *modern* women in Arzu are now thought to have indolent bodies that just "sit at home." In this context, "sitting" (*oturma*) denotes relaxation or comfort and the verb "to sit" (*oturmak*) means to live or dwell in a place with others. Interestingly, the activity of sitting is perceived in many ways, ranging from the way in which women are now thought to be comfortably settled in their homes to the way in which they, in comparison to men, are thought to be freed from the land. Sitting has now come to mean the opposite of work or the other of work. The use of the term "sitting," especially in reference to what women do, is employed by older generations to indicate women's changed routine habits. Its use not only expunges women's household work and the record of their movements but establishes a fixed image of what women do in households. That is, for women to be known just to sit not only conjures up and controls a present and a future but implies that they are positioned, immobile, that they have an abode. It is only in settled places where women are seen to have a particular place to inhabit, where their apparent sitting habits are considered to liberate them from the constraints of contemporary agricultural demands.

This traditional view of settlement suffers from a number of shortcomings and lacunae. I would like to interrupt this timeless portrayal of women's sitting habits with another image of settlement. Mobilizing this image gives it greater depth and opens up new dimensions. When I think of women's sitting habits, I think about their household work routines, where their daily child care, domestic, and productive activities establish rhythms, regulate the cycles of repetition, and thus order and partition time. The daily chores of planning and preparing meals, taking care of children, husbands, and sometimes the elderly, the weekly tasks of preparing butter, cheese, and yogurt, making bread, washing laundry, housecleaning, and the seasonal demands of garden work, household wall plastering (*siva*), indoor painting, and labor-intensive farmwork (such as hoeing) are the main activities performed by women in Arzu throughout the year. These activities, however, may be performed with changing frequency and intensity, depending on alterations in household size, the use of household technologies, and the presence of in-marrying women. In any case, it is women's movements through household space, exemplified by their planned work routines, that command them. There is *the* time to wash, cook, feed, sew and mend, and to tend to household members' demands and expectations. Like Marx's conception of labor time, the household work routine quantifies time; it portions out the time for certain duties and therefore classifies, estimates, and ranks temporality (cf. Grossberg 1996:179).[7] Thus the activities that occur in the settled space of households fix the meaning of time: time is planned, ordered, and calculated. Women's time is occupied by the spatial routines of the household.

In addition to time and mobility constraints, the obligations imposed on women by older household members (especially on young brides) have disciplinary outcomes. From the very beginning, and upon her arrival in the extended household,[8] a newly married woman is generally not permitted to visit her natal family until forty days after her wedding. It is assumed that after this period a bride (*gelin*) will be settled into her new abode (see also Delaney 1994:161). If she does not already know how to present herself in front of her newly acquired relatives and neighbors, she is taught to show respect to those older than her, instructed to talk and dress appropriately in front of guests, and trained to sit properly. She is also expected to do various household chores, and this work is often concluded with an examination by a mother-in-law who will judge the level of her performance and authorize the necessary improvements. However, while this form of power surveys, supervises, and observes a *gelin*'s bodily behavior and her interactions with others, such technologies of power rarely go unnoticed. A young, newly married woman commented on her sense of spatiality: "I had a very hard time adjusting to the lifestyle here, and I am still trying to adjust. This society is very different from the one I came from. I tell you this house is like an *open-air prison* (*açik hapishane*)." Nevertheless, a well-disciplined bride is considered to be a hard worker, a polite and attentive host in the company of elders and guests, a "good" wife, and a household's mark of distinction: she reveals to others the household members' good judgment in finding a suitable bride for their son (and also for them) and for bestowing the appropriate brideprice (*başlik*).[9]

In Turkey's northwestern countryside, especially in those areas marked by the mechanization of farming and the modernization of household economies, the household is "typically" a place organized for the unpaid work of women and the caring of the bodies of men and children (feeding, clothing, and replenishing activities). This does not mean, however, that women do not transform the settled domain of the household and its timely duties; nor does it mean that this is the only site of women's activity. The spaces within households are much more complex when we consider women's relationship to them. In the context of Turkish rural society, Sirman reminds us that "all social structures open up particular spaces of operation for socially positioned individuals, [and] we should investigate what this space consists of for women and what women do within this space, as well as the means available to them for enlarging its boundaries" (1991: 201).

UNSETTLING: WOMEN'S "NOMADIC" SPACES AND UNDIRECTED TIME

Settled spaces can be displaced through peoples' alternative notions and practices of space. They can give way to new spaces that create new images and new modes of thought. In this process of transformation, one may not have to go far to change one's place or to change places (see Braidotti 1994:

5). In fact, rural women in Turkey and elsewhere have been known to occupy the household not simply as a central site of domestic duty, of social and generational reproduction, but as a nomadic space for socializing and participating in female gatherings, neighborly visits, and informational exchanges.[10] Unlike settled spaces, nomadic spaces do not divide or disseminate populations in a network of relations; they are not cellular or rank-ordered, as there is no partitioning of places for individuals and no individualized places. They do not have the rules of conduct that define for us the meaning of "knowing how to act" or "how to respond" as found in the disciplinary space of households. Instead, these sites offer the potential for creating alternative modes of behavior because there is no one state of affairs given completely, no one set of principles to follow, and no one way to act. It is in these liminal places that place seems to matter most while the place located in the center of things grows ever so predictable and familiar (see Stewart 1996:42). As I discuss below, the most central of locations can be transformed, however intermittently, into places where there is no hierarchical ordering of people and no regulated routines.

In rural Turkey, as in other areas of the rural Middle East and Mediterranean, it is common for women to leave their natal households upon marriage and move to their husbands' parents' home. These women are known as *gelin* ("the ones who come"). Except for unmarried women, and the occasional *kiz kaçirma*,[11] every woman is a *gelin*. This term, however, furnishes a subtle negativism; it not only highlights the foreignness of women who marry into the community but draws attention to their flight of passage and minority status. Women, more than any other group, are expected to abandon their homeland and former identity and to enter into a new place of habitation upon marriage. In fact, married women are said to have come from the "outside" (see also Delaney 1991). I remember when I first heard an older woman identify both herself and her daughters-in-law as *yabanci* ("outsiders," "strangers"), a term referring to those who originate from another community, are descended from other ancestors, and are distinguished from the indigenous, local people (*yerli*). This comment struck me as I imagined over one-half of the community population not really belonging but merely living on the boundaries of the social group. It also alerted me to the stories of spatiality and the tropes of proximity and distance[12] that continually weave relations among people, places, and things.

What does it mean to come from the outside, to be a stranger? I posed this question to myself and to others when the opportunity arose. Is it a position of transmigration, of signaling a capacity to be transferred from one place to another, to be subjected to the twists and turns of social life, to be marked by a sense of loss or separation from a homeland? I recollect the story that Aysel told about a flock of wild (*yaban*) sheep who were labeled *yabanci* because of their "history of lacking a home environment and of being fed in the forest by a lazy *çoban* [shepherd]." I recall the tales about the groups of *çingene* ("gypsies") that traveled to the region to work as farm laborers (for a few weeks every year during the hoeing and planting seasons) and lived in plastic tents positioned beside the main road and isolated from nearby communities. I was warned to stay away from them because "they steal." "They are wanderers," I was informed, "who never stay for long." This statement left me wondering about the large number of rural migrants who settled on the periphery of Istanbul in shantytown houses called *gecekondus* ("built overnight"): were they outsiders too? The numerous experiences and stories of being an outsider were all too familiar to me for I too was an outsider: a Western-trained researcher, with dual citizenship and Turkish "roots," who moved from a permanent place of residence to a temporary abode in another nation. From the perspective of those who consider themselves conventionally naturalized (native, provincial), I had a denaturalized status: I lacked a direct kinship connection to community residents and did not belong to the community from the beginning.[13] However, while this outside(r) status has been and continues to be applied to women in largely exclusionary and sedentary ways, it has a means of not standing still: it tracks the places where one has been, sketches one's territorial crossings, and charts one's historic departure and arrival. We could say then that an outsider's disposition delineates an inventory of passages, of movements: it is nomadic. It compels, even as it rearranges, the relations it interrupts. Grosz goes further and suggests that "the outside or the exterior is what both enables and resists the movements of territorialization and deterritorialization" (1995:131).

Rather than reifying women's outsidedness in tropes of tragedy and isolation or depicting women as the victimized other, perhaps we can unsettle this view by looking at the ways in which women politicize and make use of this imposed outsider status (cf. Abu-Lughod 1993:116–21). I consider it essential to see how women displace their patterns of regulated activities and move out of the disciplinary domain in which they find themselves working and living in most of the time. This is an understanding that works toward exploring how women bring about change in and through time and space configurations. Such a disposition emphasizes the permeability of boundaries and the potential to change places. There is a critical, perhaps a wishful thinking, side to my position: that there must be ways for women to deterritorialize or break up those spaces in which they find themselves settled in order to challenge their patterns and practices of settlement. This position, as Braidotti would say, "is the intense desire to go on trespassing, transgressing" (1994:36). The vital, though unsettling, value of this position is that it makes you increasingly aware of the construction of gendered culture, the creation of spatial boundaries, and the rhythms and ordering of time.

The ability to transform the household's disciplinary space into a nomadic one is influenced by a particular conception of time quite different from modern time. Modern time is directed and planned. It is dominated by those spaces where things are produced and invested: time recorded on measuring instruments, time spent working, time assessed in terms of value, money, and the production of commodities (Lefebvre 1991:95–96). However, a time that is not administered or managed is one that allows women to displace the household and its habitual routines. Minh-ha (1991:19) suggests that "displacement involves the invention of new forms of subjectivities, of pleasures, of intensities, of relationships." I would add that in order to engage in this process of change, an undirected conception of time is necessary. When undirected time trespasses on social spaces (as opposed to the control of time by movements in "modern" spaces), then there is the potential for women to have visions and wishes and to tell stories. Such reflections on social life are not only politically valuable but also migratory: they incorporate a notion of the future and a distancing of the past. As I illustrate below, women populate the household's threshold, a space of "outside belonging" that challenges their regulated positions and designates a profound manner of shared nomadism for women. Their contacts with female neighbors in the form of economic cooperation, informational exchanges on domestic decision making, local healing remedies, bride searches, as well as their discussions on household politics and conflicts (especially those between women and their in-laws), highlight their sharing of outside differences. Especially when they engage in activities that have little to do with being settled or under the rule of authority figures, they reach an ability to do things differently: to unfold autobiographical histories, to tell stories, and to disappear from household duties and time-bound routines for a while.

There are particular times when, and spaces where, women embrace change and fluidity rather than fixity. The *kabul günü* ("reception day") is a good example of a female gathering that takes place in the nomadic space of households and involves activities separate from those that characterize the settled space of households. As a visiting pattern practiced in other regions of Turkey,[14] the *kabul günü* (locally referred to as simply *günü*) is a well-organized event. Once a host receives permission from her husband to hold such an affair, she is responsible for inviting individual women to her home on the designated reception day. These invited guests are typically young married women from varied social class groupings but from similar ethnic backgrounds. Such visits generally take place in the household of a designated host about twice a month, especially during the spring and summer months, and include twenty to forty women. More important, however, the reception day creates a space to challenge those master narratives that "speak a war of positions" (Stewart 1996:97) and locate women in traditional reproductive and caring roles. It is a time for women to talk openly about their lives as *gelin* and to highlight the issues and struggles they face as women who have entered the community from the outside. It is for these reasons that men and mothers-in-law are not invited to such events for they are often perceived as the source of tension and conflict.[15]

Women's narratives during reception day events reflect an untiring distaste for settlement. The themes of these narratives range from issues of marriage, family life, and restricted spatial mobility to those of education, economics, and community politics. An important thread running through these stories is the way in which women tell them from another point of view or from a nomadic disposition. To clarify the use of this concept in this particular context, the term "nomadic" refers to an alternative mode of thinking and awareness that allows women to question common cultural assumptions and sedentary views of life. By "disposition," I am not only referring to women's outside(r) status, which certainly uproots them as well as grants them a particular character, but to their ability to challenge their place of settlement. It is for these reasons that these stories are worthy of reproducing here, if only to get a sense of women's "comings and goings."

Reception day events take place in a nonauthoritarian space and in an untimely manner. They are infused with critical accounts of the past, present, and the future, of stories pertinent to women's lives. On one occasion a newly married woman, who had a grade five education and was dissatisfied that she did not have more, spoke of gender as a site of struggle and of the injustice that families impose on their female children. Her narrative not only moves uninterruptedly from one vantage point to another, from outside to inside, and vice versa, but it elaborates a description of the territories that are crossed in a woman's journey. It also alerts us to a conception of the "way things are managed" and "the way things could be managed."

There are no limits for men. More opportunities are provided to men, and there aren't enough opportunities given to women. I always argue about this point with my father. He rented a car and took my brother to school every day. He could have done the same thing for us [her three sisters]; at least he could have sent us to *orta okul* [middle school], but he didn't. If you ask him why, he will say "even if my daughters earned a higher education, their husbands wouldn't let them work." So, because he would have to spend all that money on us for nothing, he thinks women's education is pointless. There are a few women here who finished university, but they aren't allowed to work. My uncle's daughter finished a two-year university program, and she was the district governor's secretary. Later on she got married, and they [her husband and his parents] wouldn't let her work. They said to her, "stay at home and do the housework; later on you will have a baby, and you will look after your children instead of hiring a babysitter." So they don't allow her to work.

Like this woman's story, other narrative accounts emphasize women in transit and their experience of what it means to be displaced, or what Minh-ha calls "living in-between regimes of truth" (1991:21). Hayriye, born at the beginning of the 1970s and raised in a farming community several hours' drive from Arzu, told the story of her marriage to a local man, her move to his parents' house, and the difficulties of living "here." She began by recounting her life as a farm girl, the close friends she had back home, and her love for her natal family whom she rarely sees now. She highlighted the intricacies of her engagement and arranged marriage to a man whom she described as having completed both high school and the mandatory military service, a rare accomplishment in the eyes of most people, given that he had come from a poor family that did not own much farmland or technology. After asking her if she would talk about her move to Arzu, her storied recollection turned to her difficulties of adjusting to a new place, a new family, a new way of life. With confidence in her voice, she said: "When women marry and come here, they leave their families and their friends behind. Sometimes it is many days later, even weeks later, when you find out about the things that have happened back home. My family is far away from here. As you know, I can't just go and visit them. Last year I visited my family once during *bayram* (a religious holiday). . . . I am obliged to be here: to look after our house, to prepare the food, to feed the animals, to help my mother-in-law." After the other women joined in the conversation, telling their own experiences of moving to and settling in the community, Hayriye posed the question:

What do I have here? Of course, I do have my children and my husband, but I cannot do the things that I would like to do. I cannot always go where I want without first getting permission (*izin*). Before I can visit my relatives or even visit my neighbors, I must ask my husband and his parents. . . . This life is not what I had really expected. It was not my wish to live in the countryside with my in-laws or to do what they demand from me. But what choice do I have now? . . . Still, I have made a life for myself here. I guess you could say that I have adjusted. I have friends, I have my neighbors. . . . I have wishes too. When I was a little girl my mother used to tell us that "our wishes are our possessions" (*tek varlığımız dileklerimiz*).

What kinds of things do you hope for, I asked. With much enthusiasm, she replied by saying that "someday, I wish to move to [a nearby town] and have our own house, with a garden, like we have here. . . . I would like my children to have a high school education and maybe go to university. *İnşallah* (if God wills)."

Shared by many women, these alternative views of another place and another time interrupt an attachment to settled ways and evoke new visions. The yearning for a different kind of life or the telling of a wish foregrounds the notion of dislocation. Each is a form of reflection on the temporality of existence conveyed through a present translation of an experience in the past.[16] Through their ability to seize what is taken for granted and unravel it to new and varying levels, women are able to think differently and recognize other ways in which they can live outside their routine lives. This is an important feature of women's shared narratives and experiences in nondisciplinary spaces. Having similar household positions and perceptions of relocation and adjustment, their outside(r) standing is, and has been, critical for invoking the positive effects of reception gatherings, especially the development of a collective awareness of their relations with others. As Grosz claims, "the marginalized position of the exile, at the very least, provides the exile with the perspectives of an outsider, the kinds of perspective that enable one to see the loopholes and flaws of the system in ways that those inside the system cannot" (1993:69).

Women's shared reflections and narratives in less formal gatherings than those of reception days also express a dynamic mode of questioning and of rethinking one's positionality. In fact, the most common and near-daily gatherings take place when women visit their female neighbors, usually during the day—and between mealtimes—when their husbands and fathers-in-law are laboring in the fields, purchasing goods from the town market, or participating in activities within the all-male coffeehouse. In these gatherings, the disciplinary, household space becomes transformed into a nomadic one, a place where women exchange information, share ideas, and tell numerous stories of their settled lives, restricted travels, and their past experiences. During one household gathering, an older woman, reflecting a historical knowledge of shifting grounds, recounts and recasts how women's travels from one home to another required justification. Her story also reveals that "sitting" is not a woman's choice.

In the old days, women weren't able to go out and visit friends. When I first came here [forty-five years ago], women used to look outside from their doorsteps. They weren't able to see one woman on the street. Women were always in the garden. If they really had to go out and visit someone, they used to wear a veil and cover themselves. Only then, in the company of other people, could they go out, pay the visit and come back again in the company of the same people. Only the old people (büyükler) in the family visited neighbors, and if you wanted to go with them, you had to follow them. We always had to sit at home.

In remembering the stories that her sixty-three-year-old mother-in-law told her, a younger women echoed similar sentiments of the past in the context of the changing present. Her story, only partially recapped here, locates women's agency in shifts and transitions and highlights the complexity of women's place in a specific culture of time and space.

In the past, women weren't able to go out much. Now we are able to go out. For example, in the old days it was harder to go and visit someone. You first had to finish your housework and then maybe you could go and visit your friend once during the winter. Women were only able to visit one family during the winter, but they visited their neighbors frequently. My mother-in-law used to tell me that people didn't have the habit of visiting each other like they do now; now, a man can see his close friends at the coffee shop and their wives can see each other at home. Years ago, women . . . couldn't visit each other because they had to spend most of their time working, working in the fields. . . . They weren't even able to do their needlework; they had to come home from the fields, cook the dinner, get water from the fountain, do the laundry, and make bread at night after spending the day in the fields. The following morning, they would take their bread with them and go to the fields.

No matter how minute, mundane, or meticulous, these stories are mobile: they disrupt the boundaries of women's routine lives, they move in and out of history, and they compel connections among women.[17] Moreover, they are shaped and influenced by a concept of undirected time that is distinguishable but not separable from space. As Bakhtin reminds us, "time, as it were, thickens, takes on flesh, becomes artistically visible; likewise, space becomes charged and responsible to the movements of time, plot and history" (1981:84). The importance of this time, the time to tell stories, occurs at those points when women's positions and locations in settled spaces become interrupted. Undirected time not only marks change but is *about* change. The trespassing of undirected time over space envelops a fluid and fragmented sense of space where women can challenge the practices of their settlement. It is for this reason that expressing new visions and telling wishes are so significant: they are not tied to a present but are constantly on the move.

Living on the edge, so to speak, potentially enables rural women to alter the "spectatorship" of the center[18] and traverse disciplinary boundaries. Although women are the ones who have been brought in from the "outside," they are the ones who have also brought with them new questions and who have dealt with their social and spatial displacement in ways that introduce change. Over the past several decades, especially since the modernization of farming, women are seen as the ones responsible for slowly challenging "Ottoman" women's dress codes, movements, and positions. In the face of authoritarian regimes, arranged marriages, and "forced" migration, women, as I have shown, do question the norms and confront the practices of their settlement. They have struggled to develop ties with others by establishing cooperative female networks: farmwork groups, reception day assemblies, neighborhood gatherings. As an important feat for women, these networks permit them to exchange private information on the economic affairs of and conflicting demands within their households, to question, through storytelling, their rank within the hierarchical order of things, and to develop different ways of envisioning their lives with others and of initiating social change. These changes range from breaking down the barriers of women's household isolation to devising new strategies and ways of knowing that permit women to assess and negotiate the forms of control imposed on them. Thus women's lived materiality of being "outsiders in the inside" has in effect politicized their disposition. Through their shared activities in unsettled places, women are able to think differently and produce alternative accounts of their experiences, for they are the ones who have the great capacity to import new qualities and strategies into community life and to remind us of the other, perhaps not so visible, dimensions of dwelling. It would be erroneous to assume, then, that women merely operate within institutional frameworks and cultural value systems without interrupting them.

A PARTING NOTE

The metaphors of nomad, migrant, and exile have been used by analysts to convey a sense of process, flow, and transversality in the spatiality of social life and to cross the meanings of center and margin, inside and outside, private and public. The conventional views of women's space and time have emerged within those universal frameworks such as modernization, disciplinary regimes, and the institutionalization of social life. However, in order for us as analysts to highlight the diffuseness of women's place and politics, we need to be able to deal with the constraints of those settled and tradition-bound perspectives that have a habit of keeping us in our place, of encouraging us to stay focused on those dominant social structures without ever recognizing their openings. By ignoring these constraints, we face betraying peoples' struggles in the specific ways in which they practice and live them and in the places in which they surface. This is why, in Kirby's words, "we cannot afford to naturalize the boundary, though we must analyze boundaries that have been naturalized in order to break down their rigidity. We cannot afford to reify the distinction between 'inside' and 'outside,' though in formulating a politics, we cannot abandon either space but must continually traverse the difference" (1993:189). We should, therefore, not underestimate the numerous effects that materialize when women change places and thereby create an "alternative geography,"[19] a heterogeneous place from which to challenge the practices of settlement. As I have suggested in this essay, it is here, in a space for telling, that women's politics of telling forge a critical awareness among women. These displacement practices force us to reconsider how disciplinary spaces are lived, how women refuse to sit still, and how important these nomadic alliances are in the processes of social change.

ACKNOWLEDGMENTS

This research was supported by a grant from the Social Sciences and Humanities Research Council of Canada. I am grateful to Selma Eren for her valuable contributions to this research project, Alper Özdemir for arranging and processing some transcribed materials, and the Turkish authorities for granting me permission to carry out the field research component of this project. I would like to thank Sema and Zeynep and Ender G. and Tulu G. for their generosity and hospitality during my stay in Turkey. A special thanks to Daniel O'Connor and Lynne Phillips for their comments on this chapter. Most of all, I remain deeply indebted to the women and men in northwestern Turkey whose struggles and stories around gender and culture made this analysis possible. A version of this chapter was presented at the European Sociological Association Conference (University of Essex), Colchester, England, August 1997.

NOTES

1. For more extensive discussions on these issues in specific areas of the rural Middle East, see, for example, Keddie (1990), Moghadam (1993:104–9), Ghorayshi (this volume), and Ilcan (1996a, 1996b).

2. These practices often have a reserved place in the popular discussions of "the" Islamic Middle East.

3. See Barrett and Phillips (1992) on the value of destabilizing modern social theories and practices for the purpose of formulating new feminist visions.

4. See Ilcan (1998b) for more on disciplinary and marginal spaces.

5. See Grosz (1995) on women and dwelling.

6. The ethnographic materials in this chapter derive from field research carried out in an agricultural community (Arzu, pseudonym) in the region of Trakya (Thrace) or "European" Turkey during the summer of 1996. In Arzu (pop. 235) and in the surrounding area, local inhabitants identify themselves as Sunni Islamic, reckon descent in patrilineal terms, support arranged marriages and virilocal residence, and live mainly in three-generational households. Their major economic activities include capital-and labor-intensive agricultural work, household reproductive work, and some animal husbandry. Moreover, there exists a strict gender division of labor. Men are largely responsible for capital-intensive farmwork, market and commercial transactions, and the repairing and upgrading of farm equipment. Women do most of the labor-intensive agricultural work, household-related chores, child care activities, and the feeding and caring of farm animals.

7. See Grossberg (1996:179) on how the timetable controls movements through space.

8. I use the term "household" to refer to those people who live together as a domestic unit as well as a dwelling unit. Household membership in this region, as well as in other areas of Turkey, is generally based on kinship through marriage and descent.

9. Disciplinary strategies characterize the domain of family households not only at the community level but at the level of the nation-state. This is evident in state policies and civil codes pertaining to matters of family, gender, and property relations in Turkey (see N. Arat 1996:403; Y. Arat 1996:29). The government's monitoring of parental and conjugal relations in claims of citizenship and its regulation of license marriages, property inheritance, divorce, and child custody procedures are among the most controlling tactics used to authorize aspects of family life, sexuality, and reproduction and to partition people into certain locations.

10. See also Tapper and Tapper (1987) and Sirman (1990, 1995) for more on female gatherings in Turkey.

11. The literal translation of this term is "girl kidnapping." It mainly applies to couples who have "run away" to get married without parental approval.

12. See Ilcan (1998a) for a more elaborate discussion of spatial proximity and distance.

13. See Simmel (1950:402–8) for a theoretical discussion of the phenomenon of the stranger as a condition and symbol of social relations.

14. For a discussion of this visiting pattern in cities and towns of Turkey, see B. Aswad, "Visiting Patterns among Women of the Elite in a Small Turkish City," *Anthropological Quarterly* 47 (1974):9–27; P. Benedict, "The Kabul Günü: Structured Visiting in an Anatolian Provincial Town," *Anthropological Quarterly* 47 (1974): 28–47.

15. Sirman (1995:212) also notes that rural women's gatherings are important for discussing issues not generally broached in "mixed company."

16. See Bell (1994) on dreaming, time, and dislocation.

17. See Hanson and Pratt (1995) for an interesting discussion of women's "mobility stories" in contemporary Worcester, Massachusetts.

18. See Minh-ha (1993) for more on the hegemonic unification and representation of occupied territories.

19. See Shields (1991) for a compelling analysis and discussion of the "alternative geographies" of modernity.

REFERENCES

Abu-Lughod, L. (1993). *Writing Women's Worlds: Bedouin Stories*. Berkeley: University of California Press.

Arat, N. (1996). "Women's Studies in Turkey." *Women's Studies Quarterly* 1–2: 400–411.

Arat, Y. (1996). "On Gender and Citizenship in Turkey." *Middle East Report* (Jan.–Mar.):28–31.

Bakhtin, M. (1981). *The Dialogic Imagination*. Austin: University of Texas Press.

Barrett, M., and A. Phillips. (1992). "Introduction." In *Destabalizing Theory: Contemporary Feminist Debates*, ed. M. Barrett and A. Phillips, 1–9. Stanford, Calif.: Stanford University Press.

Bell, V. (1994). "Dreaming and Time in Foucault's Philosophy." *Theory, Culture & Society* 11:151–63.

Blunt, A., and G. Rose, eds. (1994). *Writing Women and Space: Colonial and Postcolonial Geographies*. New York and London: The Guilford Press.

Braidotti, R. (1994). *Nomadic Subjects: Embodiment and Sexual Difference in Contemporary Feminist Theory.* New York: Columbia University Press.

Delaney, C. (1991). *The Seed and the Soil: Gender and Cosmology in Turkish Village Society.* Berkeley and Los Angeles: University of California Press.

———. (1994). "Untangling the Meanings of Hair in Turkish Society." *Anthropological Quarterly* 67 (4):159–72.

Erman, T. (1997). "The Meaning of City Living for Rural Migrant Women and Their Role in Migration: The Case of Turkey." *Women's Studies International Forum* 20 (2):263–73.

Foucault, M. (1979). *Discipline and Punish: The Birth of the Prison.* New York: Vintage Books.

Göle, N. (1991). *Modern Mahrem. Medeniyet ve Örtünme.* Istanbul: Metis Yayinlari.

Grossberg, L. (1996). "The Space of Culture, the Power of Space." In *The Post-Colonial Question: Common Skies, Divided Horizons,* ed. I. Chambers and L. Curti, 169–88. London and New York: Routledge.

Grosz, E. (1993). "Judaism and Exile: The Ethics of Otherness." In *Space and Place: Theories of Identity and Location,* ed. E. Carter, J. Donald, and J. Squires, 55–71. London: Lawrence & Wishart.

———. (1995). *Space, Time, and Perversion: Essays on the Politics of Bodies.* London: Routledge.

Hanson, S., and G. Pratt. (1995). *Gender, Work, and Space.* London and New York: Routledge.

hooks, b. (1990). *Yearning: Race, Gender, and Cultural Politics.* Boston: South End Press.

Ilcan, S. (1996a). "Fragmentary Encounters in a Moral World: Household Power Relations and Gender Politics." *Ethnology* 35 (1):33–49.

———. (1996b). "Moral Regulation and Microlevel Politics: Implications for Women's Work and Struggles." In *Women, Work and Gender Relations in Developing Countries,* ed. P. Ghorayshi and C. Belanger, 115–31. Westport, Conn.: Greenwood Press.

Ilcan, S. (1998a). "The Marginal *Other*: Modern Figures and Postmodern Dialogues." In *Postmodernism and the Ethical Subject,* ed. B. Gabriel and S. Ilcan. Ottawa: Carleton University Press. (in press).

———. (1998b). "Occupying the Margins: On Spacing Gender and Gendering Space." *Space and Culture* 1 (3): (in press).

Kandiyoti, D. (1988). "Bargaining with Patriarchy." *Gender and Society* 2 (3):274–89.

Keddie, N. (1990). "The Past and Present of Women in the Muslim World." *Journal of World History* 1 (1):77–108.

Khouri, D. (1996). "Drawing Boundaries and Defining Spaces: Women and Space in Ottoman Iraq." In *Women, the Family, and Divorce Laws in Islamic History,* ed. A. Sonbol, 173–87. Syracuse: Syracuse University Press.

Kirby, K. (1993). "Thinking through the Boundary: The Politics of Location, Subjects, and Space." *boundary 2* 20 (2):173–89.

Kocturk, T. (1992). *A Matter of Honour: Experiences of Turkish Women Immigrants.* London and Atlantic Highlands, N.J.: Zed Books.

Lefebvre, H. (1991). *The Production of Space*. Translated by Donald Nicholson-Smith. Oxford and Cambridge: Blackwell.

Melman, B. (1996). "Transparent Veils: Western Women Dis-Orient the East." In *The Geography of Identity*, ed. P. Yaeger, 433–65. Ann Arbor: University of Michigan Press.

Minh-ha, T. (1993). "All-Owning Spectatorship." In *Feminism and the Politics of Difference*, ed. S. Gunew and A. Yeatman, 157–76. Halifax: Fernwood Publishing.

———. (1991). *When the Moon Waxes Red*. New York and London: Routledge.

Moghadam, V. (1993). *Modernizing Women: Gender and Social Change in the Middle East*. Boulder, Colo., and London: Lynne Rienner Publishers.

Mohanty, C. (1991). "Under Western Eyes: Feminist Scholarship and Colonial Discourses." In *Third World Women and the Politics of Feminism*, ed. C. Mohanty, A. Russo, and L. Torres, 51–80. Bloomington: Indiana University Press.

———. (1992). "Feminist Encounters: Locating the Politics of Experience." In *Destabilizing Theory: Contemporary Feminist Debates*, ed. M. Barrett and A. Phillips, 74–92. Stanford, Calif.: Stanford University Press.

Ong, A. (1995). "Women out of China: Traveling Tales and Traveling Theories in Postcolonial Feminism." In *Women Writing Culture*, ed. R. Behar and D. Gordon, 350–72. Berkeley: University of California Press.

Probyn, E. (1996). *Outside Belongings*. New York and London: Routledge.

Shields, R. (1991). *Places on the Margin: Alternative Geographies of Modernity*. London and New York: Routledge.

Simmel, G. (1950). *The Sociology of Georg Simmel*. Translated and edited by K. Wolff. New York: The Free Press.

Sirman, N. (1990). "State, Village and Gender in Western Turkey." In *Turkish State, Turkish Society*, ed. A. Finkel and N. Sirman, 21–52. London and New York: Routledge.

———. (1995). "Friend or Foe? Forging Alliances with Other Women in a Village of Western Turkey." In *Women in Modern Turkish Society*, ed. S. Tekeli, 199–218. London and Atlantic Highlands, N.J.: Zed Books.

Starr, J. (1989). "The Role of Turkish Secular Law in Changing the Lives of Rural Muslim Women, 1950–1970." *Law and Society Review*, 23 (3):497–523.

Stewart, K. (1996). *A Space on the Side of the Road: Cultural Poetics in an "Other" America*. Princeton, N.J.: Princeton University Press.

Tapper, N., and R. Tapper (1987). "The Birth of the Prophet: Ritual and Gender in Turkish Islam." *Man* 22 (1):67–92.

5

Reconstituting Households, Retelling Culture: Emigration and Portuguese Fisheries Workers

Sally Cole

Nazaré is a fishing town and tourist destination 150 kilometers north of Lisbon from which more than 200 families emigrated during the late 1970s and early 1980s to work in the commercial fishery on the north shore of Lake Erie in southwestern Ontario, Canada. Nazaré is also, these emigrants say, "not only a place on the map; it is a space in the heart; it is a way of life." Calling themselves *nazarenos*, these men and women carry with them an image of Nazaré as: a fishing way of life that they define as a legacy of Portugal's proud maritime history and a product of the country's North Atlantic coasts and landscapes; an oppositional consciousness derived from a history of social discrimination and objectification by a landowning elite and urban bourgeoisie; and a women-centered set of household relations that incorporate endogamous and uxorivicinal marriage and residence patterns and a gendered division of labor defining women as workers and as managers of household resources. *Nazarenos* emigrate in order to reproduce this "storied space" of Nazaré, which they see as fundamentally located in the reconstitution of households whose members earn their livelihood from fishing. Thus they emigrate to places around the world where they can find remunerative employment in fishing. The majority see emigration as temporary, as a sojourn that will enable them to return and retire in the geographical place of Nazaré.

In her moving cultural history of the devastated landscapes of the Appalachian coal mining camps of southwest Virgina, Kathleen Stewart, in her book, *A Space on the Side of the Road*, encourages us to understand history not as "an accomplished fact" or master narrative (of "progress" or "exploitation," for example) but as what she describes as "an occupied space of contingency and desire in which people roam" (1996:90). Stewart locates history instead in the images that people mobilize in the stories they tell—in their "just plain talk"—about the places and "things" of their world. The element of desire is a crucial explanatory variable in culture-making which, according to her, is undertaken through practices of re-membering and retelling. For culture, in Stewart's terms, is "a space of imagination, critique and desire produced in and through mediating forms . . . [and] performed and imagined in precise practices of retelling" (1996: 9). In this chapter, following Stewart, I explore the spaces of desire in the practices of transnational culture-building of Portuguese emigrants in Canada. Specifically, I consider gender and household relations to be, in Stewart's terms, primary mediating forms of culture and the reconstitution of households in emigrant contexts to be a practice of "retelling culture." Much as Stewart's Appalachian coal miners invest cultural desire in their re-memberings of the ruins and "things" of an apparently ravished and abandoned landscape, Portuguese migrant fisheries workers in transnational spaces invest the everyday practices of constituting households and making a livelihood with historical memory and the desires and longings of culture. Emigration for *nazarenos* is a search over a global landscape for the possibility to maintain a way of life based on fishing and to reconstitute households—the relations of everyday life—as they are remembered in the rural fisheries of Portugal. Thus emigration as a search for that desired space is itself a practice of retelling culture.

Fieldwork and the oral recording of life stories of Portuguese emigrants on Lake Erie and in Nazaré between 1990 and 1995 revealed that both men and women see the household as the focal point around which transnational reconstitutions of *nazareno* culture revolve.[1] The household is at once a physical place within which men and women carry out the work of production and social reproduction and a symbolic time-space that ties *nazarenos* to a historical past and a presently distant place. In the relations of everyday emigrant life, the household is the idiom through which *nazarenos* express and measure their closeness to the physical and symbolic space, Nazaré. Thus, on the one hand, the household is a receptacle of romantic nostalgia for Nazaré and a locus of emotions that, over centuries of emigration, Portuguese have coded as *saudades*.[2] In these terms, the emigrant household is what some might call a "resting place of identity" (Hanson and Pratt 1995:22). On the other hand, because households are defined by the articulation of relations of production and reproduction in everyday life, they are necessarily continually constituted and reconstituted and are thus dynamic and continually restored spaces. That households in emigrant contexts are not only places of re-membering but spaces of desire and imagining render them primary analytical sites for theorizing the relations of culture and economy.

Although the men and women in this study understand the household and the gendered division of labor to be central to the practice of and desire for a *nazareno* way of life, they also experience households as internalizing differentiated gendered (and aged) spaces. That is, whereas households as units are important mediators of relations of the exterior world, their interiors incorporate different spaces for different household members. Households thus embody both unity and difference and, as a result, contradiction and tension. Cross-cultural research over the past two decades has revealed that the household is the social institution that mediates the structural tensions of political and economic conditions and within which individuals mobilize as cultural actors and makers of their own destinies. This research has also revealed that, whether engaged in subsistence production or structured on wage-based consumption, households do not always represent the shared and unified interests of their members. Despite the effort and desire of members to construct the household as a unit, forces external to the household often impact in ways that divide individuals within households. These divisions usually occur along age and gender lines (Grasmuck and Pessar 1991; Harris 1981; Hartmann 1981; Young 1978). This study documents the efforts of one group of men and women to mobilize the household as a resource in the struggle to make a livelihood, to reconstruct a way of life, and to retell the story of Nazaré.

HOUSEHOLDS AS STORIED SPACES

Households based on fisheries production emerged in Portugal in the nineteenth century as a direct result of social stratification and inheritance practices. In efforts to control population density and increase agricultural productivity, landowning households had begun to consolidate property in the hands of a single heir. Where, formerly, properties had been divided equally among children, increasing numbers of sons and daughters were being left landless or land-poor. Massive emigration was one response, but in coastal areas some men and women moved to the state-owned shoreline where they squatted and began to develop a new pattern of subsistence based on the exploitation of seasonally available maritime resources and on efforts to reclaim the sand dunes for gardens through the use of fertilizer produced from seaweeds harvested and dried by women. The temporary or serial migration of male members of these households—to work in fisheries in Brazil or in the annual cod fishery off the coast of Newfoundland—emerged as a necessary part of the household subsistence strategy and, over generations, as a cultural expectation and masculine gender role. High rates of male emigration diluted men's kin ties and tended to strengthen women's kinship ties as they intensified matrifocal relations of social and economic support and uxorivicinal postmarital residence patterns. With the likelihood that sons would emigrate, parents developed a preference for a daughter, usually the youngest, to care for them in their old age and to inherit the house upon their death. Women also often inherited boats, fishing gear, and gardens. And, in the frequent absence of men, some women also became boat owners, captains, and crew in the local fishery. These relations of residence, property, and inheritance, in conjunction with women's economic roles as producers of seaweed fertilizer, subsistence gardeners, and fish-sellers, created the "matrifocal" (Brøgger 1987) or "women-centered" (Cole 1991) households that characterize Portugal's maritime communities. Local adages such as: "ser mulher é ser trabalhadeira" ("to be a woman is to be a worker") and "a mulher é a governadora da casa" ("the woman is the manager of the household") affirm women's economic importance. Women characteristically describe themselves as "a comandante da família" (the commander of the family).

Central to the relations of maritime production, the social construction of woman as worker and manager is further mobilized in the development of an oppositional class consciousness, for it exists in strong contradistinction to the ideal of woman as dependent *dona de casa* (housewife) that prevails in wealthy agricultural and urban bourgeois households. Strategic inversion of local symbols of status helps consolidate the "culture of opposition" that close-knit fishing communities give birth to in efforts to define autonomous (and counterhegemonic) social spaces. Recruited, as they are, from the lowest strata in a local hierarchy based on land ownership, fishermen and women in Portugal, as in other predominantly agricultural nations of Europe, tend to be subordinate socially, economically, and politically to their landowning peasant neighbors and kin. This history has generated highly endogamous societies and ethnic subgroups whose members are active in the construction of cultures of opposition rooted in the relations of production and of everyday life. As the point where social and economic production daily intersect, the household has become both a repository for and a refuge from symbolic class struggle. In addition to legitimating women's economic importance in the gendered division of labor, members of landless fishing households positively contrast their own values of communality, egalitarianism, and generosity to what they describe as the privacy, avariciousness, and selfishness (*egoísmo*) of landowning, agricultural households. They further declare themselves direct descendants of Portugal's sixteenth-century maritime explorers reliant on their courage, hardiness, and skill at extracting the communal resources of the sea without the security of land-ownership. This construction of self and other developed in a social context in which landowning peasant farmers describe fishermen and women as "ill-bred," "dirty," "lazy," and "drunkards" (*mal-educados, porcos, preguiçosos y bêbados*) (Cole 1991:42–54).[3]

In Canada, an oppositional consciousness rooted in the historical development of Portugal's rural fisheries is mobilized as a resource for emigrant survival. For in transnational contexts, fishermen and women retell the story of Nazaré when they maintain the continuity between emigrating to fish on Lake Erie and Portugal's historic prominence in maritime exploration and as they reconstitute household spaces where women's economic production is esteemed and the values of communality, egalitarianism, and generosity are upheld.

THE LAKE ERIE FISHERY

Wheatley (pop. 2,000), Leamington (pop. 12,500), and Kingsville (pop. 5,500) are neighboring towns located in a 40 kilometer stretch along the north shore of Lake Erie about a 45 minute drive east of Windsor and Detroit. Seventy-eight "tugs" (gillnetters and trawlers) fish from the ports of Wheatley and Kingsville primarily for perch, pickerel, and smelt. Approximately 600 men (one-third of whom are Portuguese), working in five- and six-person crews, are employed on the boats. Seven processing plants employ about 500 workers year-round (more in peak season), mostly women, more than one-third of whom are Portuguese. The largest and oldest is Omstead Foods in Wheatley, founded in 1911. In addition to fish products, the Omstead plant cooks and freezes a variety of vegetables and, in peak season, may employ as many as 600 workers. Since the 1970s, several new plants have been built including, in 1984, Italian-owned Lake Erie Foods, which employs eighty workers and, in 1986, Portuguese-owned Pressteve Foods which employs sixty. Four other smaller plants each employ an average of thirty workers.

Before World War II, the Lake Erie commercial fishery was a masculine industry both on the boats and on shore. Fish was packed in the round, on ice, sold whole, and picked up by American packer steamers and transported by truck to New York and Chicago. Employment of women began with labor shortages of men during World War II and continued in the postwar period as the industry changed from packing to processing. In the late 1940s, with the development of refrigeration technology, Omstead's had begun to produce fish sticks, fillets, and other frozen foods. The marketing of frozen convenience foods expanded in the 1950s along with the elaboration of standards of housework and the male breadwinner-female housewife ideal held by increasing numbers of North American middle-class households. Relying as it did on hand filleting, industrial fish filleting became linked to women's food preparation in the home and the fish plant itself became understood as a woman's workplace.[4] In 1950 Omstead's employed thirty women as filleters. By 1972, two-thirds of workers in fish processing and packing were women, mainly Portuguese and Italian immigrant women; by the 1990s, all employees except mechanics and equipment operators were women.

The conditions of work within this new women's space were significantly different from the conditions of women's work in Portugal's rural household-based fisheries. Women who effectively had been self-employed in Nazaré as fish-sellers, boat owners, employers, and managers of a household economy become pieceworkers in mechanized plants where their comportment is supervised and the knowledge and skills needed to maintain the cooking and freezing technology is held by men. The women are paid per kilogram of fillets, the piece rate depending on the species and availability of fish—conditions over which they clearly can have no control. Although the women were once partners with their husbands in a household enterprise in Nazaré, in the Canadian context, women's wage work is seen as an extension of their domestic work in food preparation in the home and viewed by their employers as secondary to the wage earnings of their husbands. Men, on the other hand, have reproduced labor relations similar to those in the Nazaré fishery in that they are paid on a system of shares. Under the share system in the Lake Erie fishery, 50 percent of the boat's earnings go to the boat owner and 50 percent is shared among the crew members.

1970: *NAZARENOS* "DISCOVER" LAKE ERIE

Like other men from Portugal's coastal communities, numbers of *nazareno* men have annually signed on for the six-month voyage to the centuries-old cod fishery on the Grand Banks off the coast of Newfoundland. A masculine rite of passage, at about the age of fourteen, young men would join the "White Fleet" and make as many voyages as they needed until they had cash enough to invest in small boats to take up fishing locally in Portugal and to marry and establish households of their own. Some men continued this seasonal round, making as many as forty voyages during their lifetimes (Cole 1990). During the Salazarean regime, men could avoid the compulsory military service by signing on for six years in the state-run cod fishery. In the 1960s and early 1970s when military service had meant active combat in the so-called Colonial Wars in Mozambique and Angola, more *nazareno* men opted to join the cod fleet. The life of a cod fisherman was arduous, dangerous, and poorly remunerated, however, and the men actively sought alternatives. Throughout the 1960s, a few men each year would decide not to return to Portugal at the end of the season and instead migrated up the St. Lawrence River to Toronto. Here they found work in restaurants, hotels, and in food services at the airport—far from fishing. By the late 1960s, there was a thriving Nazaré Club in the Canadian city.

In the spring of 1970, four *nazarenos* rented a car and drove down to the port of Kingsville on Lake Erie. One of these men, Manuel Costa, explained: "We heard there was fishing on the lake. We wanted to see if we could get work fishing because, really, we are fishermen. We from Nazaré are a fishing people. We went to the docks, told the boat owners that we wanted to fish, and asked if there were any jobs. They said 'Sure,' and so we fished through May and June. There were lots of spaces on boats, lots of work back then." The men returned to Kingsville the following season with their wives, who at first found work as pickers for local farmers but were soon integrated into the fish-processing sector. Over the next few years word spread among *nazarenos* about the available work for both men and women and, among Canadian employers, of the availability of skilled and industrious workers. Manuel explained: "Employers wanted us to work for them. There were no quotas [on fish] back then. We could fish as much as we wanted. We wanted to earn as much as possible, and we were prepared to work day and night. We were there to work, to fish. That's all we wanted to do." When fish prices fell during the 1970s, Canadian fishermen began to sell their boats, and a few enterprising Italian and Portuguese immigrants, who had generated capital (through diverse means but often through construction), began to buy into the industry. They actively sought *nazareno* workers, and by 1982 there were more than 200 *nazareno* families living in Leamington and working in the commercial fishery.

Margarida Gonçalves, who came to Canada in 1973 with her mother and two brothers to join her father, began work as a filleter in 1979 when she turned seventeen. She describes the *nazareno* household strategy:

The whole family worked in fishing—the fathers worked on the boats; the mothers worked making and mending nets or filleting fish; and sons and daughters quit school just as soon as they could to join their parents. We all worked for the household, and this way we could earn sometimes as much as $80,000 in a year with the whole family [mother, father, daughter, and two sons] working. It was a family operation. The whole purpose of the family coming in the first place was to work in fishing. We were here to fish, and we planned to return to Nazaré. And that's the way it's been with the *nazarenos* for ten, fifteen years now. Kids never questioned their parents. As teenagers we all wanted to get out there and earn money. And most of the girls knew they'd be marrying soon anyway. Some families used to send their daughters back to Nazaré for the summer with a mission: she was to find a husband. She would come back engaged, and then the family would find work for her fiancé on a boat and bring him over. That's just starting to change a little now—but still most girls don't finish high school and most still get married in their teens.

Emigrating to work in the Lake Erie fishery enabled husbands to bring their families with them and enabled wives and teenaged children to earn wages to contribute to the household. In Canada, *nazarenos* seek to maintain the household ideology of the Nazaré fishery by symbolically constructing the household as a production unit that recruits labor from within its own ranks, whose members contribute their earnings to the household, and whose resources are managed by the wife and mother. The men consider that the more they fish—the longer hours they put in and the greater volumes of fish they catch—the more work they give directly to their wives, daughters, and mothers who are paid on piece rate in the plants. Husbands and wives, sons and daughters see their work as directly interconnected and mutually beneficial to their households. It is this reconstitution, both material and symbolic, of the *nazareno* household that mobilizes household and gender relations as images of Nazaré in transnational retellings.

AÇORIANOS AND *TRÁSMONTANOS*

When *nazarenos* began to settle in the Lake Erie communities in the 1970s, they found a resident population of about 1,500 Portuguese who had, in the 1950s, emigrated from the islands of the Azores, *os açorianos* (approximately 300 families), and from Trás-os-Montes, the interior mountain province of Portugal, *os trásmontanos* (about 40 families). Important differences among these three groups serve to maintain the heterogeneity of Portuguese-speaking immigrants in the region and to highlight the particular characteristics of the *nazareno* migration. As in Portugal, the occupation of fishing and the social organization of household and gender relations separate *nazarenos* from their compatriots.

Azoreans came to Canada in the early 1950s in response to Canada-Portugal joint government initiatives to recruit labor to work on Canadian farms and on the national railroad after the war. As Wheatley resident Tony Perreira remembers it: "I arrived in Halifax by ship in March 1954 along with my brother-in-law and 100 other men. A Portuguese government official came with us. We were a kind of cargo that Portugal was exporting to Canada." His experience is typical.[5] In his first year his jobs included building greenhouses, planting tomatoes, picking tobacco, working in a bowling alley, and washing cars. By the end of his second summer, through a fellow *açoriano*, he had secured employment in a wood products company in Wheatley where he worked for the next twenty-seven years. By 1975, the company employed 120 men, 75 percent of whom were *açorianos* from Tony's hometown, Faial da Terra. Once settled, the men had brought over their wives and children, the women quickly finding jobs at the Omstead plant. Many second-generation Azoreans, women and men, continue to work for Omstead's; others commute to manufacturing and service sector jobs in the city of Windsor. *Açorianos* return rarely, if at all, to Portugal. They are committed to building their futures in Canada, serve on the local town council, and intermarry with members of other ethnic groups in the area including Italians and Anglo-Canadians. They emphasize family values, the Catholic church, and a strong work ethic in the raising of their children, most of whom find blue collar jobs immediately upon finishing high school.

Trásmontanos are concentrated in Leamington. Although few in number,

as founders and managers of the Portuguese Club, they are prominent locally as the official "brokers" of Portuguese culture. Unlike *açorianos* who
were recruited, *trásmontano* men and women migrated independently and
for a variety of reasons. Some took up greenhouse farming, but most work
in the manufacturing sector. Upwardly mobile, they emphasize higher education for their children, both sons and daughters, several of whom have
graduated from university. Some have invested in rental-income properties
and have become landlords in Leamington. Unlike *açorianos*, who are
firmly committed to a future in Canada, and *nazarenos*, who plan to return
permanently to Portugal, *trásmontanos* build retirement homes in Portugal
with the intent of living part of the year there and part of the year in
Canada. *Trásmontano* Miguel Borges explains: "We work for the education of our children. I have worked so hard. When my daughters finish
university, I'll quit. I'll go back to Vilar [his community of origin] when I
want, come here when I want."

WORK, ETHNICITY, AND HOUSEHOLD IN TRANSNATIONAL RETELLINGS

In work, intraethnic relations, and household and gender relations, *nazarenos* retell the story of Nazaré in their everyday lives in Canada. Work
in fishing brought them to Lake Erie. As briefly outlined above, local historical and economic conditions intersected with *nazareno* patterns of emigration and offered attractive labor and lifestyle possibilities through work
in the commercial fishery. The historical moment of their arrival coincided
with low fish prices in the early 1970s and with the expansion of the auto
industry in Windsor, which lured the sons of fishermen. The resultant labor
shortages opened up positions for *nazarenos* in the fishery. When aging
Anglo-Canadian fishermen began to sell their boats and licenses at low
prices, some Portuguese were positioned to become boat owners and employers. To pay off their loans, new owners (who were primarily Portuguese and Italian) intensified their effort in fishing by increasing hours and
days of fishing, and in 1984 the Canadian government introduced a quota
system to stop overfishing and manage fish stocks. The immediate impact
of quotas was that it was no longer possible for owners to increase their
earnings by increasing production. Instead, their incentive became to decrease the costs of obtaining their allocated quota (Berkes and Pocock
1987). They sought to reduce the costs of production by reducing labor
costs, by reducing the size and number of crews, and by attempting to
reduce crew shares from 50 percent to as low as 42 percent. In the processing sector, owners sought to reduce costs to compensate for what they
anticipated would be reduced volumes of fish by cutting the piece rate and
thus reducing women's income-generating potential.

The attempts to reduce the crew's share and to cut the piece rate affected both men and women and directly challenged *nazareno* emigration strategy. The earning potential and future of *nazareno* households in Canada were threatened by the actions of boat and plant owners, some of whom were themselves not only Portuguese but also fellow *nazarenos*. Men on the boats and women in the plants united in a series of strikes that resulted in the formation in 1987 of the Great Lakes Fisheries and Allied Workers' Union (now Local 444, Marine Division, Canadian Autoworkers Union). Unionization heightened *nazareno* sense of difference from other Portuguese in Leamington and crystallized latent class conflict within the *nazareno* community itself. Intergenerational differences within *nazareno* households were also heightened as some parents refused to participate in the union. In these cases, parents remembered the assistance employers had given them in their first years in Canada: Portuguese employers had often paid for air tickets to and from Nazaré or helped families to find housing or obtain social services and landed immigrant status. In most cases, however, *nazarenos* targeted the new-found wealth and apparent changed lifestyles and values of their Portuguese employers in attempts to affirm the egalitarian ethos and share system that they remember as central to life in Nazaré. *Nazareno* owner-employers had themselves come from the same poor fishing households as their workers. Slashing the tires of employers' Mercedes or vandalizing their ostentatious homes in Leamington was, from the workers' point of view, a public remembering of *nazareno* communality and culture.

Nazarenos also actively "occupy" (in Kathleen's Stewart's terms) the symbolic space of Nazaré in their management of intraethnic relations with *açorianos* and *trásmontanos*. As Manuel Costa tells us, *nazarenos* see themselves as "a fishing people." Emigration is understood as "following the fish," that is, following the possibility of making a livelihood in fishing. When fishing in one location fails, *nazarenos* will move to another. They understand that when working in the Lake Erie fishery is no longer a rational economic strategy for the household, they will move elsewhere on the globe. Unlike *açorianos* and *trásmontanos* who take whatever jobs they need to earn a living, who work in multiethnic settings and intermarry with members of other ethnic groups, and who envision their futures in Canada, *nazarenos* remain determined to work in fishing and locate not only their pasts but their futures in the symbolic and storied space of Nazaré. Rarely do *nazarenos* invest in their children's education or in boats and licenses to advance in the Canadian fishery. Capital is accumulated less for private gain than for public affirmations and re-memberings of Nazaré that include: investment in boats, small businesses, and retirement homes in the town of Nazaré; return visits to Nazaré, especially at Christmas; designing costumes and staging communal events to celebrate Carnival in Leamington; teaching children the folkloric dancing of Nazaré; and, for a few years, supporting a Nazaré Club in Leamington.

The risks and dangers of maritime occupations further separate *naza-renos* from their Portuguese compatriots and strengthen notions of inter-dependence and communality. On 16 September 1983, three men drowned (three others swam to safety) when the Jorge B, a vessel owned by a fellow *nazareno*, sank in Lake Erie a mile from shore. In a public ceremony their bodies were flown home for burial, and the collective outpouring of grief among *nazarenos* was intensified by a universal perception of the great sadness of dying away from Nazaré. Communal grief was subsequently further intensified by the difficulty the widows have had in receiving any compensation. The tragedy is frequently remembered in everyday conver-sation—particularly the employer's perceived lack of aid and generosity to the widows—further heightening *nazareno* consciousness of their separate-ness from other Portuguese in the region, mobilizing *nazareno* resolve to return finally to Nazaré, and crystallizing incipient class tensions in rela-tions with employers.

Household and gender relations are a third sphere that *nazarenos* ne-gotiate in diasporic retellings of Nazaré culture. The households of Lake Erie fisheries workers appear to resemble those in Nazaré. As Margarida described, fathers and sons work on the boats; mothers and daughters work on shore; all contribute their income to the household. As in Portugal, *nazarenos* are highly endogamous, and the homes of the fisheries workers are clustered together on a few streets in Leamington. And, as in Nazaré, socializing is public and sex-segregated: men in the taverns and cafés; women on the street and in the donut shops and bakeries. Women are not strongly identified with domestic work, and, like men, they enjoy social-izing outside the home.

Açorianos and *trásmontanos* negatively measure *nazareno* gender and household relations against their own and are especially critical of *nazareno* women who, they say, spend too much time outside the home and do not aspire to the *dona de casa* (housewife) role that is ideologically dominant for women in *açoriano* and *trásmontano* households (although they too are wage workers). They also vividly described isolated instances of male phys-ical dominance in *nazareno* households. For *açorianos* and *trásmontanos*, the home is the center of family life and socializing takes place in private homes, not public spaces. For *nazarenos*, however, work—not home—is the center of family life, and socializing in donut shops and bars is time spent talking about work—for both men and women. Not incidentally, the local critical commentary of *açorianos* and *trásmontanos* reproduces middle-class ideals of gender roles in the larger Canadian society while, at the same time, bearing a marked resemblance to the historical stereotyping and stigmatization of fisherfolk in Portugal. "You'll never meet a more ignorant people," one Portuguese employer in Leamington told me. An Azorean woman who had worked almost twenty years at Omstead's, de-scribing her *nazareno* co-workers, said: "Nazarenes are impolite, uneducated, rough. The women are domineering. The men are drunkards. We Azoreans would rather have nothing to do with the nazarenes."

Household and gender relations are clearly focal points of cultural practice and consciousness. At the same time, they serve as barometers of change in social and economic relations. Subject to external critique and judgment, insiders simultaneously are experiencing tension and contradiction in relations within the household. Both men and women are ill at ease with emergent changes in household organization and uncertain of the implications of the changes, particularly the shift away from women-centeredness. For, increasingly, in the emigrant context, husbands and fathers consider themselves to be, and are considered by their wives and daughters to be, the decision makers in the family. Household members also describe men as having more authority within the household in Canada than they had in Portugal. In contrast to fishing communities in Portugal where women always speak for the household and men are subordinate to women (Brøgger 1987; Cole 1991), in the Canadian research, *nazareno* men invariably spoke for the household and women would only speak or agree to be interviewed when their husbands were not present.

Two conditions may help explain this reconstitution of gender relations within households in the Canadian context. First, as *bacalhoeiros* in the centuries-old seasonal migration to the Newfoundland cod fishery, most *nazareno* men have prior experience of Canada and with Canadians. It was also men who had "discovered" the Lake Erie fishery. *Nazareno* men are, as a result, often more at ease living in Canada than are women. More men than women are comfortable speaking English. Women who in Nazaré dominated social life, public and private, defer to husbands' and fathers' greater knowledge in interactions with the wider Canadian society. Men, for example, navigate the household's interactions to obtain banking and health care services. Women and men thus collaborate in awarding men greater authority within the household because of their perceived greater familiarity with Canada. Second, in the share system of remuneration in the Lake Erie commercial fishery, men effectively have reproduced *nazareno* labor relations and some have bettered their positions as boat owners and employers. *Nazareno* women, however, are no longer working as managers of household-based fisheries. They are wage workers in the industrialized processing sector subject to lack of control over their time, wages, and working conditions. In the eyes of their employers and in the wider context of Canadian society, their work in fish processing is ideologically linked with women's unpaid domestic work in the home. The wages women earn as pieceworkers in the plants are inferior to and directly dependent on male production on the boats. In the plants, women work under the supervision of male managers and owners; men also control the technological skill and knowledge required to operate the plants. Women's working conditions in the fish plants thus parallel those of women who work in the home and are dependent on men as primary wage earners and household heads. This local (and global) construction of women's industrial work poignantly affects everyday relations between men and women within *nazareno* emigrant households. These external constraints challenge emigrant efforts to reconstitute a *nazareno* world in Canada.

LISETTE AND FERNANDO'S RETELLING

I met Lisette in the Lake Erie Bakery owned by a *nazareno* couple, Aora and João. Before opening the bakery, Aora had worked twelve years as a filleter in the fish plant where her women customers still work. When they first came to Canada, João had worked as a member of a fishing crew. He later bought his own boat, but after several years of misfortunes had recently had to sell the boat. I had taken to going to the bakery about mid-morning, several days each week in order to be present when the women came either at the end of a workshift or to gather for morning coffee on the days when they had not been called in to work. There were five *nazarena* women who usually sat together and who gradually welcomed my company. I had been introduced to them by João who explained that I was "writing a book of stories." He said that I spoke Portuguese, that I had "heard his story," and that "it's easy: everybody has a story." The women, initially, were nervous—and so was I. But over the next few weeks we became comfortable with one another. The women appreciated that I knew the coastal fishing towns of Portugal, including Nazaré, that I had previously written about women's hard lives as workers and household managers, and that I myself was a working woman and had to "suffer" by being away from my husband and children in order to do this "writing work." The women were at different stages in the life cycle and in different economic circumstances. But there was a closeness between them generated through their years as co-workers at one of the local fish plants and as compatriots from Nazaré but also because they all have energetic approaches to constructing their lives. They seemed to enjoy recounting the drama of their lives not only to me but to one another. João likened the storytelling in the bakery to public confession, saying I was "como um padre" ("like a priest").

Maria Virginia had left her husband on their twentieth wedding anniversary a few months before. She had rented a small apartment for herself and had left him in the house with their teenaged children. She was adjusting to her new status with difficulty but with the help, she said, of her *nazarena* (women) co-workers. Thirty-eight-year-old Maria Julia had been widowed with four sons when the *Jorge B* sank in 1983. She supported her household through work as a filleter, but when there was no fish she had no income and was desperately poor. She had received no compensation from her husband's employer, a compatriot, and was helped by her *nazarena* co-workers and by her older sons, who now work on the boats. Aora hired Maria Julia as a cleaner both in the bakery and in her home. Irene was a happily married woman with grown-up children whose husband had come to fish on Lake Erie initially on a seasonal contract. A few years later, with the aid of his Italian Canadian employer, he had obtained landed immigrant status and brought his family to join him in Canada. The couple, happy with the conditions of their employment, loved Canada and planned to stay. Mila was working in Canada in order to return to Nazaré to live in the house she and her husband had built there. It had been her husband's idea to emigrate, and Mila had reluctantly agreed to join him, bringing their two children. She worked as a filleter for a few years but had been unhappy and, unable to persuade her husband to return to Nazaré, had returned herself with the children. After four years of living apart, she had rejoined her husband in Canada because she wanted "a minha lar unida" ("my family united"). They had had another baby "to make me happier," but she's still longing to return to Portugal to live. When we talked in the spring of 1991, she had been laid off from the plant because of the slow season. She was distraught to be without work. "I know my children would go [to Portugal] with me, but I'm waiting for my husband. I don't want to divide the family again. In the meantime, I have my friends [indicating her co-workers at the table]." Mila was hoping the decline in fishing would help convince her husband that it was time to move back to Nazaré.

It was Lisette, however, who dominated the group whenever she was present, and I came to understand that she represented a local success story and a cultural ideal for *nazarena* women in Leamington. Lisette was a strikingly beautiful, large-boned woman with shoulder-length naturally wavy dark hair. She was always well dressed when she came to the café. She wore a black trench coat, a long flowing burgundy paisley skirt, lots of gold jewelry, and black suede high-heeled shoes with gold bars across the back of the heels. Lisette was in her early thirties and had two daughters, then ages nine and eleven. She and her husband had emigrated to Canada as a young married couple ten years before. Both from fishing families, they had come during the mass emigration of *nazarenos* to Leamington in the early 1980s with the express purpose of saving capital to invest in building a fresh fish restaurant back in Nazaré and working in the expanding tourist industry there. They had pursued this goal together, he on the boats and she as a filleter, and were preparing to return permanently to Nazaré for the official opening of their restaurant, The Rosamar (named after their daughters, Rosa and Maria). "Já tenho a vida arranjada" she explained. The other women nodded to me in affirmation: "She has her life/livelihood all organized."

A year later in March 1992, I spent several weeks in Nazaré and regularly ate meals at The Rosamar Snack-Bar e Restaurant. With its walls covered with blue-and-white ceramic tiles and decorated with fishing nets, models of fishing boats, and black-and-white photographs of Nazaré and *naza-renos* in days gone by, the restaurant is like many others in Nazaré that cater not only to foreign tourists but, and perhaps more important, to urban bourgeois Portuguese who come for fresh fish meals, healthy sea air, and a renewed closeness with Portugal's historic past as a maritime nation. Bearing little resemblance to my memory of her in Canada, Lisette, now working with her mother in the restaurant's kitchen, looked much like her mother and other women of fishing households in Nazaré. Her lovely long hair was held back and covered in a tam. She wore a plain gray fitted skirt, covered with an apron. Her sweater sleeves were rolled up, and on her feet she wore the ubiquitous *chinelas* (flip-flops) worn by *nazarena* women. She was very busy and effervescently happy: "I'm very happy here. I'm very busy in the restaurant. Business is going well. Moreover, I'm close to my family again and my beautiful homeland ("Mais, eu é ao pé da minha família e da minha linda terra"). My husband misses Canada more than I do." Lisette plans that her two daughters will soon be able to assist her and her mother in the business.

For Lisette's husband, Fernando, the story is different, however. Fernando's role in the enterprise is to greet customers and to serve those who seat themselves at the bar rather than at one of the fifteen white-clothed tables. Behind the bar, Fernando talks of *saudades* (reminisces nostalgically) for his fishing days on Lake Erie, expresses a disinclination for his present work as a restaurant owner, and plans his future emigration to work on an industrial trawler in Germany, which, since Portugal's 1992 entry into the European Community, has become the new destination for Nazaré's fishermen.

CONCLUSION

One story that is told here is of households that were women-centered in the small-scale fisheries of Portugal becoming increasingly male-headed in Canada where both men and women work in the paid labor force. This story contributes to the literature on the impact of women's waged labor on immigrant households (Di Leonardo 1984; Iacovetta 1986; Lamphere 1987; Zavella 1987). The Lake Erie case contrasts with the documented rise of female-headed households particularly in Latin American and Caribbean contexts, where men increasingly are marginalized in the informal economy and women are sought as cheap female labor in the export-led industrialization that tends to characterize these regions (Safa 1995). Emergent changes in the structure of emigrant *nazareno* households and in the character of gender relations have been described here as due in part to: men's and women's often different histories of emigration and men's prior experience in Canada; the different labor relations in which men and women are engaged in the Lake Erie fishery; and the gendered cultural construction of their work in the Canadian context.

But *nazarenos* are also described here as reinterpreting this script in diverse and creative ways, mobilizing culture as an inexhaustible resource. Lisette remembers *nazareno* households as women-centered production units, and, working on a transnational stage, she seeks to reconstruct her own household in this image. Her husband Fernando's retelling of *nazareno* culture, on the other hand, draws on the masculine history and experience of emigration. For them (as for the ethnographer), culture is continually imagined and reenacted through the practice of everyday life. For the fishermen and women of Nazaré, culture is not an end in itself and is never finally "gotten right" (Stewart 1996:5–6), but is always "in-filled with desire" and, ultimately, an ongoing process of reconstitution and retelling.

ACKNOWLEDGMENTS

This research was funded by a grant from the Social Sciences and Humanities Research Council of Canada.

NOTES

1. Field research was conducted between 1990 and 1995 during more than a dozen field trips ranging from one week to two months in duration. Participant-observation included: visiting the fish plants and interviewing workers, union stewards, and plant owners; talking to crew members on the docks in Wheatley and Kingsville as they returned to shore with loaded boats; spending mornings in the Portuguese bakery on the main street in Leamington where women gathered on days when there was little or no fish to fillet; and evenings at Tim Horton's donut shop, which between 8 and 9 p.m. becomes, according to local people, "Little Nazaré," as women and their small children gather at the end of a day's work. In addition, I recorded eighteen individual life stories (nine women and nine men) and nine detailed household case histories (three from each of the three internal communities—*nazarenos*, *açorianos*, and *trásmontanos*). In the spring of 1992, in Portugal, I interviewed *retornados* (returned or retired emigrants from Lake Erie) in Vilar de Perdizes (Trás-os-Montes) and in Nazaré.

2. On the importance of *saudade* in Lusophone cultures, see, for example, Brettell (1986) and Feldman-Bianco (1992).

3. For cross-cultural and historical perspectives on fisherfolk as stigmatized and subordinate populations in Europe, see Löfgren (1979:98), Nadel (1984:104), and Smith (1977:8).

4. Understanding transformations in gendered conceptualizations of workplaces is aided by recent writings of feminist geographers like Doreen Massey, who urge us not to think of places as static and bounded but rather as "articulated moments in networks of social relations and understandings" (1993:66). Places (including workplaces) are locales of dynamic social relations that are linked to wider sets of

local and global relations and that are transformed with changes in and among these wider sets of relations.

5. The pattern of Azorean immigration to Canada has been well documented. See, for example, Anderson and Higgs (1976).

REFERENCES

Anderson, G., and D. Higgs. (1976). *A Future to Inherit: Portuguese Communities in Canada*. Toronto: McClelland and Stewart.

Berkes, F., and D. Pocock. (1987). "Quota Management and 'People Problems': A Case History of Canadian Lake Erie Fisheries." *Transactions of the American Fisheries Society* 116:494–502.

Brettell, C. (1986). *Men Who Migrate, Women Who Wait: Population and History in a Portuguese Parish*. Princeton, N.J.: Princeton University Press.

Brøgger, J. (1987). *Pre-Bureaucratic Europeans: A Study of a Portuguese Fishing Community*. Oslo: Norwegian University Press.

Cole, S. (1990). "Cod, God, Country, and Family: The Portuguese Newfoundland Cod Fishery." *Maritime Anthropological Studies* 3, (1):1–29.

———. (1991). *Women of the Praia: Work and Lives in a Portuguese Coastal Community*. Princeton, N.J.: Princeton University Press.

Di Leonardo, M. (1984). *The Varieties of Ethnic Experience: Kinship, Class and Gender among California Italian Americans*. Ithaca, N.Y.: Cornell University Press.

Feldman-Bianco, B. (1992). "Multiple Layers of Time and Space: The Construction of Class, Race, Ethnicity, and Nationalism among Portuguese Immigrants." In *Towards a Transnational Perspective on Migration*, ed. N. G. Schiller, L. Basch, and C. Blanc-Szanton, 145–174. New York: The New York Academy of Sciences.

Grasmuck, S., and P. Pessar. (1991). *Between Two Islands: Dominican International Migration*. Berkeley: University of California Press.

Hanson, S., and G. Pratt. (1995). *Gender, Work and Space*. London and New York: Routledge.

Harris, O. (1981). "Households as Natural Units." In *Of Marriage and the Market: Women's Subordination in International Perspective*, ed. K. Young, C. Wolkowitz, and R. McCullagh, 49–68. London: CSE Books.

Hartmann, H. (1981). "The Unhappy Marriage of Marxism and Feminism: Towards a More Progressive Union." In *Women and Revolution*, ed. Lydia Sargent, 1–41. Boston: South End Press.

Iacovetta, F. (1986). "From Contadina to Worker: Southern Italian Immigrant Working Women in Toronto, 1947–62." In *Looking into My Sister's Eyes: An Exploration in Women's History*, ed. J. Burnet, 195–222. Toronto: Multicultural History Society of Ontario.

Lamphere, L. (1987). *From Working Mothers to Working Daughters: Immigrant Women in a New England Industrial Community*. Ithaca, N.Y.: Cornell University Press.

Löfgren, O. (1979). "Marine Ecotypes in Preindustrial Sweden: A Comparative Discussion of Swedish Peasant Fishermen." In *North Atlantic Maritime Cultures*, ed. R. Andersen, 83–109. The Hague: Mouton.

Massey, D. (1993). "Power-Geometry and a Progressive Sense of Place." In *Mapping the Futures: Local Cultures, Global Change*, ed. J. Bird et al., 59–69. London and New York: Routledge.

Nadel, J. (1984). "Stigma and Separation: Pariah Status and Community Persistence in a Scottish Fishing Village." *Ethnology* 23 (2):101–115.

Safa, H. (1995). *The Myth of the Male Breadwinner: Women and Industrialization in the Caribbean*. Boulder, Colo.: Westview Press.

Smith, M. E., ed. (1977). *Those Who Live from the Sea: A Study in Maritime Anthropology*. American Ethnological Society Monograph 62. St. Paul, Minn.: West Publishing Co.

Stewart, K. (1996). *A Space on the Side of the Road: Cultural Poetics in an "Other" America*. Princeton, N.J.: Princeton University Press.

Young, K. (1978). "Modes of Appropriation and the Sexual Division of Labor: A Case Study from Oaxaca, Mexico." In *Feminism and Materialism: Women and Modes of Production*, ed. A. Kuhn and A. Wolpe, 124–54. London: Routledge and Kegan Paul.

Zavella, P. (1987). *Women's Work and Chicano Families*. Ithaca, N.Y.: Cornell University Press.

PART III

Colonialism, Community, and Kinship

6

Shadow of Domination: Colonialism, Household, and Community Relations

Max Hedley

In this chapter I identify and discuss some of the complex issues surrounding the colonization and social transformation of First Nation communities in Canada (Carstens 1991; Dickarson 1992; Henriksen 1973; Moore 1993). My interest here is with an examination of the social circumstances associated with the emergence of the symptoms of social disorder. I should stress that the patterns of social disorder are not the focus of attention. Instead, the social and cultural changes with which such problems are associated are at issue. Expressed in general terms, concern is with changes in control over everyday life that occurred on a reserve community in southwestern Ontario,[1] and in linking the character of these changes to the legacy of the colonial experience.

My interest in this topic was aroused during conversations I had with two young members of Walpole Island First Nation during the mid-1980s. The first arose during an hour spent relaxing on the bank of the St. Clair River on a summer afternoon while casually discussing life on the island. Conversation turned from the erosion of beaches and the threat to water quality caused by industrial activity to the loss of life on the water. A further turn and we were talking about accidents, suicides, and the problems of youth generally. Awareness of such misfortune was not new, for it has been documented statistically and received a generous share of media attention. However, it is quite another experience to listen to someone for whom statistical tabulations and distant media accounts are translated into personal experience. A further conversation with another young man followed a similar pattern but concluded with the statement that the com-

munity had always been like this. This turned out to be a commonly held
view. However, the idea was flatly contradicted in interviews with members
of an older generation. On the contrary, they were quite definite in suggesting that the loss of social stability, and the social problems associated
with this, were post–World War II phenomena.

This latter view receives support from the nineteenth- and early
twentieth-century reports of the Indian agent. Agents had a formal interest
in the profligacy of their charges and generally included comments about
religious practices and moral demeanor (hygiene, marriage, and drinking)
in their annual reports. We find that references to incidents suggestive of
social disorder on Walpole Island are virtually nonexistent. Instead, the
reports portray the community in a very favorable manner. In the 1892
report the agent points out that: "Divine service is held in both churches
every Sunday, and the morals of the people are improving, especially in the
matter of drinking. In this particular there is a great change for the better,
there being not more than three habitual drunkards on the reserve at this
time, and they are becoming ashamed to be seen drunk" (Canada, Annual
Report 1892, 14, pt.:2). While the report is enthusiastic about the improvement, it sheds no light on the earlier conditions that are used to measure
the "great change for the better." Five years earlier a comment by the agent
about the state of temperance and morality also fails to identify any difficulties. He states:

with the exception of a few who drink and get drunk, and will continue to do so
as long as intoxicants are manufactured and sold, the people of the Walpole Island
Reserve are as little addicted to the use of intoxicants as the same number of people
of any community in Canada, with as many well-behaved men and women as can
be found in the same numbers anywhere, and it is only necessary for any person
to attend a church service on Sunday, or a social gathering on a week day, to be
convinced of the truth of this statement. (Canada, Annual Report 1887, 14:34)

These reports may well have been self-serving, for their contents do have
a bearing on the perceived competence of the agent. Moreover, interest in
the morals of the people, including temperance,[2] reflect an ethnocentric
concern rooted in a Western worldview. Nevertheless, one would suspect
that any significant problem would have been noted. Even earlier reports
do not provide any information to suggest that social disorder was an issue.
On the contrary, the community is regarded in a very favorable way. In
other words, the agent's reports support the contention that community
life on Walpole Island was relatively stable despite the extensive changes
brought about by the processes of colonization. In fact, the first suggestion
that drinking and morality were issues of concern for the community is
found in the early twentieth century. Ironically, this refers to the disruptive
influence of outsiders ("whites") who were using Walpole's beaches for

drinking and dancing on the Sabbath (Nin.Da.Waab.Jig 1903–13). The general point to recognize is that there was a prolonged period of social stability during which there appears to be no evidence that suggest the "evils of liquor" were a source of difficulty or that the community faced any generalized problem of social disorder. This leads one to ask why social disruption was absent, or at least insignificant, during one period of time yet particularly evident during another. This question becomes more interesting when it is recognized that the way of life was radically transformed during the course of the nineteenth century.

APPROACH

I suggest that the problems of the post–World War II years resulted from a loss of local control over cultural reproduction that was associated with the transformation in household and community relations. To develop this argument I will identify those key features of the reserve community of the 1930s that allow us to appreciate the character and degree of local control as well as the reasons underlying its transformation. At this time, social and cultural reproduction occurred within the context of an agrarian economy that was organized on a household basis. The household economy was of relatively recent origin, for it had emerged in the process of colonization during the second half of the nineteenth century and remained relatively stable until the 1940s. Recognition of the emergent nature of the agrarian economy should ensure that we neither succumb to the temptation to adopt essentialist concepts of indigenous society and culture (or colonialism for that matter), or ignore the complex ways in which the lives of First Nation peoples carry the hegemonic mark of their colonial history (Berkhofer 1979; Thomas 1994). First Nation peoples were never simply passive in their response to the vicissitudes of colonization. They were active agents, albeit under constraint, in the constitution and reconstitution of their communities (Carstens 1991). Consequently, timeless and homogeneous representations of indigenous peoples have more to do with colonial domination, and resistance to it, than the realities of peoples' lives that they purport to convey (Bhabha 1994:115; Escobar 1995:7–8). Phrased differently, the boundaries between "traditional" indigenous society and colonial society, whether attributed to "traditional" culture or administrative fiat, were less well defined and more porous than our conceptualizations generally allow.

It may seem somewhat paradoxical to suggest that people retained any direction over their lives when we acknowledge the extensive control the federal government exercised over reserve communities. The paradox is more evident when we admit that the social relations of the agrarian economy unambiguously reveal the influence of colonial policy. Yet the impact of colonialism on earlier (traditional) lifeways did not prevent people from reconstituting their control over everyday life. However, I suggest that critical changes resulting from colonial policy and incorporated into reserve life were implicated in the erosion of control over social and cultural reproduction during the postwar years. In this respect, it is the postcolonial constitution of the household that is at issue, for it became the basis upon which the "new" rural culture emerged. The analysis proceeds from a historical examination of selective features of the household economy as it emerged during the nineteenth century to a discussion of aspects of rural society in the 1930s that further our understanding of local control and the way this is linked to the household economy.

MUNICIPAL INSTITUTIONS AND THE LOSS OF LOCAL POWER

Following Confederation in 1867, the federal government directed its policies toward achieving the civilization or assimilation of Aboriginal peoples. The object of the policy was to eradicate any vestiges of traditional practice and to "lead the Indian people by degrees to mingle with the white race in the ordinary avocations of life" (Canada, Annual Report 1871:4). To this end, it pursued policies that sought to destroy local patterns of leadership, religion, language, and any other cultural practice that was perceived to be incompatible with their civilizing mission. This is readily apparent in the years immediately following Confederation (Titley 1986). At this time the federal government began in earnest to impose the institutions of government on reserve communities and thereby formally to circumscribe the realm of jurisdiction within which native peoples could participate in the governance of their communities. Specifically, an attempt was made to impose a municipal type of administration in an effort to undermine traditional forms of self-government and therefore reduce the power of Aboriginal peoples to pursue objectives of their own design. The Superintendent of Indian Affairs points out that the legislative acts of 1868 and 1869 were "intended to afford facilities for electing, for a limited period, members of bands to manage, as a Council, local matters—that intelligent and educated men, recognized as chiefs, should carry out the wishes of the male members of mature years in each band, who should be fairly represented in the conduct of their internal affairs" (Canada, Annual Report 1871:4). The legislation was designed to establish municipal institutions and thus substitute "a responsible," for what was described as "an irresponsible," system of local government (1871:5). We may note the irony of dismissing supposedly "irresponsible systems" of government and replacing them with a "responsible" and "representative system" that excluded the participation of women (1871:4). After all, it was "young intelligent men, who feel the injustice of being excluded from any voice in deliberations which materially affect their interests" (1871:5).

More than a change in the form of government was at stake. The manner in which municipal institutions were structured provided a means whereby the authority of traditional leadership was undermined, local jurisdiction circumscribed, and ultimate political control transferred to the Department of Indian Affairs. The pervasive nature of these controls gives substance to the suggestion that the department was "a miniature government" that had extensive controls over the lives of reserve populations "who were systematically deprived of the opportunity to influence government" (Hawthorn 1966:207, 368). Municipal government enhanced the control of Indian Affairs over the reserve communities. The loss of power and jurisdiction meant that councils became more a vehicle of delivering government policy than a means of formulating and furthering the objectives of First Nation peoples. They could and did resist the implementation of policy initiatives and administrative decisions that they did not approve, but were increasingly constrained to construct their objectives within the framework established for them.

RELATIONS OF PRODUCTION: PROPERTY

For many First Nation peoples, including those on Walpole Island, the policy of assimilation included an attempt to foster an interest in agricultural production. However, it was not just engagement in the cultivation of the land that was sought. The ideal model of an agricultural enterprise was associated with a combination of commercial and subsistence production and definite forms of social organization, relations of production, and distribution. The settler household, rather than any communal alternative, was considered desirable. The rights of private ownership of the land was central to this model. Ideally, ownership of the land provided household members with a claim to the product of their own labor and the right to deploy this in any manner they desired. Existing practices, which would include communal alternatives, were represented and dismissed in a perfunctory fashion. The latter is evident in a comment made to Parliament by the Superintendent of Indian Affairs: "Very many, however, prefer trafficking one with another, often to the injury of their families, to being limited to a life interest. Their old system is now exhibiting its fruits, and we find families, consisting of active young men, actually without any land, while on the other hand a few cunning unscrupulous persons have by jobbery acquired possession of two or three times as much land as the proper quota" (Canada, Annual Report 1871:5). Here traditional practices are homogenized through their representation in the singular, dismissed as a barrier to change, and identified as a source of injustice. That is, other peoples' practices are symbolically transformed into an unjust and irrational residue of a past age.

The solution was to replace traditional systems of tenure with a private property regime. To this end, the Enfranchisement Act of 1869 included provisions to establish a system of individual ownership rights to reserve land. The aim was to create a secure tenure system in which land could be inherited by descendants, encourage the development of a commitment to the land that paralleled that of settlers, and to ensure that First Nation peoples appreciated its advantages (Canada 1978:53; Canada, Annual Report 1871:5). The new system allowed an individual owner to deploy the land in accordance with his or her own interests, though ownership rights could not be transferred to a nonband member. However, it could be sold, willed, or given to other band members. One consequence of this was that land could not be used as a lien against debts incurred to non-band members.

The cultivation of a taste for private ownership of reserve land was a fundamental part of the policy of assimilation. A private property regime was very different from earlier practices in which access to resources was determined through communal relations. In agriculture a private property regime not only conferred ownership, but also denied nonowners access to the land. It also created the possibility that rights might be lost to others through indebtedness, though a degree of protection was offered in that nonband members could not obtain ownership. Conversely, the arrangement meant that band farmers could not use their land to raise capital from nonband members. However, the creation of a regime in which land could be purchased, sold, or lost established a new basis for the emergence of social inequality within First Nation communities.

WALPOLE ISLAND FIRST NATION: EARLY NINETEENTH CENTURY (BKEJWANONG FIRST NATION)

It is useful to begin with an overview of agricultural practices during the early nineteenth century to appreciate the nature of the changes that occurred and the influence of federal policy. Walpole Island was established as a sanctuary during the late eighteenth century. Unlike the usual land cession treaties, the area occupied by the people of Walpole Island First Nation was never relinquished from Indian possession (Surtees 1983). It remains unceded land. During the early nineteenth century the Aboriginal inhabitants of Walpole Island remained politically autonomous despite the presence of a colonial government and the influence of an expanding capitalist economy. In fact, it was not until after the War of 1812 that their value as allies of the imperial power lost its significance. Aboriginal people in the region were nomadic and relied extensively on fish and game for subsistence, though this was complemented by horticulture and commercial engagement in the fur trade. Agricultural settlement in the region was associated with a steady diminution of the resources that used to sustain traditional lifestyles. Hence it is not surprising to find that Aboriginal people shifted the focus of their economic activity. By the 1840s agriculture had become an important means of self-provisioning, though hunting, gathering, and fishing remained significant.

By the 1850s the range of crops grown and the cultivation techniques employed were similar to those of settlers in the surrounding area (Nin.Da.Waab.Jig 1987:30; Taylor 1984:26; Van Wyck 1992). However, it is not so much the technological similarities as the differences in social organization and relations of production between native and settler agriculture that should be stressed at this point. While a lack of information severely limits discussion of this question, a few general comments can be made. Settlers, engaged in subsistence and commercial agriculture, worked within a private property regime in which land was owned or rented and operated by members of a household for their collective benefit. The latter comment should be qualified, because we know that women were less than equal in terms of ownership rights, and that debts allowed the benefits of labor to be transferred to others (Cohen 1988). At least ideally, the owner-operator settler household allowed those who worked the land to reap the rewards of their own labor. In contrast, the social organization and relations of agricultural production and distribution on Walpole Island were based on a different cultural model. Agricultural land seems to have been part of a communal property regime in which rights of access were acquired through membership in the community rather than by private ownership.

Residents of Walpole Island were organized into distinct bands composed of a group of relatives. Members of these bands are described as working within a common enclosure on plots of land that were allocated by the "inferior chief" in accordance with their needs (Nin.Da.Waab.Jig 1987:30; Taylor 1984:26; Van Wyck 1992:176). Moreover, there is evidence to suggest that social relations, at least among those working within a common enclosure, were marked by communal redistribution of the product of labor (Van Wyck 1992:181). In other words, the limited evidence available indicates that access to agricultural land, and presumably other subsistence and commercial resources, was regulated in terms of Aboriginal institutions. This leads us to believe that the people of Walpole Island remained nominally independent despite the presence of a colonial government and the changes occurring in the economy of the region. Consequently, community life, including agricultural practices, could be regulated in terms of their own institutions and values, despite the emergence of constraints linked to their involvement in the new political and economic relations that were emerging in the region.

THE HOUSEHOLD ECONOMY (CIRCA 1860–1940)

By the end of the nineteenth century, agriculture occupied the central place in the reserve economy. Other resources were significant, but cultivation for both subsistence and commercial exchange was vital. The shift ensured continuing self-sufficiency despite the diminution of resources due to settlement in the region. Residents of Walpole Island cultivated the same range of crops as other farms in the region and took advantage of the commercial opportunities that were available. The latter included the sale of wood (fuel and lumber), hay, fish, furs (muskrat), farm products, and a variety of crafts. Extensive gardens and other local resources were used for self-consumption. Household members also engaged in wage labor when it was available.

The main characteristics of the new local economy were visible in the 1860s and 1870s, clearly in place by the late nineteenth century, and remained prominent until the 1940s (Hedley 1993). However, neither the distinct organization of agriculture of the earlier period, nor the autonomy this implied, survived. This is not surprising, given the long-term and pervasive influence of Indian Affairs and the policy of assimilation. As we have seen, there was little room for alternative forms of agricultural organization for the property-owning homestead or for Aboriginal institutions generally, given the ethnocentric presumptions of this way of thinking about the development of Aboriginal communities.

The communal relations of the 1840s had been lost as agriculture came to be organized on a household basis. More specifically, the organization of agriculture generally corresponded to the model of the self-sufficient settler household mentioned above (Hedley 1993; Van Wyck 1992:232). Households, consisting of a nuclear or extended family, were the focal point of production, distribution, and consumption in that they drew on their own labor and resources to meet their own needs. As with settlers, households were in possession of the land they cultivated, though the institutions of private property were not fully in place on the reserve until the land was surveyed in the early twentieth century. Even before the survey, there is evidence to suggest that land could be purchased and sold (Van Wyck 1992:245). However, the market for land was limited by the provisions of the Indian Act, which restricted transactions to band members. This protected land from outsiders but did not preclude its loss to other band members. Not all of the land was individually owned. The major part of the reserve remained common land, though it was held in trust by the federal government. The resources found on common land were available to households, though there was a degree of administrative regulation (permits for lumber, hay) and locally devised customs (trap lines were respected and horses and cattle grazed freely on common land) that regulated access.

An example drawn from an account of a woman (ET) who was living in her aunt's household during the 1930s provides a glimpse into the organization of Walpole households and the extensive range of activities in which its members were engaged. Her observations span the period of transformation in household and community relations. They illustrate the nature of the traditional household and the impact of redeployment of household labor, and allow us to gain some insight into the changing nature of household and community social relations.[3] While a specific household cannot be construed as the mirror image of another, the example can serve to illustrate some of the essential characteristics of agrarian economy during the 1930s and the changes that occurred.

ET's aunt's family was deeply involved in the traditional self-sufficient household economy. They cultivated corn and oats (three acres), cut hay, maintained an extensive garden including potatoes, peas, and tomatoes, and raised cows, horses, and pigs. This particular household had an orchard in which cherries, peaches, pears, and apples were grown. In addition, the household would harvest a variety of resources from band-owned land. These included wild plums and raspberries, hazelnuts, hickory nuts, and walnuts, as well as wood for fuel and building. Many of these items had to be preserved for use during the winter. Also, her uncle would hunt muskrats, rabbit, duck, fish, squirrel, pheasant, and raccoon, so there was no problem getting meat on the table. What they could not or did not produce themselves they often obtained through an extensive network of exchange relations (trade or barter) with others. Like other households on the reserve during the Great Depression, reliance on externally produced commodities was limited to a few items such as lard (intermittently, because they did make their own), flour, baking powder, sugar (when locally produced maple sugar was not available), salt, kerosene oil, perhaps an axe and other implements, and clothing (usually obtained through barter). The little cash available was obtained through selling small quantities of furs, wood, some farm products, items such as quilts and baskets manufactured by the household, and casual wage labor when it was available. Members of the household were engaged in a labor-intensive regime, for it took the work of all family members to maintain the material basis of their existence.

Throughout the period in question, households were involved in market relations. Household members were small-scale commodity producers who relied on the sale of various items, and the occasional sale of their labor, to gain access to externally produced goods that were incorporated into their lifestyles. As small-scale commodity producers, they can be seen as part of the class structure of Canadian society and subject to cyclical variations and long-term changes in the national and global economy. Some nineteenth-century evidence for the impact of this involvement is seen in discrepancies in farm size (a process of differentiation), exclusion of some from access to the land, the reliance of destitute band members on charity, and the presence of discrepancies in average farm size between Walpole Island and the surrounding region (Hedley 1993:193; Van Wyck 1992:

252). A more relevant example is the general movement into wage labor in the 1940s associated with the decline of the household economy. I return to the previous example to illustrate the consequences of this.

Reserve households had a limited capacity to generate income through commodity production.[4] However, economic expansion in the region provided an opportunity for people to enter or reenter the workforce as wage laborers. ET's uncle was one of those who took the opportunity to engage in seasonal work. As she explained it, "my uncle quit farming and he went sailing. There was good money in it I guess, for what they were getting then" (Nin.Da.Waab.Jig 1982–84). She also points out that "our family life kind of went to pieces" at that time. A major reason for this was that wage work reduced the labor available to complete the traditional array of household activities. The shortage was compounded because the seasonal nature of work corresponded to the period in which the demand for household labor for agriculture was at its highest. As she put it: "I don't think my uncle had much time off, maybe, just like one day and one night and then he'd have to be back to work on the boat again. And that one day and one night off, well, they'd like to spend with their wives, and their family and didn't [leave] them much time. Then they'd have to be back on the job again. That's not enough time" (Nin.Da.Waab.Jig 1982–84).

This work schedule did not allow enough time for any significant participation in the established round of household activities. However, as was the case earlier in the century, the absence of males did not necessarily lead to the immediate abandonment of farming. In this particular instance, her aunt and grandmother attempted to continue with their work, though the work regime became more difficult. ET observes: "I think it was twice as hard 'cause what the man (had usually done) around the home, the women had to do. They could plant, weed the garden and things like that. But as far as plowing and all the heavy work, that was pretty hard. Well it just sort of broke down the family, that's all I could say (Nin.Da.Waab.Jig 1982–84). Well, my aunt did (the work) for awhile, but it was too hard. And my grandmother was getting pretty well along in years, but she'd still go out there and work. But the gardens kept getting smaller and smaller" (Nin.Da.Waab.Jig 1982–84).[5]

Despite an increase in cash income, and the continuing engagement of women in subsistence activities, the household was described as being "hard hit" during the winter because the seasonal nature of employment meant that there was no income during the off-season. ET describes their situation this way: "Yeah, well they figured that it was easier to work eight or nine hours a day than to put in a full day's work, but they never realized that in the winter they would be really hard hit by that time, because they didn't (have) anything that they could fall back on. Whereas years ago, they always had the farm. And so as a result, they didn't have enough food to last them all winter" (Nin.Da.Waab.Jig 1982–84). In the absence of a social welfare safety net, or communal relations that would ensure their reproduction, the household was obliged to draw on a range of traditional practices during the winter months. In particular, this involved a heightened reliance on fishing, trapping, and hunting to feed the family during the winter months.

Involvement in the wage economy also undermined the economic value of participation in community relations. As noted earlier, households in the traditional economy were heavily engaged in exchange (barter) relations. While households engaged in the local agrarian economy were broadly similar in the range of activities they followed, there were differences in emphasis that allowed benefits to be derived from exchange. The decline in household production meant that the basis for exchange diminished. For the household in question, there was less available to trade with neighbors. One conclusion that can be drawn from this is that exchange relations were premised on the ability of individual households to maintain their economic place in the community. (Also, decisions to enter into wage labor were made in terms of the interests of household members.) This further supports the idea that the household economy was very different from the communal economy of the early nineteenth century. That is, the structure of interests in the household economy constrained people to focus on their own self-interest and therefore contained the imprint of the colonial project. However, this should not be taken to imply that people were precluded from engaging in altruistic activity (Hedley 1995:123).

Within the rural economy, the household, conceived as the organization of production and distribution based on family or extended family labor, was the focal point of material and, as we shall see, social and cultural reproduction. Members of households were embedded in the capitalist economy through relations of commodity exchange and work. They were also constrained by an administrative structure through which the power of the federal government had abrogated the political autonomy of an earlier era and continuously pursued a policy of assimilation. A significant aspect of the latter was the creation of a new property regime that allowed for the ownership of land by households and regulated, to some degree, access to resources on common land.

To this point I have focused attention on economic production. In fact, one might want to conclude that the changes that occurred are little more than a shift between occupations. Such reasoning rests on an analytical and ideological distinction drawn between work and social life generally. In this view, work is portrayed instrumentally as a means of completing a particular task. Yet work is always more than an instrumental activity, for it is conducted within the framework of definitive social relations and unavoidably imbued with cultural meaning. This is particularly obvious in the household economy, where work was intricately entwined with control over the reproduction of social and cultural life. In this respect, as we shall see, the social relations of work provided a significant context in which the young acquired their social and cultural competence, and which facilitated their involvement in the continuous creation of household and community life. ETs' references to the breakdown of family life offers a clue to the magnitude of the change that took place.

SOCIAL AND CULTURAL CONTROL IN THE HOUSEHOLD ECONOMY

Political decisions of the Indian bureaucracy established the parameters of personal and collective freedom and constrained the type of development that could occur. Within these parameters the "new" household economy harbored a realm of control over everyday life. One should be wary of suggesting this because the details of local culture have also been the focus of intervention as government and missions have sought to leave their mark on the customs and practices of First Nation peoples. Thus, even in the more intimate arena of everyday life, we are referring to a long-contested terrain of interpersonal relations and subjectivity. Moreover, the form that local control (empowerment) takes is itself a function of the historical distribution, as well as the use of and resistance to colonial power. The position of women in the household provides an indication of the degree and nature of local control over social relations and culture (subjectivity).

As mentioned earlier, women were denied political rights during the period of the household economy. They could not participate in provincial or federal political processes. Moreover, they were excluded from formal participation in band government, for they could neither vote nor be elected to office. However, their position in the household economy gave them considerable influence, or potential influence, over everyday life. This was most clearly expressed by a woman responding to the observation that women were denied political participation in municipal affairs in the past: "I think women had a lot more say (in the past) because they had control of the families. They had control of the children. You shaped the thoughts of your child. Now, mothers don't even worry about what (their children) think or what they do. (The children are taken to) day care as soon as they can get in there" (Nin.Da.Waab.Jig 1982–84). In this instance the loss of control over the young was attributed to attitudes of mothers. Mothers were perceived to be lacking interest in rearing children and to pass the task on to others by sending them to day care as soon as possible. While attitudes may well become part of the problem, there is more to it than this. The power or influence was not simply a function of the ability of adults to impose sanctions but relates to the total social context in which all were involved. It was engraved in the very interstices of the way of life itself. An indication of this is provided by DJ's next comment which refers to the context in which children acquired their traditions. In this example, the focus is on traditional teachings and sexuality, though we might note that the reference to Christianity is indicative of a dynamic tradition:

And you know, our teachings, like we were Christians but a lot of the old teachings were still prevalent. Well, I said it isn't so much it [sex] was considered dirty it was, rather being, like, realistic. It was not encouraged there, in fact, it was definitely discouraged in the young. So even the parents were taught not to be so demonstrative. . . . And it sort of carries over from the past. Because you had to keep things down. Like a lot of the families lived in the one house, maybe two or three families, so you could never expect to have had children growing up like this. . . . there were a lot of things that young people were taught that is not being taught now. So while the women . . . didn't go to vote or anything, they still had control of the family. A lot more than they do now. (Nin.Da.Waab.Jig 1982–84)

Whether through personal example, sanction, or stories, the household provided a context in which the young were drawn into the ways of an older generation. In fact, the labor-intensive household economy captured the attention of all its members in a welter of daily and seasonal routines. Sometimes routine chores were described as easygoing, while at other moments they seemed endless. As explained by ET, who was sixteen at the time: "Well, I'll tell you one thing though. My grandmother told us, well you know, she didn't come right out and tell you what to do, she said, well, this should be done today. Now, we have to put so much up today, we should get so much done today. And we'd work like the dickens to get that much done. Whether we did or not, I don't remember, but I do know we did work" (Nin.Da.Waab.Jig 1982–84). All members of the household were involved; there do not seem to have been any strict schedules or close supervision of activities. You saw what needed to be done, and you did it. The context provided little choice, for the work was required for the reproduction of the household. All members of the household were engaged in its activities, and the tasks did not vary much from those of neighboring households.

It was not just household relations that provided an intense social context. Reserve life was characterized by a high degree of sociability. Though the household was the focal point of individual reproduction, its members were connected with other households through patterns of exchange (goods and services) and cooperation in economic production and social life generally. It was a time when households were dependent on each other for material support, exchange of labor, and cooperation in the organization of the community's social life generally (Hedley 1993:204; Nin.Da.Waab.Jig 1987; Van Wyck 1992).

Logging bees provide an example of the way sociability was built into the social organization of reserve life. The putative purpose of a logging bee was the collection of wood for use as fuel during the winter. Yet when people talk about them, it is the social aspect of the occasion that is drawn to the fore. A logging bee seems to have been open to anyone to attend and could attract as many as twenty-five households, though numbers do not seem to have made any difference to the way the task was performed. More important were the communal meals and the celebrations, which included dancing, singing, games, and storytelling, that marked the end of the day's work. In the work bee, distinctions between practical activity (work) and celebration (leisure) are elided, that is, distinctions or boundaries between work and pleasure are blurred and there is both pleasure in work and work in pleasure (preparing meals/preparing wood). The logging bee was also a social event in which the order of the community was revealed through engagement in common activity. It was a context in which the ideological equality of the community was revealed, for, at least in principle, any household was free to attend, and all participated equally in the activities of the occasion.[6] Moreover, through the participation of males and females of all ages in "work," communal meals, dancing, singing, and storytelling, one finds an affirmation of cooperation, mutual reliance, the division of labor between men and women, young and old, patterns of authority, and the equality and independence of households. It was also a context in which traditions were conveyed through recounting stories about the old days. In general, the work bee provided a social context in which the order of things was implicitly acknowledged.

For the young, the path to adulthood, at least for those who did not go to boarding schools, was paved by the relational context of household and community. They learned about the social world through participating in a social context that members of the community created and controlled. Through work, work bees, church socials, and other social activities, they were involved in relationships with adults and learned the patterns of appropriate behavior. There was little choice, for life on the island entailed commitment to the rural economy. The experience of the young was heavily influenced by adults who, within the parameters of the community, controlled the reproduction of household and community relations and local culture in a situation where all were living under similar social and economic circumstances.

A NEW WORLD

The range of household practices in the past clearly indicates the importance of material production for the reproduction of the way of life. However, there should be no doubt that there is more to the traditional pattern of rural life than this. Nevertheless, it is hard to avoid the conclusion that a key factor in the social transformation that occurred was the transfer of labor from the household to the wage sector. In an economic sense the adoption of wage labor could be seen as a substitution of one source of income for another in a strategy sometimes benignly referred to as occupational dualism or pluralism. However, the new adaptation proved to be far more than this for, as we have seen, the household regime was always more than a round of economic activity. The entry into wage labor led directly to the impoverishment of the relational context through which rural culture was reproduced. The effect is better described as corrosive, rather than immediate, because it invoked a series of intentional and unintentional consequences that were cumulative in their effect. Particularly significant, and definitely unintended, were the changes in household and community relations that transformed the social context in which the young learned their place in the social world, and that increasingly rendered redundant the knowledge and practices acquired within the traditional regime. For some, the ideals of an earlier age persist, but the relational context of their realization is lost. One can aspire to live in accordance with traditional ideals, but without the emergence of alternative patterns of sociability that reconstitute local control, the problems of asserting cultural control remain personal. It is not that knowledge of the past is necessarily lost, but that the veracity of older models was grounded in their place within a specific historical, social, and cultural context (Hedley 1995:130–32).

We can acquire a glimpse of this issue from some additional comments made by ET that refer to a time when she was engaged in rearing her own children during the 1950s. They point to a source of difficulty for women in maintaining control over children in the post-traditional context:

I taught my children to go to bed at 8:30 every night. The older ones could stay up till nine after they got to be thirteen or whatever. There they had to have a lot of homework done. Then they could stay up a little later until nine o'clock. But I had it out with one of the teachers at the school there. They told the teacher, but we have to go to bed at 8:30 every night. And the teacher said, why should you have to go to bed at eight thirty every night. You should be able to stay up till nine o'clock. Well not children of mine. When they came home and told me that I was furious! I went right to the school and I told that teacher, I raise my children the way I want to, and I don't want you disrupting my household. I said, those children . . . need their sleep while older ones need some quiet time for homework. (The teacher apologized but) by then it was too late, the damage was already done. Young kids don't forget anything like that, you know, they figure, oh well, my mother's mean. (Nin.Da.Waab.Jig 1982–84) (ET: 16–17)[7]

This comment points to a source of threat to parental influence and authority in a context where household activities are more isolated from each other than in the past. In the emerging postwar circumstances, the influence that people had over their children was more easily challenged by the influence of other social interests that fill the social void by new distinctions and divisions. For an older generation this is epitomized by the emergence of a generation gap that had no place in the traditional order. The basic problem is that the countervailing power rooted in control over household and community relations was lost. The postwar years witnessed a proliferation of agencies and programs that sought to intervene in the affairs of individuals and families. Moreover, one should remember that the possibility of people reconstituting control over their circumstances was limited by the formal constraints imposed on the governance of their community.

CONCLUSION

I began by asking why the symptoms of social disorder became an issue in the postwar years. The usual answers, such as cultural shock or too little or too much assimilation, are difficult to sustain, if for no other reason than that the people of Walpole Island had already undergone a remarkable transformation of their lifeways during the nineteenth century and had accomplished this without any significant expression, at least in the agent's reports, of social disorder. Instead, I formulated the question in terms of the loss of control over the reproduction of social and cultural life.

The particular developmental trajectory that led to the emergence and subsequent transformation of the household economy contained the imprint of Walpole's colonial experience. It involved the formation of a unit of social and economic reproduction that was tied to commodity production, casual wage labor, and subordinate to the political relationships established by the federal government. That is, a long-term effect of colonization was the creation of an institution, the household, that was enmeshed in translocal economic and political relations and that became the focal point of people's self-interest. From this perspective, the household is not a universal category, though we are tempted to treat it this way, but one that wears a particular cultural veil.

From this discussion it should be clear that one should not underestimate the importance of engagement in economic relationships because they were vital to the reproduction of the household and its transformation. Yet to focus exclusively on material production alone would miss the full significance of involvement in household and community relations for the creation and reproduction of social and cultural life, and would inhibit our understanding of the changes that occurred. The relations of work are at the same time cultural relations interwoven into, and part of, distinct ways of life. This is particularly evident in the household economy, where the transparency of the boundary between cultural and economic activity is readily discerned. Household and community relations are constituted intersubjectively through human activities that, in turn, are unavoidably meaningful and carry connotations that are both intentional and occluded. They may embody conceptions of authority, time, loyalties, personal space, gender, ideas of right and wrong, a taste for the order of things, and a sense of one's position in the ongoing flow of social life.

Discussion of Walpole Island First Nation provides an instance of hegemony in which the experience of domination was incorporated into local culture. What was once an alien institution became an integral part of local culture and a source of new loyalties and interests. It provided the social context from which the people of Walpole Island weaved a dense web of relationships that allowed them to retain considerable control over material and cultural reproduction. Unavoidably, the shadow of domination was woven into the very web of household and community relations that emerged. While offering a basis for control over everyday life, the new order was premised on inequality, for the members of rural households were incorporated into a wider social world, marked by hierarchy and inequality, which they did not control. They were both without political power and tied to an individualistically organized agrarian economy in a way that ensured their subsequent marginalization as commodity producers (Hedley 1993). This is not meant to suggest any simple determinism that denies local agency. Control over material and cultural reproduction was retained within the household economy until it was subverted by a mass entry into relations of wage labor. Decisions to abandon the rural economy were made by individuals. However, the fact that such decisions could be made on an individual or household basis was itself a testimony to the legacy of colonial domination, for responsibilities and loyalties were clearly structured in terms of individual and household interests. There was no possibility of a collective devised alternative in a context where political power had been usurped by the federal government. It was only in the mid-1960s that Walpole Island First Nation began to regain a measure of political control through the removal of the Indian agent. In doing this, they entered a prolonged struggle to retrieve their political powers and find ways of addressing the many problems that others could not resolve.

NOTES

1. I have been associated with Walpole Island First Nation since the early 1980s as a member of a community-based research unit called Nin.Da.Waab.Jig. The structure and aims of Nin.Da.Waab.Jig have been described elsewhere (Hedley 1986). The reserve occupies the Canadian portion (approximately 32,000 hectares) of the delta formed by the entry of the St. Clair River into Lake St. Clair. The current population of the reserve is approximately 2,000 people whose tribal origins are Chippewa (primarily), Pottowattomie, and Ottawa. More detailed accounts of Walpole Island First Nation can be found in Hedley 1992, 1993; Nin.Da.Waab.Jig 1987; Van Wyck 1992.

2. Conceivably, references to the evil effect of liquor represent stereotypical views that might have had some relevance prior to the 1840s. At this time there is evidence to suggest that liquor was used by settlers to induce Aboriginal people on Walpole

Island to surrender their rights to the land (Van Wyck 1992:167). This could not be done, at least legally, for land could only be alienated through the Crown. The practice did occur on Walpole Island, though the land was eventually returned.

3. Specific comments about the 1920s and 1930s are drawn from interviews conducted with older residents of Walpole Island First Nation. These were conducted between 1982 and 1984 as part of an oral history project developed by Nin.Da.Waab.Jig (see Hedley 1986 for details). The woman in this interview (ET) was born in 1923 and lived on Walpole Island until she was five or six years of age. She then spent a year in a boarding school before moving to Detroit to live with an aunt. Her contact with the island was maintained through periodic summer residence until she returned to live with another aunt at the age of sixteen. Within three years she had left the reserve again, but returned permanently in the early 1950s.

4. Farmers faced a problem raising capital from nonband members because the tenure system did no allow them to use the land for collateral (Hedley 1993). See Van Wyck (1992:295–305) for a detailed examination of the problems faced by a particular household in trying to develop a farm after World War II.

5. The process is more intricate than described here. One aspect of the division of labor in this household was the responsibility of the uncle for plowing the land with the use of horses. This had an immediate impact on the size of the farm, for the three acres put aside for corn was lost and the amount of land cleared to plant vegetables reduced. The loss of corn meant that the ability of the household to maintain livestock was lost, for it was a major source of winter feed for horses, pigs, and cattle.

6. This is not to suggest an idealized version of household or community in which conflict and exclusion are absent (Hedley 1988; Phillips 1989). In the case of a logging bee, all might be invited, but this does not mean that all would feel free to attend.

7. Schools have long been a means by which the influence of First Nation peoples over newer generations has been contested. This role is more apparent when the schools were used to undermine language and practices that have their roots in precontact realities.

REFERENCES

Berkhofer, R. F. (1979). *The White Man's Indian*. New York: Vintage.

Bhabha, H. (1994). "Remembering Fanon: Self, Psyche and the Colonial Condition." In *Colonial Discourse and Post-Colonial Theory*, ed. P. Williams and L. Chrisman, 112–23. New York: Columbia University Press.

Canada, Department of Indian Affairs. (1868–1930). *Annual Reports*. Sessional Record of Canada, Ottawa.

Canada, Indian and Northern Affairs. (1978). *The Historical Development of the Indian Act*. Treaties and Historical Research Centre, Policy Research and Evaluation Group.

Carstens, P. (1991). *The Queen's People: A Study of Hegemony, Coercion, and Accommodation among the Okanagan of Canada*. Toronto: University of Toronto Press.

Cohen, M. G. (1988). *Women's Work, Markets, and Economic Development in Nineteenth-Century Ontario*. Toronto: University of Toronto Press.

Dickarson, O. P. (1992). *Canada's First Nations: A History of Founding Peoples from Earliest Times*. Toronto: McClelland and Stewart Inc.

Escobar, A. (1995). Encountering Development: The Making and Unmaking of the Third World. Princeton, N.J.: Princeton University Press.

Hawthorn, H. B. (1966). *A Survey of the Contemporary Indians of Canada—A Report on Economic, Political, Educational Needs and Policies*. Vols. 1–2. Ottawa: The Indian Affairs Branch.

Hedley, M. (1986). "Community Based Research: The Dilemma of Contract." *The Canadian Journal of Native Studies* 6 (1):91–103.

———. (1988). "The Peasant Within: Agrarian Life in New Zealand and Canada." *Canadian Review of Sociology and Anthropology* 9 (1):67–83.

———. (1992). "Native Peoples in Canada." In *Profiles of Canada*, ed. K. Pryke and W. Soderland. Toronto: Copp Clark Pitman Ltd.

———. (1993). "Autonomy and Constraint: The Household Economy on a Southern Ontario Reserve." In *The Political Economy of North American Indians*, ed. J. H. Moore, 184–213. Norman: University of Oklahoma Press.

———. (1995). "A Little Free Time on Sunday: Women and Domestic Commodity Production." In *Ethnographic Feminisms: Essays in Anthropology*, ed. S. Cole and L. Phillips, 119–37. Ottawa: Carleton University Press.

Henriksen, G. (1973). *Hunters in the Barrens: The Naskapi on the Edge of the White Man's World*. St. John's: Institute of Social and Economic Research, Memorial University of Newfoundland.

Moore, J. (1993). *The Political Economy of North American Indians*. Norman: University of Oklahoma Press.

Niezen, R. (1993). "Power and Dignity: The Social Consequences of Hydro-electric Development for the James Bay Cree." *Canadian Review of Sociology and Anthropology* 30 (4):510–29.

Nin.Da.Waab.Jig. (1903–13). *Minutes, Regular and General Council Meetings*. Reference no. 2111. Wallaceburg, Ontario.

———. (1982–84). *Oral Interviews*. Reference no. 323 PENI. Wallaceburg, Ontario.

———. (1987). *Walpole Island: The Soul of Indian Territory*. Walpole Island, Ontario.

Phillips, L. (1989). "Gender Dynamics and Rural Household Strategies." *Canadian Review of Sociology and Anthropology*, 26 (2):294–310.

Surtees, R. (1983). Indian Land Surrenders in Ontario 1763–1867. Ottawa: Indian and Northern Affairs Canada, Research Branch.

Taylor, J. F. (1984). *Indian Band Self-Government in the 1960s: A Case Study of Walpole Island*. Ottawa: Indian and Northern Affairs Canada, Treaties and Historical Research Centre.

Thomas, N. (1994). *Colonialism's Culture: Anthropology, Travel and Government*. Oxford: Polity Press.

Titley, B. (1986). *A Narrow Vision: Duncan Campbell Scott and the Administration of Indian Affairs in Canada*. Vancouver: University of British Columbia Press.

Van Wyck, S. M. (1992). "Harvest Yet to Reap: History, Identity, and Agriculture in a Canadian Indian Community." Ph.D. dissertation, University of Toronto, Toronto, Canada.

7

Weaving and Mothering: Reframing Navajo Weaving as Recursive Manifestations of *K'e*

Kathy M'Closkey

Feminist political economists have remarked on women's absence in most analyses, especially in the domains of politics and economics. Women vanish because of the faulty epistemological lens of androcentric researchers. Until the 1970s, women's domestic work was seen as "natural"; it was perceived as a constant throughout history, an unchanging set of necessities that did not require analysis. Many scholars now recognize that colonization, Westernization, and international capitalism restructured traditional economies in a way that had a profound impact on women's economic activities (Mies 1986). The process of transforming colonized peoples into producers and consumers of commodities served the colonial powers' need for both raw material and markets (Leacock and Etienne 1980:19). The appropriation of the Aboriginal textile market by traders and manufacturers of trade blankets epitomizes this process for the Navajo people.[1]

However, to highlight only the political economy component of this story would perpetuate an attenuated understanding of the *qualitative* values expressed in the process of weaving. Rather than viewing the Navajo rug primarily as a commodity, emphasis is shifted to encompass the weaver *and* her rug and the maintenance of relationships vital to Navajo culture. Today these relationships are jeopardized by free trade, globalization, and the volatile investment market for *historic* weaving, all of which drastically reduce the demand for textiles created by thirty thousand contemporary Navajo weavers. These recent events exacerbate the systemic poverty of the Navajo people. However, it is difficult to perceive the extent of the threat because of the manner in which textile production by Navajo women has been marginalized in the anthropological literature.

Historically, textiles have been marginalized in the domains of commerce, art, and religion. Because of a number of unquestioned assumptions grounded in Western logical dualisms, textile production by Navajo women has fallen between the paradigmatic cleavages in the social sciences. The development of ideas related to gendered spheres of productive and nonproductive labor, art and craft, and sacred as opposed to secular spheres—all differences that reflect binary oppositions—provided the context to marginalize the importance of weaving in perpetuating Navajo lifeways.[2] Currently, historic Navajo weaving is tethered to gallery aesthetics and subsumed under the purview of the museum curator. In this chapter I address the shortcomings of current perspectives and reveal an alternative interpretation based on archival evidence and interviews with contemporary Navajo weavers. This view delineates how weaving perpetuates *K'e*, or proper kin relations as directed by the Navajo creation story.

As a weaver for two decades, I approach this subject from a perspective missing from the prolific literature on the Navajo. Over the years, a number of anthropologists and popular writers have developed a coherent body of literature considered as "the history of Navajo weaving." Reflecting the asymmetry of gender relations as constituted historically in the West, weaving was perceived as (a) women's domestic activity engaged in for practical purposes, (b) nonsacred because materials were borrowed from non-Navajo sources, and (c) dominated by a handful of male traders who altered designs influenced by consumer preferences. In 1987, anthropologist Gary Witherspoon estimated that more than one hundred thousand Navajo women had woven more than one million blankets and rugs over the last two centuries. To a weaver like myself, these are astonishing figures. However, there is a large gap between the magnitude of production and the dearth of knowledge concerning the conditions under which these women labored. Not only have weavers' economic contributions been airbrushed from history, but researchers (with the exception of Witherspoon 1975, 1987) have failed to recognize the critical role that weaving played in relation to *cultural* survival.

Much of the evidence that reveals the sustained impoverishment of the Navajo people lies buried in unresearched trading post records. This chapter incorporates information extracted from the Lorenzo Hubbell Papers (1876–1966). The Hubbells were the most powerful trading family to the Navajo for decades; they owned or controlled more than thirty businesses on or adjacent to the Reservation.[3] The senior Hubbell is deemed the "czar" of Navajo trade and the "father" of the Navajo rug. The original trading post located in Ganado, Arizona, is now a national historic site operated by the United States Park Service and visited by thousands of tourists annually. An analysis of the Hubbells' business records reveals a story that differs substantially from that in the published literature. The following information provides some historical context for a discussion of these records.

The Navajo, or Diné, comprise the largest group of First Nation peoples in North America. More than 75 percent of the population of 250,000 occupy a 20 million-acre Reservation in the southwestern United States. According to their creation story, they evolved through four underworlds before emerging in Dinétah, a mountainous region now known as southern Colorado and northern New Mexico. Archaeologists suggest a different genesis, in which the ancestors of the Navajo crossed the Bering "land bridge," ultimately migrating along the western edge of the great plains nearly one thousand years ago. Ethnologists note that the Diné share an Athapaskan heritage with the Dene of northwestern Canada.

Some of the most magnificent scenery in the southwest United States is located on the Navajo Reservation. Although much of the region is classified as desert, Navajo country is crosscut by the Chuska and Lukachukai mountain ranges, Monument Valley, and Canyon de Chelly. Although the region is rich in nonrenewable resources, systemic poverty prevails. Per capita income remains at one-quarter the national average; unemployment or underemployment is the norm. More than half the housing is substandard, and less than 50 percent of the homes have basic utilities (Downer 1990). Many Navajo survive in pockets of despair reminiscent of third world poverty (*U.S. News & World Report* 1994). This portrait painted by contemporary authors is a far cry from descriptions published in mid-nineteenth-century reports.

Before the Civil War, the Navajo were christened "Lords of the Desert" by the U.S. cavalry. Eyewitness reports described their vast herds of sheep and horses (stock was acquired from sixteenth-century Spanish explorers), abundant gardens, cornfields, peach orchards, and finely woven blankets. Van Valkenburgh and McPhee (1974:42) describe how the Navajo blanket was the most valuable trade item in an extensive intertribal trade network: "The Navajo blanket can well be called the mother from which all external Navajo trade of today developed. Before the inception of the American system of trading, the woollen goods manufactured by the Navajos was the most important medium for external exchange with the Pueblos, Havasupai, Apache, and Utes as well as the New Mexicans." By mid-century, the federal government was intent on subduing the "wild tribes" to open the region for "settlement." In 1864, the U.S. government sent Kit Carson to Navajoland. His "scorched earth" strategy destroyed their fields and orchards and scattered their flocks. More than eight thousand Navajo were forcibly marched four hundred miles eastward into New Mexico territory. For four years, they struggled to farm in a region rendered hostile by alkaline water, insect plagues, and failed harvests (Roessel 1983b). In 1868, after one-quarter of the population had perished from malnutrition and disease, the federal government designated less than 4 million acres of their former territory as their Reservation. Thus the Navajo were allowed to return to their beloved canyon country, but it comprised only one-quarter of the area they had previously occupied (Vogt 1961:315).

Shortly thereafter, Navajo self-sufficiency was undermined in part as licensed traders fostered a dependency on expendable commodities. By 1890 there were forty posts on or adjacent to the Reservation. Large accounts were drawn against weavers' production, assuring a continuous supply of textiles while destroying women's bargaining position. Traders reaped double benefits from two-way commodity trade, as they engaged in "credit saturation" facilitated by geographic isolation and territorial monopoly.

Weavers not only lost control of the marketing of their textiles because of trader interference, but they also lost the market to commercial manufacturers such as Pendleton Woolen Mills. Trade blanket manufacturers appropriated the form, materials, and Navajo designs and, through traders, sold tens of thousands of mechanically woven blankets to many Aboriginal peoples formerly provisioned by Navajo weavers (Kapoun 1992). Thus commercial blanket manufacturers capitalized on the Navajos' unawareness of copyright protection. This is why the Navajo wearing blanket became a *rug* around the turn of the century. The niche for the hand-woven Navajo wearing blankets had vanished.

Analysis of the Hubbells' business records refutes the following assumptions that have dominated the literature on the Navajo for decades: (1) traders "saved" weaving by developing off-Reservation markets (Amsden 1975:179; Dedera 1990:36; Kent 1985:85); (2) traders were primarily responsible for design changes in Navajo patterns (Amsden 1975; Boles 1981; James 1988; Kent 1985; Rodee 1981); (3) selling blankets by weight declined after 1900 (Kent 1985:83; Rodee 1981:9); (4) machine-woven trade blankets were far cheaper than their hand-woven counterparts (Amsden 1975; James 1974; Kapoun 1992:35; Maxwell 1984:60; Weiss 1984: 19; Wheat 1984:19); and (5) traders' greatest profits lay in wool (Adams 1963:175; McNitt 1962). All of these assumptions are suspect. Because the Hubbells controlled a significant portion of Navajo trade, their business records provide a barometer of the regional economy. In pursuing this kind of research, one experiences how the construction of "history" occurs through continued emphasis and recycling of particular forms of information.

Reservation traders working for wholesale merchants such as the Babbitt Brothers headquartered in Flagstaff, Arizona, were issued directives on how to acquire blankets and rugs from weavers for the lowest possible "price" (Akbarzadeh 1992:301). Weavers were never paid in cash but were granted book credit to pay down their accounts owing. If a weaver had no debit, she was issued "seco" or tokens, redeemable only at that particular post.

While working with the Hubbell archives, I discovered a list of words on the inside back cover of one of the earliest ledger books (Box 321 ~ 1883). Translated from English into "trader" Navajo, 30 percent of the words dealt directly with weaving. The first four words were as follows: "blanket," "good," "bad," "to [sic] much." Given the tremendous devaluation of weaving, it appears that regardless of quality, the weaver wanted "too much." She had little choice but to exchange her blanket for food-stuffs and household goods. The following vignette illustrates difficulties women encountered when exchanging their textiles. It was written by Mrs. Churchill, the wife of a U.S. government Indian inspector (12/28/04, Box 16 #6), while they visited the Hubbells: "There are several hogans near the store, and one woman came to the store while we were there with a blanket. Mr. Hubbell was not willing to pay the price she asked. She said she could get much more at Gallup (60 miles distant). She told him he had three partners in his business; he asked who they were and she replied 'cold, rain, and mud.' If it wasn't for them, she could get her price."

The economic importance of women's textile production was more diverse and complex than existing literature suggests (cf. Bailey and Bailey 1986; Weiss 1984). My analysis of the Hubbells' business records revealed hundreds of women expending thousands of hours of labor annually weaving fleece from their flocks into textiles. I calculated that women had from twenty-five to fifty hours of labor embedded in every pound of hand-spun weaving they produced.[4] Data extrapolated from archival sources demonstrates that weavers' workloads tripled after 1890. Not only were women compelled to accelerate weaving, they had to barter for cloth by the yard and sew much of their families' clothing by hand. They averaged 2 cents per hour in book credit for decades. The fruits of weavers' domestic labor ensured far greater financial security for traders in comparison to raw wool. Evidence in the Hubbell papers suggests that traders seldom realized more than 2 cents per pound on the sale of Navajo wool. Weaving fleece into textiles provided a more secure means of diversification for traders faced with continual price fluctuations in the international wool markets (Wright 1910). Consequently, many traders did not risk putting all of their entrepreneurial eggs in one basket. Had Hubbell continued to market only wool, he would have lost his shirt and his empire. Instead, his empire expanded significantly after the turn of the century. And it was the marketing of Indian "curios" that enhanced his fame, expanded his influence, and augmented his bank balance.

My analysis revealed that the Hubbells' profits in "wool woven into blankets" averaged more than twelve times their wool profits for decades. The Hubbells shipped 208 *tons* of weaving from Ganado, Arizona, between 1892 and 1909. Although the Navajo population increased 50 percent between 1885 and 1915, textile production increased *800* percent over the same period. Yet Weiss (1984:83) reports that 85 percent of the Navajo population was "destitute, moderately poor or average" in 1915. Such an assessment is not difficult to understand, given the surfeit of weaving on the market. The acceleration of textile production in tandem with the usurpation of the market by trade blanket manufacturers had created a glut. Analysis of evidence contained in Hubbell's business records revealed that, due to a shortage of "Moroccan" kidskin at the end of World War I, Navajo goatskins (prepared by women) were selling for more per pound than hand-spun and woven Navajo *rugs*. Furthermore, my analysis of additional information contained in government documents and in two "classic" texts (Amsden 1975; James 1974), corroborates the sustained impoverishment of the Navajo people regionally in tandem with the escalation in textile production. According to government records, weavers' production was valued at one million dollars annually by 1930, yet published statements describe women as weaving "part-time for pin money." Thousands of Navajo women were perceived as dark-skinned housewives toiling within the domestic sphere. Although the cost of living quadrupled for the Navajo people between 1900 and 1928, the exchange value of their weaving stagnated at 1902 levels. Thus "the more they wove, the poorer they became."

WEAVING AND MOTHERING

Given the magnitude and extent of production (and exploitation), why would Navajo women continue to weave? The Navajo creation story provides a number of clues. *Dine Bahane'* comprises a rich, extensive, and complex belief system that provides a charter for human behavior. It defines meaningful social relationships among members of the community and between the community and the entire cosmos. The order inherent in the cosmos was meant to serve as a pattern for proper behavior in both general and specific ways (Griffin-Pierce 1992:87). Such harmony epitomizes the pattern of *hózhó* (beauty/balance) manifest everywhere in the universe. It governs male-female relations and cosmic relationships such as earth and sky, night and day, summer and winter, and mortals and supernaturals (Zolbrod 1984:11). Major mythical figures set examples for the personal growth and maturation of Navajo men and women. Changing Woman, the mother of all Navajo, reminds Father Sun that: "As different as we are, you and I, we are of one spirit. As dissimilar as we are, you and I, we are of equal worth . . . there must always be a solidarity between the two of us . . . there can be no harmony in the universe as long as there is no harmony between us" (Zolbrod 1984:275).

The *K'e* (right and respectful relations with others and the nonhuman world) that exists between mother and child provides the foundational concept and form for all relationships in Navajo social life. Motherhood in Navajo culture is identified and defined in terms of life, particularly its source, reproduction, and sustenance. Mother and child are bound together by the most intense, diffuse, and enduring solidarity to be found in Navajo culture. The relationship of Changing Woman to her children provides the major conceptual framework for the Navajo cultural definition of motherhood as life is created in and sustained by mothers (Witherspoon 1975).[5]

As Mother Earth provides sustenance for her children, human mothers nurture their children. Changing Woman taught Navajo women to weave so they would not suffer from the cold as they would have clothing (Roessel 1983a).

In a text published by the Navajo Curriculum Center, weaver and grandmother Ruth Roessel (1981) incorporates an entire chapter on Holy Peoples' instructions on child rearing: "Navajo women are basic to the understanding of Navajo life and culture. We women are the heart and center of our society. If there is no teaching of Navajo life to our children, there will be no future for the Navajo people. We, the Navajo women, must know the role and traditions of Navajo culture so that we can carry and pass it on. Countless generations ago, when things were out of hand, Changing Woman came and taught the Navajo the right ways. We now need to bring her teachings to our children." Kindness, respect, hard work, generosity, and helpfulness are important values inculcated into children at an early age through example and explicitly taught during *Kinaaldá*, the puberty ceremony for girls. Navajo mothers show their daughters how to cook, spin, and weave. These activities and other family responsibilities are learned by doing, observing, and helping (Parezo 1996:25). Through weaving, women reflect many Navajo values including that of industriousness on the part of the mother who works hard taking care of her family (Sunrise in Kent 1985).[6] Literature on the Navajo frequently references comments indicating how hard Navajo women work.

However, the creation story also cautions that excessive activity in any field is to be avoided as it is contrary to maintaining *hózhó*. The ideals related to *hózhó* are threatened when women accelerate weaving to avoid impoverishment. Mrs. Dorothy Begay, a grandmother from the Rough Rock area of the Reservation, recalls: "We were taught to weave all day and even at night, carding and spinning the wool for the next rug. Once the rug was completed and sold, you would be ready to begin another one. Young girls and women did this into the late hours of the night. Even then, we were able to get up before the sun rose, when it was still dark, and herd sheep. We were always told that herding sheep and weaving rugs were the ways we would survive in this world" (McCarty 1983:12). Evidence of the dilemmas created by overwork are reflected not only in comments made to me by weavers I interviewed, but in letters that a number of Navajo wrote to the Hubbells between 1902 and 1966 (Box 124). Several women remarked on how they needed food and cloth in preparation for a ceremony to cure them from illness caused by excessive weaving. "What the women weave is part of the environment . . . it's in their hearts. If you take something from the environment, you must give something back. Navajo weaving is all about relationships . . . we are like children in our relation to Mother Earth . . . the weaver respects the sheep, as she uses their wool in her weaving" (Harry Walters, Navajo philosopher).

Many Aboriginal peoples extend kinship to all of nature. Rather than using the environment as a means to an end, there is a reciprocal relationship—survival will not occur (or continue) without acknowledging this relationship. Steve Darden (1991) reflects the reciprocal relationship between *K'e* and Navajo cosmology: "Gardens are for feeding the family and for giving to others who are hungry. We help everyone because we all come from our earth . . . plants are one offspring of the Earth Mother and Sky Father. Utilized to perpetuate life, they are symbolic of the essence of life. . . . Father Sky embraces Mother Earth, much as a husband his wife. Water flows throughout the world and embraces the earth, propagating life . . . wood is rooted in Mother Earth, the womb. She nourishes our wood and cares for it." Human reciprocity may only occur within the context of human/environment reciprocation: "Life grows out of the land, woman grows out of the Earth . . . the Beautyway. . . . Women change the world . . . rear sheep, shear . . . all the movements and tensions into a rug" (Annie Kahn, 1992).

Thus weaving is part of an ecological nexus. Navajo weaver and educator Ruth Roessel (1992) describes the process: "The spindle represents the turning of the values . . . with the soft goods, with the jewels . . . you have five fingers . . . all the values go through your fingers to your family. Family members [are] important . . . they help each other. My mother always wove, and raised her children through her weaving . . . it makes you a person, it makes you who you are . . . this is art, this is life. The warps are like a curtain of black clouds . . . a hope for rain . . . weaving is to call the rain . . . all tools have spiritual names, even the loom."

As Ruth's eloquent statement attests, through their weaving, Navajo women unite the two fields of ritual and work as weaving is accompanied by songs, stories, and prayers. Weavers' "mapping" of the domain of textile production includes a cosmological realm. The upright loom is associated with emergence, growth, and ascendance. Such concepts are embedded in Navajo thought:

The Navajo term *ketl'ool*—derived from *ke*, meaning "feet," and *tl'ool* meaning "root system"—expresses the concept of having a foundation for one's life in the earth . . . the central root . . . extends . . . back to Asdzaan Nadleehi, "Changing Woman"—who is Earth Mother herself. Developing from this main root is the complex web of kinship relations . . . including clan relations, the extended family. . . . Tied to this system are material goods, familiar surroundings and livestock. This webbing of the earth, of ancestors, of clan and familiar surroundings all constitute a Navajo home, enabling those within it to flourish and thrive (McNeley 1987:163–64).

Yet researchers have labeled the social relations and practices of female Navajo weavers and male ceremonial chanters dualistically (Reichard,

1950, 1968). This is because of the covert assumption that "whatever is sacred is never sold." Anthropologists have drawn boundaries between information to be included in the fields of "economics," "art," or "religion," thereby determining what will be excluded. The categories constructed through language utilized by social scientists and applied to Navajo material culture have fractured our ability to perceive patterns. Adherence to such a research regime informed by an epistemology that splits cultural pattern from commodity has had devastating consequences for the Navajo people.

The patterns of relations that brought Navajo rugs into existence are fractured through adherence to dualisms. Cultural theft has been sanctioned in multiple ways. Currently a way of life is being sold to the highest bidder as historic Navajo textiles fetch record prices at Sotheby's and other international auction houses.[7] Such activities are midwifed by the bifurcation between the sacred world of religion and the secular or profane world of commodity production as conceived by social scientists. Based on my interviews with weavers, the dualism perceived to be operative that severed sacred and profane is neither generated nor sanctioned by the Navajo people.

Complex patterns of Navajo relations were occluded through the epistemological lens of the colonizers and later the ethnographers. The myth of the origin of the loom and weaving tools as revealed in the creation story is frequently referenced at the beginning of texts on Navajo weaving. Authors then describe the *facts* and relate how everything was borrowed: the loom from the Pueblos, sheep from the Spaniards, and dyes from the Anglos. What is suppressed, overtly or covertly, is the acknowledgment of women's provisioning as a core component of K'e. The bifurcation of sacred and profane thrust Navajo weaving into an alien field. It became completely disassociated from what ethnographers have designated as Navajo religion (Reichard 1950). In a recent issue of *Cultural Survival Quarterly*, Alfonso Ortiz (1996:27–28) remarks: "Native American religions embody a lot of practical knowledge, teachings which serve to put believers in rapport with their environments in a very deep and abiding way. This practical dimension of Native American religions has never been seriously studied, as the romantic tradition surrounding them in American scholarship has always drawn attention to their mystical and spiritual dimensions, and away from the practical tasks that they also perform." Ortiz's remark is most relevant to addressing the shortcomings of the perceived bifurcation between the male activities of sandpainting created to restore harmony and health and female weaving tasks. Both activities are necessary complements to properly perpetuate Navajo lifeways as evoked by *hózhó*. Both sets of activities are recursive processes, sacred forms of reciprocation, that stress continuative renewal and reanimation. Both sets of activities contribute to survival. Thus cyclical interdependence is continually expressed by both chanters and weavers.

The repetition and redundancy of recurring patterns suggest a commonality of form in which Navajo textiles map expressions of fundamental formal relationships. The aesthetics of Navajo weaving is an aesthetics of *holism* rather than an aesthetic that is isomorphic to the rug. I suggest viewing a Navajo rug as a metaphor of Navajo cultural relations because it evokes recognition of important cultural patterns of balance, repetition, rhythm, and reciprocity. In creating her rug, the weaver perpetuates *hózhó*, the order and harmony of the system. Thus weavings are far more than autonomous commodities; they become salient manifestations of *K'e*.

ACKNOWLEDGMENTS

The author wishes to thank the editors of the volume and acknowledge support of the Social Sciences and Humanities Research Council of Canada in the form of a predoctoral fellowship.

NOTES

1. The words "Navajo" and "Diné" continue to be used interchangeably, as the Navajo Nation government has not mandated a change.

2. For example, Western perceptions concerning Aboriginal textile production are informed by the following assumptions: (1) The *mind/body dualism* so prevalent in Western thought was extended to the realm of art during the Renaissance. The creation of painting and sculpture became intellectual activities. The production of crafts (including weaving) was considered equivalent to manual labor and became an unpleasant activity, attractive only because a wage was involved (Immanual Kant, *Critique of Judgement*); (2) The emergence of *aesthetics* as a branch of philosophy at the beginning of the nineteenth century further undermined attitudes toward Aboriginal creations. The Western concept of beauty (central to classical aesthetics) was expressed only in the fine arts of painting and sculpture, thus excluding everything created by Aboriginal peoples globally. Eurocentric ideas about "art" formed part of the cultural baggage that provided justification for the acquisition of Navajo textiles by *weight* until quite recently (M'Closkey 1995).

3. The Lorenzo Hubbell papers include day books, ledgers, correspondence, advertisements, and catalogues covering the years 1883–1964. Four thousand pounds of the family's cumulative papers were placed in custody of the U.S. Park Service. The Special Collections Library, University of Arizona, was chosen to house the papers.

4. There are several "experiments" described in the literature on the time it takes to spin and weave a Navajo rug (Maxwell 1984). I based my estimates on that information in addition to my experience as a spinner and weaver.

5. The subsistence residential unit is organized around a sheep herd, a customary land use area, a head mother, and sometimes agricultural fields, all of which are called *shima* or mother.

6. Pearl Sunrise was the only Navajo weaver present at a conference on the topic hosted by textile scholar Kate Peck Kent at the University of Denver in 1984. In her text published the following year, Kent (1985:113–14) quotes a portion of Pearl's presentation: "The custom of spinning at every odd moment exemplifies the Navajo ideal of keeping busy, while carding, spinning and weaving itself express the value placed on patience and determination. It is important to work steadily at one's own rate and to keep at a task until finished. The Navajo believe that beauty lies within the individual, and in visualizing a pattern and then projecting it onto her loom, the weaver is expressing this beauty. Her designs will be judged good if they meet the Navajo ideals of harmony and balance."

7. Between 1985 and 1987, 1,087 Navajo textiles valued at $1.7 million dollars sold through major auction houses such as Christie's and Sotheby's. For comparison's sake, 77 non-Navajo textiles sold for $222,000, including Chilkat dancing blankets and Satillo serapes, over the same period. Meyer (1973:81) estimates that for every million dollars sold at public auctions, at least ten times that amount is exchanged in private transactions.

REFERENCES

Adams, W. Y. (1963). *Shonto: A Study of the Role of the Trader in a Modern Navajo Community*. Bureau of American Ethnology, Bulletin 188. Washington, D.C.: Government Printing Office.

Akbarzadeh, A. (1992). "The House of Babbitt: A Business History of the Babbitt Brothers Trading Company 1886–1926." Ph.D. dissertation, Department of History and Political Science, Northern Arizona University, Flagstaff, U.S.A.

Amsden, C. A. (1975). *Navajo Weaving, Its Technique and History*. Salt Lake City: Peregrine Smith, Inc. (Originally published 1934.)

Bailey, G., and R. Bailey. (1986). *A History of the Navajo. The Reservation Years*. Santa Fe: School of American Research Press.

Boles, J. (1981). "The Navajo Rug at the Hubbell Trading Post, 1880–1920." *American Indian Culture and Research Journal* 5 (1):47–63.

Darden, S. (1991). *Time among the Navajo*. Edited by Kathy E. Hooker. Santa Fe: Museum of New Mexico Press.

Dedera, D. (1990). *Navajo Rugs: How to Find, Evaluate, Buy and Care for Them*. Flagstaff: Northland Press. (Originally published 1975.)

Downer, A. (1990). "Life on the Reservation and Historic Preservation." In *Preservation on the Reservation*, ed. A. L. Klesert and A. S. Downer. Window Rock: Navajo Nation Papers in Anthropology 26:201–06.

Griffin-Pierce, T. (1992). *Earth Is My Mother, Sky Is My Father*. Albuquerque: University of New Mexico Press.

James, G. W. (1974). *Indian Blankets and Their Makers*. New York: Dover Publishing Company. (Originally published 1914.)

James, H. L. (1988). *Rugs and Posts. The Story of Navajo Rugs and Their Homes*. Tucson: Southwest Parks and Monuments. (Originally published 1976.)

Kapoun, R. (1992). *The Language of the Robe*. Salt Lake City: Peregrine Smith.

Kent, K. P. (1985). *Navajo Weaving: Three Centuries of Change*. Santa Fe: School of American Research Press.

Leacock, E., and M. Etienne, eds. (1980). *Women and Colonization*. New York: Praeger.

The Lorenzo Hubbell Papers. (1876–1966). Documents, personal correspondence, journals, ledgers, and day books. Special Collections Library, University of Arizona.

Maxwell, G. S. (1984). *Navajo Rugs, Past, Present and Future*. Palm Desert, Calif.: Desert Southwest Publications. (Originally published 1963.)

M'Closkey, K. (1995). " 'Trading Is a White Man's Game': The Appropriation of Navajo Women's Weaving." In *Ethnographic Feminisms*, ed. S. Cole and L. Phillips, 97–118. Ottawa: Carleton University Press.

McCarty, T. L. (1983). *Of Mother Earth, Father Sky*. Chinle, Ariz.: Rough Rock Press.

McNeley, G. (1987). "Home: A Family of Land and People." *Dine Be'iina'. A Journal of Navajo Life* 1 (1):161–64. Shiprock, N.M.: Navajo Community College Press.

McNitt, F. (1962). *The Indian Traders*. Norman: University of Oklahoma Press.

Meyer, K. (1973). *The Plundered Past*. New York: Atheneum.

Mies, M. (1986). *Patriarchy and Accumulation on a World Scale*. London: Zed Books.

Ortiz, A. (1996). "American Indian Religious Freedom." *Cultural Survival* 19 (4): 26–29.

Parezo, N. (1996). "The Diné [Navajo]: Sheep Is Life." In *Paths of Life*, ed. T. Sheridan and N. Parezo, Tucson: University of Arizona Press. pp. 3–33.

Reichard, G. (1950). *Navajo Religion: A Study in Symbolism*. Bollingen Series 18. New York: Pantheon.

———. (1968). *Navajo Shepherd and Weaver*. Glorieta, N.M.: Rio Grande Press. (Originally published 1936.)

Rodee, M. (1981). *Old Navajo Rugs: Their Development from 1900 to 1940*. Albuquerque: University of New Mexico Press.

Roessel, R. (1981). *Women in Navajo Society*. Round Rock, Ariz.: Navajo Curriculun Center.

———. (1983a). "Navajo Arts and Crafts." *Southwest* 10:592–608. Alfonso Ortiz, ed. Washington, D.C.: Smithsonian Institution.

———. (1983b). "Navajo History, 1850–1923." *Southwest* 10:506–22. Alfonso Ortiz, ed. Washington, D.C.: Smithsonian Institution.

———. (1994). Verbal presentation. "Navajo Weaving since the Sixties." Heard Museum. Phoenix, Ariz. March 10–13.

U.S. News & World Report. (1994). "The Worst Federal Agency" (28 Nov.): 61–64.

Van Valkenburgh, R. F., and J. McPhee. (1974). *A Short History of the Navajo People*. New York: Garland.

Vogt, E. (1961). "The Navajo." In *Perspectives in American Culture Change*, ed. E. H. Spicer, 278–336. Chicago: University of Chicago Press.

Weiss, L. (1984). *The Development of Capitalism in the Navajo Nation: A Political Economy History*. MEP Publications 15, Studies in Marxism. Minneapolis.

Wheat, J. B. (1984). *The Gift of Spiderwoman: Southwestern Textiles, the Navajo Tradition*. Philadelphia: University Museum, University of Pennsylvania.

Witherspoon, G. (1975). *Navajo Kinship and Marriage*. Midway Reprint. Chicago: University of Chicago Press.

———. (1987). *Navajo Weaving: Art in Its Cultural Context*. Flagstaff: Museum of Northern Arizona, no. 37.

Wright, C. (1910). *Wool Growing and the Tariff: A Study in the Economic History of the United States*. Cambridge, Mass.: Harvard Economic Studies.

Zolbrod, P. (1984). *Dine Bahane. The Navajo Creation Story*. Albuquerque: University of New Mexico Press.

8

Gendered Kin and Conflict in Kenya

Judith M. Abwunza

The examination and analysis of kinship and marriage structures have a long history in the cross-cultural research of Africa. More recent gender analyses[1] feature women as powerful actors in these structures, networking, negotiating, and politicizing in areas formerly analyzed through androcentric perspectives. The lesson we have learned is that cultural aspects played out on the ground are always contextual and rely on empirical analyses involving *all* members. This chapter discusses cultural aspects of kinship harmony and conflict in order to portray people's lives by including gender as an analytical concept. The scene is Kenya, East Africa.

The chapter includes a brief overview of precolonial and colonial times to allow an informed examination of current economic "alliances." The first section discusses alliances combining kinship, marriage, and bride-wealth structures, followed by a discussion of the "alliances" found in residence and wage labor expectations. The conflicts and contradictions in these alliances in contemporary times are conspicuous. I conclude by challenging the commonly held view of Kenyans and the Kenyan state that alliances provide a traditional source for economic support. The chapter illustrates that there are no easy solutions to the difficult circumstances that are placing people at economic risk.

About 200,000 Avalogoli,[2] who are the topic of this chapter, are established in Maragoli, western Kenya. They live in a patrilineal,[3] patrilocal,[4] segmentary society[5] and rely on agriculture and proceeds from wage labor. Logoli people are heavily dependent on genderized and politicized kinship, and affinal (relatives by marriage) structural relationships that extend to the community are influenced by historical and current conditions. Historically, somewhat idealized kinship and affine alliances provided well-being through relatively efficient survival strategies, though these were by no means utopian relationships; conflict did occur. In contemporary society, kinship, affine, and community economic strategies, affected by former colonial practices and today's state economic policies, appear to be deteriorating. The interference with economically adaptive structures, evidenced by their long history and people's survival within them, is placing people in situations of debilitating poverty. Capitalist relations of production, with its hallmark of individual accumulation, threatens what is considered the "traditional" way of collective survival benefits for all members through reciprocity. Whether invented (Hobsbawm 1983:9, Ranger 1983:248–49) or reinvented (Oberholtzer 1995), "traditional life" and its hallmark of adherence to the collectivity are still believed by the Avalogoli to be the ideal.

Reciprocity was and is the ideological and practical mode of exchange among this subethnic group. This mode of exchange involves the continuing obligation to share proceeds by way of a culturally imposed plan of action that aims at allowing all members to survive within an ideal of kinship co-residence and kin and affine cooperation. We may call this ideal a collectivity in contemporary society; it approximates a precolonial "kin corporate mode of production" (Sacks 1979:122) or, as defined in neo-Marxist anthropology, a lineage mode of production, referring to a subsistence-oriented system "where domestic groups that are the primary producing units are grouped into corporate lineages or clans with substantial collective rights and interests" (Keesing 1981:513). Among the Avalogoli, the collectivity, as a vestige of authority, depends on the patterns of relationship within kinship groups where all are seen as "children" of the ancestors and outside kinship groups that have negotiated affinal alliances. As in many African contexts, then, Avalogoli social, economic, and political relations depend on a closely knit extended family system that confers specific rights of kinship and that, prior to missionization, included ancestral mediators between living people and a remote deity. Logoli women and men are influenced by this collective ideology. It informs the kinship, marriage, bridewealth, residence, and wage labor alliances (discussed below) that ultimately provide the foundation for reciprocal ties and that should give members access to the "good life." In this and other East African societies, the "good life" contains the ingredients of land, cattle, and children.

Before colonial contact, and to this day, Logoli people had a proper way of seeing, believing in, and living out their lives. This Logoli ideology, and its extensions through time, are perfect and defensible for those who hold it. In this context, people label this ideology "the Avalogoli way," and it is called upon to legitimize procedures or when actions not considered procedural require correction. For example, the Avalogoli way gives edicts:

fathers are to give land to their sons; sons are to provide land for their wives; wives and their families are to receive bridewealth. It is recognized that in some situations the Avalogoli way is followed and in some situations it is not, but ideally it "ought" to be since it is considered to benefit all members (the collectivity) rather than only a few.

"Traditionally," Avalogoli political structure involved a process of consensus expressed in a policy of talking until you agree. One elder woman understood its historical origins during a time "when people were still naked and before God came." Socially, the levels of obligation were consistent with a social structure of segmentary patrilineage formed into a collectivity, relying on elder (and ancestor) authority. For example, a woman in her forties says: "You were trained in such a way that you had respect for anybody, living or dead. It didn't matter whether it's your father or whose father. Your mother's sister is your mother; all old people are the mothers and fathers, and the young are their children. These are the laws" (Florence, 28 Oct. 1983).[6] Economically, this collectivity emerged in the time when their ancestor, Mulogoli, immigrated to the area and gave land to his sons for their wives to dig in order that the women could support the family and community. Land was inalienable, passing from fathers to sons for women's use; it was "family land."[7] To be a member of the social group, the sons and daughters had to fulfill obligations to parents: "Logoli sons are to know again their father. Whatever they get, they are to be friends to father . . . give to your father" (Muhavi, 21 July 1984). Daughters provided bridewealth cattle and other goods to facilitate the marriage of their brothers and bring wealth to their parents; "daughters are important, they never forget parents, girls think of and care for parents in their old age" (Asava, 22 July 1984). This cycle of giving and receiving extended throughout the community, in the form of food (i.e., millet for cassava and to *silika*, i.e., reciprocal group work), by working for one another in groups, building houses, or digging land. Gradual increases in population were accommodated through what has been called predatory expansion among these segmentary lineages or, in other words, wars for land against neighboring groups of people, in this case with the Luo and Nandi.

During British colonial times in Kenya, all indigenous ethnic groups suffered similar inequalities. They were alienated from their land, and their conscripted labor for European farms and domestic work was reinforced by pass laws. Additionally, there was the establishment of reserves and laws against cash crop production and trade by Africans. Colonialism also introduced into capitalism the concept of individual accumulation. Logoli people, however, conformed to colonial circumstances by retaining a notion of the collectivity through reciprocal relations, which in turn articulated with capitalist relations. For example, a gift of food from a relative might stimulate an obligation to pay school fees for another relative. This adherence to the collectivity is relatively amazing considering the circumstances of rising population and decreasing land resources. The colonial government had a vested interest in ignoring the increasing population because the Maragoli Reserve was an important labor resource area.[8] Within the reserve, Logoli retained their living patterns in kinship territorial segments and attempted to accommodate the imposition of title deeds for land by retaining elder authority through the "native courts," the latter being an invention of tradition by the British colonials (cf. Ranger 1983). Where possible, fathers gave land to sons, "even if a small piece was divided among many sons." Sons and their families provided some bridewealth to affines and resources for women to feed the family and community.

After nearly eighty years of colonialism, Logoli people ultimately joined with other groups to fight for freedom from colonial rule. Initially western Kenya's opposition to the inequalities suffered by African people began through voluntary associations introduced by the missionaries and adapted by Africans to serve political ends. The North Kavirondo Central Association, formed in 1932 with the help of the apolitical Society of Friends, began in the most densely populated areas, Maragoli and a neighboring reserve, Bunyore. It grew until it had membership from almost every reserve in western Kenya. By now these reserves were called "locations," and people within them were issuing protests against the compulsory culling of cows, demanding payment of war gratuities to dependents of Africans killed in World War I, and campaigning for tax exemptions and the lowering of taxes. Soon the protest extended to missionaries and settlers, who were accused of stealing African lands. People demanded title deeds for the location areas in order to stop further encroachment. By the 1950s a nationalistic identity had taken hold, and people demanded independence from the British.[9]

Kenya's independence in 1963 did not provide a panacea for a situation where the economic structure of capitalism remained and the population continued to increase while land continued to decrease. Today, the Avalogoli face high population density, coupled with the possession of limited agricultural land and few cattle. They are heavily dependent on inputs from the wage labor sector in a context where opportunities are severely limited. Additionally, structural adjustment policies (SAPs) imposed by the International Monetary Fund and the World Bank in the 1980s and renewed in the 1990s are literally SAP(ping) the economic resilience of people. The shift from project-oriented funds to conditional funds has placed tremendous burdens on both urban and rural populations, even though such schemes propose to assist rural populations like the Avalogoli. In brief, structural adjustment reforms are conditioned by the devaluation of currencies, increases in food prices and interest rates, alignment of domestic prices with world prices, an emphasis on tradable rather than subsistence crops, privatization of parastatals, reductions in public-sector employment and wages, decreases in budget deficits, imposition of user fees particularly in health care, and the elimination of food and fertilizer subsidies (Economic Commission for Africa 1989:18–20).[10]

Facing these economic challenges, Logoli men and women migrate to urban areas, mostly Nairobi, to look for work that is mainly nonexistent. The pattern of circular relationships intensifies; rural people are heavily reliant on urban kin and affines for financial assistance at home and support in the urban area while seeking wage labor. Urban people depend on those at home to feed and educate their children, who are sent to the rural area where food and schooling are thought to be less expensive. They also depend on small land plots not only for growing crops but for their own resting place when they die; the Avalogoli are always buried at home. The interference with the "good life" ingredients of land and cattle to provide care for children is profound. One may ask, what is left in the cultural realms to permit survival in today's circumstances of increasing economic risk? The following analysis of kin and conflict in Kenya provides some answers to this question.

Alliance structures have undergone transformations, but rhetorically they remain remarkably intact. Kinship ties are not completely fractured, as people, despite their precarious circumstances, are not willing to ignore the reciprocal requirements that allow them to remain members in good standing. Reciprocal practices are still central in kinship, marriage, and community relations. Generally speaking, all Avalogoli social activities—being born and maturing, owning land and cattle, rejoicing life and leaving it behind—are still integrated with those who have come before, those who are now here, and those who are yet to come. Relationships within *tsinyumba* ("houses" in the lineage structure) give members a sense of affiliation and continuity and are the basis of individual security. The bond between the individual and the group is still considered to provide the "good life." Achieving the good life means living up to the requirements of good Logoli people, which involves adherence to the power structure of the collectivity, the social and political realms, and to giving and receiving within the collectivity, that is, in the economic realm. This is life in the head and heart of the people; these are the cultural "oughts" that pertain to the idealized normative structure, the way people would wish things to be.

KINSHIP, MARRIAGE, AND BRIDEWEALTH "ALLIANCES"

Kinship relations are still structured by elder authority. These relations are, as the people say, "rooted in the past" and tied to the ancestor, Mulogoli, who is called "father" or "grandfather." Mulogoli and his wife, Kaliyesa, migrated to and settled in the Maragoli area around 1700. Mulogoli and Kaliyesa had four sons: Musali, Kizungu, Kilima, and M'mavi. These four sons make up the *tsinyumba tzinene*, "great houses" in the segmentary lineage structure of the people of Logoli. The sons and their children spread over the land in defined territorial segments that for the most part remain today. In contemporary society the political structure is state controlled, but elders do wield influence. Juniors do not push limits too far in ignoring their reciprocal responsibility, no matter how much they complain that "elders have big pockets that never get filled." It is not in their vested interest to lose their place in the comfort of the social group even as that social group places demands on them that are impossible to fulfill. Fathers hold on to title deeds nowadays, excluding sons from ownership, or perhaps they do not have the wherewithal to purchase land for sons. Daughters who marry into landless families have difficulty providing for their own children and affines, let alone giving to natal kin. All of this indicates the transformation of traditional alliances. But some aspects remain. The expectation of support is still strong, evidenced by an endless stream of relatives, friends, and children of friends who appear in yards expecting some form of material support. The demands are endless: money for school fees, food, clothing, or to improve living conditions. Not giving means not receiving the support of the collectivity. This translates into not being regarded as "good" Logoli people and, in the event of the human difficulties everyone faces, having nowhere to turn for assistance. Conflict occurs, arguments take place between husbands and wives, children, parents, and siblings. In actuality, most relatives and affines debate, often angrily and sometimes violently, who should provide resources and how the resources should be distributed. Still, "helping one another" is "rooted in the past," even though everyone acknowledges that in the past it was easier to help.

Today everyone needs market commodities, as scant subsistence crops are quickly exhausted. Much of the work devolves on women who have the responsibility for feeding and caring for children and other members of the family extending to the community. Women are directly responsible for this task, and they are extremely dependent on the reciprocal relations of caring and sharing in order to fulfill their obligations. They rely on kin, affines, and the community, and they base their requests on the relationships that exist in the normative structures of kinship and in marriage relationships that extend those kinship structures to affines.

In the world of Logoli women and men, gender relationships move the world. The Avalogoli still practice patrilocality and bridewealth.[11] Logoli women engage in marriage relationships structured by marriage rules specifying their own and their children's privilege via the patriliny. A wife's kin receives cash, cows, and gifts from a husband's kin, who in turn benefit from the labor and children a wife will contribute. As Staudt and Col point out for Kenya generally, "[a] woman who leaves her own kin to live with those of her husband is celebrated for her reproductive capability" (1991: 246). In Maragoli, women are also celebrated for their hard work. An aspect of their hard work, aside from the usual overwhelming activities related to providing food for the household and the community, is found in their active participation in kin-, affinal-, and community-based recip-rocal relations. Reciprocal relations provide the *vika* (steps) for a "proper" way of life. On a daily basis, goods are exchanged in covered baskets, or women trek to other yards carrying a banana stalk, hoping for school fees in return. Husbands, older children, parents and siblings, affines, and neigh-bors are approached for assistance. Those who remain members in good standing (that is, they give as well as receive) hope to be supported, how-ever meagerly, by the norms of exchange. People complain of the demands, saying "we have so little," but they do not "kill" the one asking. This means they remain polite and attentive in their refusal if they cannot man-age rather than being abrupt or "mean." Sarah says it best: "It is the same as what you people call banking. When I face problems I will send one of my children to the one I have given to, and they will give to that child. It takes away my pain [uncertainty]" (12 Dec. 1987). In many cases, those who ask and are asked are from *umuliango gwitu*, meaning "from our door" (symbolically our *inyumba*, our "house"), and from the larger net-works of affines. *Uvukwi* (bridewealth) is described as "opening the way" for marriage and the children who provide the *daraja* (bridge) for "visiting" during which the exchanges take place.

The first step to marriage legitimacy is *uvukwi* discussion. *Uvukwi* pres-tations begin the cycle of affinal reciprocity. It is said that originally the amount of *uvukwi* was the same for everyone, and payment was always completed before the marriage took place. Differentiation began when cash intruded and set up the present system of down payments, credits, and outstanding debts that may take years to complete, if at all. Currently *uvukwi* prestations take the form of cash and cattle to (in a collective sense) daughters' fathers and tea, sugar, cloth, head scarfs, and smaller amounts of cash to daughters' mothers. Since *uvukwi* may now be as much as ten cows and 46,000 Kenya shillings (Kshs.) in a context where a wage-working person earns 5 to 7,000 Kshs.[12] a month, any hope of a complete payment prior to marriage has long since disappeared. As a result, daugh-ters and sons often elope. Yet, even when *uvukwi* discussion and payment are precluded as a preliminary step to marriage, the appropriate *vika* (steps) ought to be followed after an elopement. The responsibility for initiating discussion and making payment lies with the yard within which the daugh-ter chooses to marry. If this does not take place, and in many cases today it does not, women and men from the woman's home will make visits and suggest the procedure begin. The obligations and benefits surrounding *uvukwi* are problematic for both men and women.

I recognize that Africanists have noted that bridewealth may contribute to women's oppression and influence their social control (most recently, Lovett 1996). In contrast to this position, Logoli women view their reputations as well as their economic survival as dependent on a successful and continuing *uvukwi* process. This is a normative practice that is not easy to dispel, particularly in this context where it "opens the way" for affinal reciprocal benefits on which many women heavily rely, especially during times of economic risk. In fact, if discussion and payment do not take place at all, women describe themselves as "stuck," "just there," "just a slave" after eloping.[13]

Although most research discussions surrounding bridewealth investigate men's payments and men's receipts, Logoli women are very instrumental in the process. They describe how they "work hard" either to accumulate cash and cows or to prove their cultural worth so that cash and cows may be sent. Women discuss how they will "push" to have payments made, as their parents and kin need the support, and also how without any payment they and their children are cut off from the reciprocal relations that should exist within kin and affine groups. Without bridewealth paid, all women who are not living in marriage relationships say they will refuse to send the children "there," meaning to the fathers and their relatives. Men have a great deal of the control here. Women say it is up to men to approach their patriliny and "push" to have the first cow sent to legitimize the relationship as a marriage. Collective responsibility still works to some extent as other women and men recognize the responsibility that should take place toward affines. No person wants "the way" to be closed. Daughters want to return to their natal home with gifts showing that they are "coming from people, not trees" and return with gifts to the yards where they have married, showing they are "well-loved children."

In all cases there appear to be no particular contributing variables to nondiscussion and nonpayment. It seems very contextual: not enough children produced, too many children to be able to pay, or not enough money to provide for affine responsibilities. Often when asked about this, women were not able, or perhaps not willing, to provide causes. In most cases men attributed it to a general lack of finances. However, women were adamant that *uvukwi* should be paid, and men agreed that it ought to be paid. Most people are aware that adherence to the institution of *uvukwi* is difficult given the lack of finances. Yet women assess that *uvukwi* payments provide evidence not only for their status but also for the instigation and continuance of reciprocal alliances, the gift-giving/receiving that is the mutual support found within a collectivity. These alliances permit some people to survive and thus some institutions to remain firmly entrenched. As the Women's Group from Friend's Church says: "It is the reward for parents, and the young man and his family feel very proud for having given *uvukwi*. It is another system of saying, 'this is my wife.' If not, the wife can say these are not your children. In death, her parents would demand the body and the children, even if there were ten children. Even if one cow is given, it makes the difference." Mothers and daughters recognize that bridewealth is an important context within which their lives are enhanced. Members of the Digoi Women's Group say: "Now girls are educated, the child helps at home; when she leaves to marry, the *uvukwi* will assist those at the home she is leaving. It gives strength to the married girl. She is someone with power, she is not just someone picked from the market. *Uvukwi must* be paid. Women must see it is paid; they must work hard to see that happen."

Women do have alternatives. Wives may threaten to "walk with their children," meaning to take their children and leave the relationship and to cut the husband's sons and daughters from his patriliny. Although sons cut off from their fathers may be told to get their land elsewhere, mothers choose whether or not to pursue this and they weigh the son's loss according to their own best interests in the context of land scarcity. Daughters raised in their mother's natal home will bring their *uvukwi* prestations to that home, not to those of the fathers who neglected them. Women rely on a common saying that, "Fathers will ultimately say, 'You can lose a cow from the home but not a child.' " Bridewealth is the preliminary step in the process that permits affinal reciprocal relations to begin. It "opens the way" for social and economic alliances to be activated, not the least of which are the land and wage labor proceeds on which women rely.

RESIDENCE AND WAGE LABOR ALLIANCES

Considering today's shortage of agricultural land for subsistence operations, proceeds from wage labor of some kind are a necessary condition for survival. Thus land and cash are directly connected and discussed in this section in turn. Men own land by inheritance or perhaps nowadays by purchase. As people see it, women are given access to the land for their houses and farms only through marriage; land ownership is men's responsibility: "Men are the ones to give land to their wives." Although "the Avalogoli way" is for fathers to give land to their sons, they do not always do so. Scarcity of land is reflected in the fact that most Maragoli land is still inalienable, and the few pieces that are available for sale are priced high—an average of 50,000 Kshs. for a half-acre plot before structural adjustment policies trebled the price. The purchase price for land inside or outside Maragoli requires considerable accumulation, and many fathers and sons simply do not have and likely will never have the means.

In Maragoli, where this interviewing context includes 410 women, only two women speak of "my land" in cases where they have title deeds in their name. The remainder characterize the land as "our land" or "our family's land." In reference to men, out of 245 sons, 78 are married. All sons, married and unmarried, are considered to be "living at home," even if they are away but have a place at home where they should be entitled to a piece of land for their wives to farm, currently (if they are married), or in the future (if they are not). For all 78 married sons, wives are living in their home yards, even if their husbands are living elsewhere. For the most part these married sons do not have a title deed or identifying numbers for "their" land. Title deeds are mainly held by fathers, the male elders who retain control as long as possible, creating conflict situations.[14] Only eight sons, less than 10 percent of this sample, have title deeds for their pieces of land.

In Maragoli today, most women farm on a quarter to a half acre of land. Land size was measured in fifty-two yards. Nineteen of these yards have one-quarter acre, thirteen have half an acre. Only seven yards have one acre. Others range from zero in one case to five and a half in another. Four women in one yard share a plot of one-quarter acre, one-sixteenth for each. The inequities are evident, as the small plots do not provide subsistence for women's large families, let alone for prestations or a cash crop.

Within the cultural mandate, mothers, fathers, and brothers advise women of the disadvantages of "marrying land" that has many sons. The elder, Mariam, provides an explanation.

The reasons why we had bigger land before is like this: in one household you had one son, so he got all the land, but when the sons increase so you have four, you have to divide that land into quarters. Look, I was married to the only son, I have big land, that was my luck. When I got married to that home, I had three sons. The first one had land, the second one had land, the third one had land. No serious problems because there was only one son where I married. With Abigail, there are three sons where she is married, they have sons, and she has eight sons; Freda, seven sons where she is married, they have sons, and she has one son. And there it goes, the land is gone!

When elders (men and women) are involved in marriage decisions, one of their responsibilities is to ensure that enough land is available for their daughters' future use. If women engage in *kuvahira* (elopement) rather than *urukari* (marriage, with an elder discussion taking place), then they may be held responsible for not properly assessing the situation that may develop once they begin to produce children and underproduce subsistence. Violet, for example, has three children and a husband with no land from his father for her to farm. Violet's mother asks her, "Why did you marry there? They do not have enough land for you. There they have too many sons."

Women can own land in a context of patrilineal, inalienable land rights. For example, women who are widowed or daughters who are unmarried can call on Kenya's Law of Succession Act (enacted in 1972; in operation since 1981), which "gives a widow and her daughters equal footing with male relatives in property succession" (Attorney-general Mr. Justice Mathew Muli, opening a four-day regional conference of the International Federation of Women Lawyers in Nairobi, December 1987). In Maragoli, a few widows have the land numbers, but the majority rely on assistance

from their sons' inheritance or those of their brothers-in-law if there are
no sons.

In interviews, 41 percent of women believe women should not own land,
holding men responsible by saying, for example, "Men are the ones to give
land to their wives." "Men own land; women do not." Barnard, an elder
man says, "women owning land signifies trouble in a marriage" relationship. This is in keeping with the patriarchal structure and ideology of men
as owners of production. Yet, in the interviews, 47 percent of women believe that women should own their own land, and another 10 percent give
qualified responses. "Women should own their own land if they have their
own money to buy," or "No, women should not own their own land, but
if they have money (to buy), they may." As mentioned above, 2 of 410
women purchased land and had title deeds in their names. These women
are wage laborers. Both are married but describe their marriages as "not
steady." Both had difficulty in registering the title deeds in their names.
They had to "fight" for the deed. Even though men and a lesser percentage
of women believe that women should not own their own land, 57 percent
of women believe women should or could own land. In some sense this is
a moot point, as women are even less able than men to accumulate the
funds to purchase. Yet, while men own land by inheritance and women
only access the land through marriage, women perceive there are alternatives open to them that could conceivably fracture the patrilineal land inheritance structure.

If enough land is not available, men are considered to provide supplementary support with proceeds from wage labor. Many men are "tar-
macking" (looking for work) or "losing the day" at the markets or on the
streets in Nairobi. However, only a few men have full-time jobs. Most
employed men work outside Maragoli, and by the time they pay their own
living expenses they have little left to contribute to the home. In the sample
of 410 women interviewed, 34 men (husbands) worked full-time, only 4 of
them in the Maragoli area. Their cash contribution to the household in
most cases was limited.

Women's wage work in the rural area is influenced by a number of factors, not the least of which are the same lack of wage opportunities that
men face and the overwhelming daily task responsibilities they call "home
work." Women hoe, plant, weed, harvest, fetch water and firewood, care
for animals, acquire and prepare the daily food, care for children, do laundry, and clean the house and yard. Men are not usually involved in these
tasks. The expectation is that men will engage in and contribute the proceeds from wage labor, "outside work." Yet a few women have added wage
labor to their duties and work as clerks, teachers, or nurses, and some do
agricultural labor for others for a wage or for a share of the crop in order
to provide for their families. So, although men do not do "home work,"
women are not similarly restricted from "outside work." When colonialism

brought cash and commodities to the Maragoli economy, a labor separation was encouraged between women and men in that men were directed to wage labor while women engaged in home work and farming activities. Today women resent the implication of responsibility connected to the necessity to provide more than daily food requirements from "home work" in order to survive. They also detest that there is not enough land to get the cash needed to buy food items and commodities. This view is directed to men who do not or cannot supply land or cash from wage labor. The culturally defined gender categories create difficulties, and these are made worse when men and women do not or cannot live up to role expectations.

Women's primary task as they describe it is "taking care of the entire house and yard." Today this involves a movement across the domains theoretically categorized by Westerners as "private" and "public," although neither men nor women in Maragoli use these labels, nor do they categorize value as "use" or "exchange." Women's and men's understanding of women's role demands that women "provision" (provide needs) for their family in whatever way possible. This includes the domain of the yard, ideally women's production from men's land, and ideally men's cash production from wage labor. In terms of productive value, the two domains articulate and conflict with each other. This context provides for an unrealistic delineation of labor tasks by gender that contributes to problematic conflict situations between men and women, extending to the larger kin, affinal, and community structures. Expectations are placed on all that few can fulfill. Maintaining the proper way of life is increasingly difficult.

CONCLUSION

Logoli people are at cultural and economic risk. Their lives are influenced by individual, collective, and state practices. Like many African societies they are placed in a situation of crises management in the face of a rapid increase in poverty among both rural and urban populations. They face ecological crises, land shortages, unemployment, and political conflicts. State enterprise is overextended, debt has worsened, and living conditions have become increasingly debilitating. Kenya experiences recession, ethnic violence, drought, and imposed structural adjustment policies that exacerbate poverty. A downward spiral into economic helplessness and abject poverty would seem the norm for many. In 1992 the World Bank published a survey of 182 country economies, placing Kenya as the 26th poorest (1992:218, 285). The majority of Kenyans face situations of economic crisis and devastating poverty, and for most it appears there is no good end in sight. Basic human needs have become luxury items that many cannot afford. The class situation in Kenya is such that in the late 1980s the top 10 percent of the Kenya population received 45.8 percent of household income, while the poorest received 2.6 percent (World Bank 1989). This inequity is intensified in the Maragoli context, where decreasing land resources and severe unemployment situate the vast majority of the population in poverty.

The state offers no solutions, as many of the agricultural development initiatives have failed and scarce state resources disallow any form of viable rural or urban development. In the Sixth Development Plan, 1989–93, poverty as an issue is not given explicit reference. Instead, the economic problems of the people are to be addressed by their own "gainful employment," and there is a heavy state reliance on people helping people through the traditional alliance structures of caring and sharing. As I have said elsewhere (Abwunza 1996, 1997), one could expect that people would simply give up in contexts such as these. But they do not. They continue to confront their situations with amazing resilience and are not passive in face of imposed conditions.

Today capitalism comes close to ruling the Logoli world. These people cannot withdraw from the market, and interestingly they do not have the means to do so. Supporting the normative alliance structures is increasingly expensive, thus difficult. Some people visit late at night so as to provide a little aid to immediate family and avoid collectivity obligations. Others are described as being "lost in the city," meaning they do not provide any assistance at all. But collectivity alliances have not died out completely. Edda, in response to my suggesting this (after hearing so many people say they can no longer assist others when they have no support for themselves), sharply instructed that I should pay closer attention to my observations; to the women carrying baskets of goods, balancing a banana stalk on their heads and a baby on their hip as they walk from yard to yard, giving and receiving. She tells me to go to the bus station and observe the packed buses traveling from the urban areas to see how the passengers distribute envelopes containing remittances from those in the cities and then watch them return with "food from the land." These are the people I call messengers in the kinship and affinal alliance structures. The Avalogoli are a people attempting to hold on, with a little here given, a little here received, in the ongoing system of reciprocal alliances that colonialism and neocolonialism have so far failed to destroy completely. Indeed, in these times of economic risk, a point can be made that invoking traditional economic ideologies may be the only source of survival.

Placing gender at the forefront of this context permits us to see the heavy burden placed on women as they work hard to retain the alliances that provide at least some support for members. There is no doubt that many of the societal institutions in Maragoli contribute to the maintenance of social control. They enhance what people with power, mainly men, consider "proper" gender roles and behavior, frequently at the expense of women. But women are not passive in these situations (cf. Abwunza 1997). They exhibit remarkable energy and initiative. As Stamp has pointed out, it is "an important feminist goal to render visible the agency of women. . . . Especially in the Third World, women have been treated as passive targets of oppressive practices and discriminatory structures. Such a conceptualization colludes with sexist ideologies that construct women as naturally inferior, passive and consigned to a private, apolitical world" (1991: 845). In Maragoli, women's economic efforts are always heroic, if not always sufficient. The expected reciprocity is frequently meager, and sometimes conflict is intensified. The normative notion of reciprocity, the continuing obligation to share, places a burden on everyone but most particularly on women, who are held responsible if they are unable to give and do not receive. The situation is unrealistic, even oppressive, and further compounded by state expectations of people to support others via kinship and affinal alliances. Reciprocal alliances, grounded in an adherence to the collectivity, are an unaffordable expense today. How can kinship and affinal reciprocal relations live up to expectations in the context where, as Victoria says, "in Kenya 100 Kshs. is now worth 37"? Still, one has to admire the effort, best described by Sarah who insists, "We will help each other . . . we give according to our heart and what we can; forever we have done that, we are forever exchanging" (12 Dec. 1987).

ACKNOWLEDGMENTS

Approximately fifteen years of fieldwork in Kenya have been at times financially assisted by the following: Social Sciences and Humanities Research Council of Canada (SSHRCC); International Development Research Centre (IDRC); the Centre for International Studies, University of Toronto; Department of Anthropology, University of Western Ontario; Faculty of Arts and Science, Wilfrid Laurier University. Permission to engage in Kenya research is provided by the Office of the President, Kenya. Affiliation is provided by the University of Nairobi with the Institute of African Studies and the Department of Urban and Regional Planning.

NOTES

1. See, for example: Abwunza (1996), (1995), (1990), (1988); Brown and Tiffen (1992); Cubbins (1991); Davison (1996); Hafkin and Bay (1976); Hay and Wright (1982); Hay and Stichter (1984); Mirza and Strobel (1989); Nzomo (1989); Parpart (1994); Parpart and Staudt (1989); Robertson and Berger (1986); Romero (1988); Stamp (1991), (1990), (1986); Stichter and Parpart (1988); White (1990).

2. "Avalogoli" translates as "people of Logoli." The place name, Maragoli, and people, Avalogoli, are derived from the name of their ancestor, Mulogoli. The Avalogoli are a linguistically separate subethnic group in the larger ethnic group of Baluhya.

3. Social standing and inheritance are traced through the male line, remembering that women also have rights in their natal patriliny.

4. Wives take up residence in the area of their husbands and husbands' male kin after marriage.

5. Literally societal segments, tracing from ancestors through descent lines to living people. The classic example in the African context is Evans-Pritchard's description of the Nuer (1979), whom he described as "a tribe without rulers" living in segments ranging from maximal lineages, divided into major lineages, divided into minor lineages, divided into minimal lineages. Evans-Pritchard believed these societal structures to be rare; since then they are known to be found all over sub-Saharan Africa (and elsewhere) until colonials imposed chieftain and kingship associations in their efforts to establish indirect rule (cf. Ranger 1983). In Maragoli the former elder "talking until you agree" policy was replaced by the British early in the 1900s by imposition of a paramount chief from another society, the Avawanga. In the 1930s the first Maragoli chief was appointed, Paul Agoi. The political structure of chief, assistant chief, and headman remains in independent Kenya (see Abwunza 1993 and 1990 for an extensive chronology of political structures).

6. All quotations result from field interviews, 1983–94.

7. A common way to indicate ownership.

8. Simply put, the more people, the more servants and laborers available for colonial purposes. The pattern of what I call circular relationships was established in colonial times, when men were recruited or forced to work on settler farms or in the cities as servants, returning to the farms women worked once a year during their leave or more frequently, depending on their location. The urban men (nowadays people) were expected to provide wage labor proceeds to the home area and expected to get subsistence proceeds to support them in the city; hence a circular relationship of dependency between a home area and a working area developed (see Abwunza 1997 and 1985).

9. See Abwunza (1993 and 1985) for a more detailed treatment.

10. Owoh (1995), Nzomo (1993), Gladwin (1993), Brown and Tiffen (1992), and Elson (1992, 1991, 1989) discuss how SAPs impact more on African women than on any other segment of the population.

11. Polygyny (husband sharing or multiple wives) is nowadays infrequently practiced. It is no longer economically viable, considering the shortage of land and escalating bridewealth.

12. The Kenya shilling-to-dollar value fluctuates. From 1985, during the period of structural adjustment policies and renewals, the rate ranged from 25 to more than 80. In 1998 the rate is approximately 40 Kshs. to the Canadian dollar.

13. In 79 percent (n = 94) of cases, women reported that discussion and payment had not been completed. This situation is intensified in urban areas where bridewealth is seldom attended to (cf. Abwunza 1996). Local knowledge among some Avalogoli and other groups, for example, Kikuyu where bridewealth has declined (Stamp 1986), points out that the "high cost" associated with Avalogoli bridewealth is unreasonable. However, local knowledge does not portray that bridewealth is oppressive for women, only expensive. See Abwunza (1997 and 1988) for a more extensive treatment where it is noted that even among the middle class, women insist that their family "must" receive "my cows" and how younger men

who complain when they have to pay insist the practice continue when they age and are in the position to collect.

14. In the late 1980s, President Moi issued a statement that he no longer wanted to see land cases in the courts. At that time the backlog of cases numbered in the thousands, the majority being cases where sons were suing fathers for land identification numbers and title deeds.

REFERENCES

Abwunza, J. M. (1985). *Mulogoli's "Posterity:" Fathers and Sons Living the Land.* Unpublished M.A. thesis, University of Western Ontario, London, Ontario, Canada.

———. (1988). "The Drama of Uvukwi: A Note from the Field." *Canadian Journal of African Studies* 22 (3):607–14.

———. (1990). "NYAYO: Cultural Contradictions in Kenya Rural Capitalism." *Anthropologica* 32:183–203.

———. (1993). "Ethnonationalism and Nationalism Strategies: The Case of the Avalogoli in Western Kenya." In *Ethnicity and Aboriginality*, ed. M. D. Levin, 127–53. Toronto: University of Toronto Press.

———. (1995). " 'Silika—To Make Our Lives Shine': Women's Groups in Maragoli, Kenya." *Anthropologica* 37:27–48.

———. (1996). "Mulugulu Avakali: City Women in Nairobi." *Journal of Contemporary African Studies* 14 (1):105–17.

———. (1997). *Women's Voices, Women's Power: Dialogues of Resistance from East Africa.* Peterborough and Calgary: Broadview Press.

Brown, M., and P. Tiffen. (1992). *Short Changed: Africa and World Trade.* Boulder, Colo.: Pluto Press with the Transnational Institute (TNI).

Cubbins, L. A. (1991). "Women, Men, and the Division of Power: A Study of Gender Stratification in Kenya." *Social Forces* 69 (4):1063–83.

Davison, J. (1996). *Voices from Mutira: Change in the Lives of Rural Gikuyu Women 1910–1995.* Boulder, Colo.: Lynn Rienner Publishers.

Economic Commission for Africa (ECA). (1989). *African Alternative Framework to Structural Adjustment Programs for Socio-Economic Recovery and Transformation.* E/ECA/CM. 15/6 Rev. 3.

Elson, D. (1989). "The Impact of Structural Adjustment on Women: Concepts and Issues." In *The IMF, the World Bank and the African Debt*, ed. B. Onimode, 64. London: Zed Books.

———. (1991). *Male Bias in the Development Process.* Manchester: Manchester University Press.

———. (1992). "From Survival Strategies to Transformation Strategies: Women's Needs and Structural Adjustment." In *Unequal Burden Economic Crises*, ed. L. Beneria and S. Feldman, 26–48. Boulder, Colo.: Westview Press.

Evans-Pritchard, E. E. (1979). *The Nuer.* New York and Oxford: Oxford University Press.

Gladwin, C. (1993). "Women and Structural Adjustment in a Global Economy." In *The Women and International Development Annual*, ed. R. Gallin, A. Ferguson, and J. Harper, 87–112. Boulder, Colo.: Westview Press.

Hafkin, N., and E. Bay, eds. (1976). *Women in Africa: Studies in Social and Economic Change*. Stanford, Calif.: Stanford University Press.

Hay, M. J., and M. Wright, eds. (1982). *African Women and the Law: Historical Perspectives*. Boston: Boston University Papers on Africa 7.

Hay, M. J., and S. Stichter, eds. (1984). *African Women South of the Sahara*. London: Longman.

Hobsbawm, E. (1983). "Introduction: Inventing Traditions." In *The Invention of Tradition*, ed. E. Hobsbawm and T. Ranger, 1–14. London and New York: Cambridge University Press.

Keesing, R. (1981). *Cultural Anthropology*. New York: Holt, Rinehart and Winston.

Kenya, Republic of. (1995). *Development Plan 1989–93*. Nairobi: Government Printer.

Lovett, M. (1996). " 'She Thinks She's Like a Man': Marriage and (De)Constructing Gender Identity in Colonial Buha, Western Tanzania, 1943–1960." *Canadian Journal of African Studies* 30, (1):52–68.

Mirza, S., and M. Strobel, eds. (1989). *Three Swahili Women: Life Histories from Mombasa, Kenya*. Bloomington: Indiana University Press.

Nzomo, M. (1989). "The Impact of the Women's Decade on Policies, Programs and Empowerment of Women in Kenya." *Issue: A Journal of Opinion* 17 (2):7–8.

———. (1993). "The Gender Dimension of Democratization in Kenya: Some Internal Linkages." *Alternatives* 18 (1):61–73.

Oberholtzer, C. (1995). "The Re-Invention of Tradition and the Marketing of Cultural Values." *Anthropologica* 37 (2):141–53.

Owoh, K. (1995). "Gender and Health in Nigerian Structural Adjustment: Locating Room to Maneuver." In *EnGENDERing Wealth and Well-Being*, ed. R. L. Blumberg, C. A. Rakowski, I. Tinker, and M. Monteón, 181–94. Boulder, Colo.: Westview Press.

Parpart, J. (1994). " 'Where Is Your Mother?': Gender, Urban Marriage and Colonial Discourse on the Zambian Copperbelt, 1924–1945." *International Journal of African Historical Studies* 27 (2):241–70.

Parpart, J., and K. Staudt, eds. (1989). *Women and the State in Africa*. Boulder, Colo.: Lynn Rienner Publishers.

Ranger, T. (1983). "The Invention of Tradition in Colonial Africa." In *The Invention of Tradition*, ed. E. Hobsbawm and T. Ranger, 211–62. London and New York: Cambridge University Press.

Robertson, C., and I. Berger, eds. (1986). *Women and Class in Africa*. New York: Africana Publishing House.

Romero, P., ed. (1988). *Life Histories of African Women*. London: The Ashfield Press.

Sacks, K. (1979). *Sisters and Wives: The Past and Future of Sexual Equality*. Westport, Conn.: Greenwood Press.

Stamp, P. (1986). "Kikuyu Women's Self-Help Groups: Toward an Understanding of the Relation between the Sex-Gender System and the Model of Production in Africa." In *Women and Class in Africa*, ed. C. Robertson and I. Berger, 27–46. New York: Africana Press.

————. (1990). *Technology, Gender and Power in Africa*. Technical Study 63e. Ottawa: International Development Research Centre.

————. (1991). "Burying Otieno: The Politics of Gender and Ethnicity in Kenya." *Signs* 16 (4):808–45.

Staudt, K., and J. Col. (1991). "Diversity in East Africa: Cultural Pluralism, Public Policy." In *The Women and International Development Annual 2*, ed. R. S. Gallin and A. Ferguson, 241–64. Boulder, Colo.: Westview Press.

Stichter, S., and J. Parpart, eds. (1988). *Patriarchy and Class: African Women in the Home and the Workforce*. Boulder, Colo.: Westview Press.

White, L. (1990). *The Comforts of Home: Prostitution in Colonial Nairobi*. Chicago: University of Chicago Press.

World Bank. (1989). *Population Growth and Policies in Sub-Saharan Africa: A World Bank Policy Study*. Washington, D.C.: World Bank.

————. (1992). *World Development Report*. Washington, D.C.: World Bank.

PART IV

Work and (En)gendered Dwellings

9

Ties That Define and Bind: Exploring Custom and Culture in Nineteenth-Century Coastal Communities in Nova Scotia[1]

Anthony Davis and Daniel MacInnes

Almost thirty years of survey and case study research on Atlantic Canadian small boat fishing communities have reported consistently high levels of attachment to community and equally high levels of livelihood satisfaction.[2] These measures of attachment and satisfaction point toward experiences and relationships that remain critical to people in defining what makes their identities and life choices meaningful.

   Our research details certain features of the histories of coastal communities and household-centered, small boat fishing families to better understand how coastal peoples have come to express "agency" in relation to "other world" preferences.[3] Specifically, we argue that notions such as "custom," "tradition," and "community" are essential to understanding the concept of agency. We suggest that agency, for both men and women, is not only embedded in and actualized through culture and custom but that it also expresses, at the same time, the contradictions, tensions, and injustices of relations of structured inequality. This is especially revealing in reference to women and men and in gendered environments. We also emphasize that these ideas have to be thought through with respect to their social structural processes and dynamic contexts. These contexts require careful examination and documentation because cultural practices can, and commonly do, express both tyranny as well as harmonious consensus.

A NOTE ON IDEAS

   The work of social historians such as Thompson (1991) and social anthropologists such as Sider (1986, 1993) enlivens our understanding of culture and cultural processes. For them, the ideas of custom and tradition explain particular qualities of the human condition within circumstances and processes that feature systematic forms of power inequity. Consequently, culture for them is an idea that must be understood, from the outset, to embody qualities shared, as in value systems and ways of living, as well as the attendant contradictions, tensions, and conflicts. Moreover, cultural qualities commonly understood as custom and tradition serve in the formation of identities, the articulation of signifying meanings, and the negotiation of contradictions and conflicts. This is the case especially in settings where the "local" exists in a subordinate political and economic relation within the larger "system."

Tradition can be and often is more mutable than custom. Whereas custom is found in the actual ways things are done, tradition expresses ideas and values about how things should be done. Consequently, tradition as spoken of in present time has the capacity to reflect visions of the past and explanations of preferences, practices, and behavior that buttress contemporary wants, desires, and claims. Both Sider and Thompson argue that custom and tradition, especially as loci of resistance to the political and economic interests of dominant systems, represent a "conservative" force in human affairs. "Conservative" in this sense means essentially the employment of custom and tradition as means of affirming identity and by so doing surviving and perhaps even resisting forces of domination.

Sider (1986) notes that one can expect to find the custom-tradition nexus embodying and expressing the degrees of freedom and autonomy in local settings. Hegemony is seated in integrating culture-transmitting institutions such as the political apparatus, church, formal education systems, and market exchange economy, and reflects the specific interests of those with power and dominance. These latter interests are especially routed through the relations and agents of economic appropriation; that is, through the continuation of the material conditions that assure the movement of wealth from the local economy and labor processes, through devices such as the bridging institutions just mentioned, into the arenas of the dominant economic and political social classes. Sider (1993:10–11) insists, however, that many patterns of living in such circumstances are but continuities that express little more than the day-to-day allowances in and patterns and outcomes of living which the dominated can squeeze from their socioeconomic position. These continuities are not to be confused with custom or tradition, the latter being much more particular to the task for people of defining who they are, what they are about, their inherent worthiness, their competencies, their dignity, particularly when these are sometimes called into question by or revealed as vulnerable to the structurally and institutionally superordinate.

According to Sider, the approach best suited to study custom and tradition, especially as these are linked with identity, culture, and resistance, is one that focuses on the provision of descriptions and analyses that, from the outset, explore the antagonisms, the contradictions. The main antagonisms identified are those between the past as represented in customary usage and traditional beliefs and the present as represented in continuities: between work as labor processes and economic production as exchange relations; between the silence that greets local benefits received from dominant institutions and the "voice" that references custom and tradition in the struggle to define and assert "rights" and control; and between the intracommunity factions that on occasion, to use Sider's expression, initiate and perpetuate "civil war" (1993:9–17).

Core aspects of the human character, experience, and organization of locality are shaped in important respects by the hegemony of a class structure and a political economy focused on socioeconomic relations of wealth appropriation and exploitation (Sider 1986). The predominance of this framework can be expected to specify, within locality and community, definitive features of social relationships, understandings, and meanings. Thus a patriarchal-centered and European ancestry-colored capitalist class system imparts, through cultural hegemonic processes, significantly different material conditions, life experiences, meanings, and identity references to women than it will to men (as well as to non-European ancestry women and men) than it will to European ancestry men and women. Indeed, these conditions can be expected as locally evident in as diverse areas as inheritance practices, the distribution of access to and control of economically productive property, social and physical mobility, and marriage patterns, in those areas of human experience best representing elemental life conditions and life chances.

In this chapter we analyze, in part, two major sources of primary data used in our larger ongoing study: last wills and testaments registered in municipal deed and probate offices and the "marriage slips" accompanying government marriage registration documentation.[4]

TIES THAT DEFINE: SOCIAL AND INSTITUTIONAL ATTRIBUTES OF NOVA SCOTIAN COASTAL PEOPLE AND PLACES[5]

The early European settlement of Nova Scotia occurred as direct expression of the imperial contest between the French and the English for control over and benefit from primary resources such as fish and furs. The French were the first to establish a permanent presence in coastal areas throughout the mid- and late seventeenth century. But, by the mid-eighteenth century, all of Nova Scotia had been wrestled from the French by the English. In the main, English-speaking colonization and settlement spearheaded by prerevolutionary immigrants from New England date from this period. These so-called planters occupied developed agricultural land that had been made available through the expulsion of the Acadian French.

Others established coastal settlements along the southwest shore between Halifax and the Bay of Fundy. Many of these early New England immigrants were fishers and fish traders who had previous experience in and knowledge of the region, mainly as participants in a summer fishery staged from temporary facilities. The communities of Little River, Woods Harbour, Port LaTour, and Baccaro originated in this context. The victory of the American revolutionists over the British and the resultant mass migration of "British Empire Loyalists" from New England to the Nova Scotia colony vastly accelerated the pace of settlement and growth throughout the southwest region.

The settlement of much of northeastern Nova Scotia followed a different pattern. Canso had been the site for an important fishery well before the turn of the eighteenth century. At different times, control over the area's fishery was militarily contested by the French, English, and New England fish merchants. Firmly in the hands of the English by the mid-eighteenth century, Canso continued developing as a base for an important "banking schooner" fishery. In addition, Canso developed further as a regional center for trade and commerce. Across Chedabucto Bay from Canso, Isle Madame was peopled by both descendants of Acadian French drawn to the island's fisheries and by French-speaking "employees" of a large fish mercantile business (Jersey fishing firms, notably the Robins). The community of Petit-de-Gras formed from this background through the late eighteenth and early nineteenth centuries. With few exceptions, coastal communities along the remainder of Nova Scotia's eastern Atlantic shore appeared later, at the very end of the eighteenth and into the early and mid-nineteenth centuries.

In sharp contrast, the peopling of the Gulf of St. Lawrence shore throughout northeastern mainland Nova Scotia and Cape Breton Island was largely defined by the systematic transport and resettlement of Gaelic-speaking Scots from the Highland and Islands areas of western Scotland. Beginning in 1772, the transport and resettlement of Scots continued through the early decades of the nineteenth century. Presbyterians settled in the Pictou County area, whereas Catholics shifted northeast to develop communities in Antigonish and Inverness counties. Cape George and its environs were established by these people and settled in this manner. This general sketch underlines the fact that many of the coastal communities included in our study developed as a consequence of notably different historical circumstances and processes. From the outset, communities have embodied distinctive linguistic, ethnic, and religious attributes. Together, because of the very low rate of immigration, these qualities define critical elements in the cultural formation and meaning of places as communities.

By the mid-nineteenth century the coastal peoples and communities examined here were well established and in many respects thriving within the sea-referenced economy of the time. On the basis of the information contained within the marriage slips, all but one of the coastal communities were associated with a notable demarcation between Catholic and Protestant religious denominations. Cape George and Petit-de-Gras were essentially Roman Catholic communities, with the former containing a substantial Presbyterian minority. Little River was almost exclusively Anglican, whereas Woods Harbour featured a predominately Anglican population while containing a notable Presbyterian minority. Port LaTour and Baccaro were Wesleyan Methodist communities (later incorporated in the United Church), tempered by the presence of sizable United Baptist minorities. Only the Canso-Little Dover community area contained a diversity of religious denominations, a quality derived from the concentration of services and businesses in Canso Town.[6] All of the other communities demonstrate a very clear affiliation with one, and certainly no more than two, religious denominations. Moreover, these affiliations remain true to the end of the twentieth century.[7]

These clear associations between community and specific religious denominations embody foundational qualities of community formation, social relations, and identity. Before the rise of present-day secularism, religious affiliations and activities framed much of personal and community life. All important life cycle events, including marriage, occurred with reference to and within religious organizations and practices. Indeed, much of marriageability and mate selection within specific community localities was determined in no small measure by affiliation with a particular religious denomination. Additionally, ministers, priests, and church elders, predominantly if not exclusively males, were high-status, authoritative personages, forming one of the loci of social power within a locality. Of course, religion was also a critical institutional means whereby locality was formally linked with and integrated into the "outside" world. As such, religious affiliations can be anticipated as key elements in the linkages between local culture, identity, and community.

All of these communities were established and developed, in the first place, with respect to the livelihood and communication advantages to be gleaned from coastal settings. This is clearly indicated in the occupational affiliations claimed on the marriage slips by husbands, as well as those associated with husbands' fathers and wives' fathers. For instance, in Woods Harbour the overwhelming majority of husbands identified themselves as fishers or seafarers. The fisher and seafarer occupations predominate in most of the communities. A similar pattern for these communities is evident in the occupational distributions of husbands' and wives' fathers. The occupational profile for Cape George is the apparent anomaly. In this community, only a select few of the husbands identified themselves as fishers, while not one claimed to be a seafarer. Instead, we discover that most of the husbands were affiliated with the farming occupation, and an even more strongly drawn association with farming characterizes husbands' and wives' fathers. But the anomaly is more apparent then real. At this point it is sufficient to note that many of Cape George's farmers were at the same time deriving a considerable portion of their livelihood from fishing.

TIES THAT BIND: LIVELIHOOD, MARRIAGE, AND INHERITANCE

Within family and community settings, livelihoods are ways of living and ways of being. Between 1851 and 1918, most fathers (87%) identifying as fishers in the recorded marriage entries had husband-sons who were also identifying as fishers; likewise the great majority of seafarer fathers had sons who were also identifying as seafarers. Half of the fathers identifying trades as their occupations had sons who also indicated trades occupations, while almost as many farming fathers had sons who also identified as farmers. Over half of the fathers in the professions also had sons in the professions. In short, livelihoods and their translation into ways of living were, for all intents and purposes, inheritable. Commonly, sons entered and followed their fathers' livelihood.[8]

It is worth noting that these patterns, more or less, hold true within each of the coastal communities included in this study. As would be expected, the communities with less livelihood diversity from the outset display an even greater relationship of fathers' occupations with those of their sons. For instance, nearly all of Baccaro fisher fathers had sons also identifying their livelihoods as fishers, and a similar pattern was found among Cape George fathers who closely identified as farmers and had sons also identifying as farmers. But remarkably strong father-son associations are found in even the more occupationally diverse communities, such as that of Woods Harbour where the overwhelming majority of fisher fathers have husband-sons also fishing for their livelihoods.

Not only did husband-sons regularly assume the livelihoods of their fathers, they also found and married women whose fathers and, by implication, families were commonly involved in the same livelihoods. In just over three-quarters of the cases where wives' fathers identified as fishers, husbands were also fishers. A similar pattern was found in the cases where wives' fathers were seafarers: husbands also identified their occupations as seafarers. Notably, similarity in occupations is also seen for each of the trades, farmer, and professional categories.[9]

The patterns evident in these marriages constitute, albeit informally, an expression of occupational or livelihood endogamy. A number of observations follow from this. To our knowledge marriages were not arranged; thus livelihoods provided specific contexts wherein the contacts and interactions occurred that eventually led to marriages. People sharing similar livelihood and family backgrounds were more likely to meet and form relationships. No doubt, the similarities in background and experience were also contributory to developing the sorts of relationships that resulted in decisions to marry. That is, being born and enculturated within livelihood-defined households would translate, for both males and females, as visceral knowledge of qualities such as the pulse, work requirements, role expectations, and relational dynamics associated with the particular livelihood concerned. In short, the livelihood household, linked through marriage and family ancestry to other households with similar backgrounds, is the site of cultural processes wherein identities and attachments are formed with respect to particular livelihoods. The family household, embedded in and expressive of these linkages, is the heartland of livelihood understood as a way of living and as an embodiment of custom.

Following from and confirming this, the second observation is that the marriage patterns evident are not simply an artifact of fishing livelihood dominance in coastal communities. Certainly, differences in marriage formations respecting fisher and seafarer livelihoods clearly testify to this. The level of intramarriage in these livelihoods demonstrates that discriminations and choices were being made. Further, additional confirmation of this is found in the indicators of endogamy within the trades and professional livelihoods. Again, when examining the patterns for these livelihoods, it is essential to recall that by the turn of the twentieth century all of these communities were well on their way to becoming fishing-dependent and defined places. The dramatic diminishment of livelihood diversity, of course, meant that endogamy was not as sustainable. Marriageable partners increasingly were found only in association with fishing livelihoods. Given this, endogamy within the trades and professional livelihoods is remarkable.

The third observation is that family- and household-centered livelihoods, understood and experienced as ways of living, expressed the likely coexistence within community settings of not one but a variety of clearly distinguishable customs and traditions. For instance, making a living from fishing and living the fishing way of life are distinct in core aspects of customs from other coexisting livelihoods. It would be erroneous to presume that coastal communities were expressive of a homogeneous local culture simply defined by shared customs.

Marriage patterns also indicate that nineteenth-century coastal communities were expressive of notable social and personal cleavages. In general, there is nothing especially surprising in this observation per se; indeed, it would be surprising had the distributions indicated otherwise. This underscores the reality of social heterogeneity in community organization, structure, and dynamics. However, the fact that social cleavages are foretold in livelihood endogamy does raise the question of the relation, within community, of livelihood to the local systems of status dynamics and class structure.

Several additional differences in the marriage patterns associated with livelihoods underscore contrasts that further confirm the diversity of background and life experiences. Our analysis of the mean ages of men and women in relation to each livelihood category demonstrates that men and women associated with the fisher and seafarer livelihoods married at a significantly younger age than did those engaged in all of the other livelihoods. Aside from these notable differences in ages at marriage, fishers' and seafarers' marriages also occurred much more frequently during particular times of the year than did those associated with the other livelihoods. For example, almost one in every two seafarers (of 327 cases) were married during the winter season. Of course, this period of the year corresponded with the time when fishers and seafarers would be least absorbed with their livelihoods' demands and would be more available for marriage. By contrast, trades, farmer, and professional marriages were distributed much more evenly throughout the year. Finally, examination of these patterns with respect to the religious denomination of spouses demonstrated a more or less similar pattern to that described for livelihoods.[10]

By comparison with farmers and professionals, fishers and seafarers married young. Fishing and seafaring livelihoods enabled and encouraged this by the simple fact that these livelihoods could be engaged in without much prior accumulation of either formal training or physical property. Young men regularly entered these livelihoods at an early age, often serving very lengthy periods of informal apprenticeship as they learned the requisite skills through accumulating experiences. Of course, being born and raised in a family reliant on the sea enhanced recruitment to and participation in fishing and seafaring. Nonetheless, these men were in livelihoods that enabled them to be making a living "for themselves," that is, more or less independent from their families, at a much earlier age than would have been the case for males within the trades, farming, and professional livelihood settings. Consequently, fishing and seafaring males would have been positioned earlier in their lives to engage in relations with women that lead to marriage. Here we examine the relation between wives' and husbands' places of residence, as reported on the marriage slips, at the time of their marriages.[11]

The primary means of transportation and communication between coastal communities during the nineteenth and early twentieth centuries was the sea. Although the sea offered the most reliable means for movement in the era before widespread use of motorized boats, considerable time and effort were required to move between places. Given these qualities, one might anticipate that most marriages would involve persons resident in the same or, at least, in physically proximate communities. Indeed, the evidence shows that in every community at least one in two and as many as three in four marriages involved persons resident within the same communities. Adding the marriages with persons resident in adjacent communities to these, at least 60 percent of all marriages are accounted for. In communities such as Petit-de-Gras and Cape George, this proportion rises to 90 percent and higher. Yet there still remain notable numbers and densities of marriages involving nonresidents from quite distant places.

From the perspective of the spouses' gender, women in Port LaTour and Baccaro were a bit more likely than the resident men to marry from within. In other settings, such as Little River and Cape George, men were slightly more likely than women to find their spouses within their own community. Given the prevalence of livelihood endogamy, the scale of intracommunity marriage evident here meant that the vast majority of families would, in very few generations, have become directly kin-related through marriage and ancestry. This would only further the sense of commonality and interconnection between families participating in similar livelihoods. This sense of commonality and interconnection was broadened through intracommunity marriages, particularly as the concerned persons were drawn from either adjacent or regional settings.

Livelihood endogamy would build solidarities between families with common backgrounds, a process that would have been only deepened through the diminishing of occupational diversity and the development of the fisheries-defined community, and fishing as "a way of life." These are among the most fundamental relations and identity references in the formation and expression of local culture and custom. Focusing on one set of communities, Port LaTour and Baccaro, enables a clearer demonstration of these patterns and their meanings for local culture and custom.

A CASE ILLUSTRATION

Port LaTour and Baccaro, established in 1763 by New England fisher, seafarer, and mercantile families, are adjacent communities in southwestern Nova Scotia. By the mid-nineteenth century, Port LaTour had developed into a thriving mercantile, bank fishing, and shipping center, whereas Baccaro remained a community of small boat fisher and seafarer families. In both communities, patterns of residence at marriage for fishers, seafarers, tradespersons, and professionals exhibit a high degree of occupational endogamy. These data also show notable contrasts in residence associations and relationships.

With respect to the fisher livelihood, women in both Port LaTour and Baccaro were much more likely than men to find their spouses from within their communities. Of those marriages involving spouses from outside the community, Port LaTour and Baccaro men and women consistently found and married outside persons drawn from different community areas.

Notably, very few marriages occurred between fishing livelihood residents of Port LaTour and Baccaro, even though these are adjacent communities. Herein lies evidence of local status dynamics differentiating within livelihoods and between fishing families. While one in ten Port

LaTour fisher husbands married women resident in Baccaro, not one Port LaTour resident woman married a Baccaro resident fisher. Moreover, although almost 8 percent of Baccaro fishers married Port LaTour women, not one of these was from a fishing livelihood background. Further, only a few of the Port LaTour fishers married Baccaro women with a fishing family background.

Men and women from fishing backgrounds in these adjacent communities, when marrying outside their communities, apparently found their spouses in places much further afield or from family backgrounds other than fishing. In all likelihood these patterns reflect intralivelihood status evaluations. Among fishers, those working aboard schooners were "the elite," while those in the small boat, day fishery were the "grunts." Intramarriage between schooner and small boat fishing families would have run the risk of transgressing the status boundaries. Baccaro fishers would not have been much sought after or especially welcomed by Port LaTour women, while Baccaro women would have little status to offer Port LaTour fishers. Even into the late twentieth century, Baccaro residents were being characterized by those in Port LaTour as "crude" and "poor." On the other hand, Baccaro residents commonly describe those in Port LaTour as "untrustworthy" and "snobs" (Davis 1985). Of course, the persistence of such sentiments simply reflects the dearth of fishing livelihood intramarriages, a situation no doubt exacerbated by these communities' experiences of the further development of fishery dependency.

Patterns further confirming these qualities are clearly evident in the distributions associated with the nonfishing livelihoods. Rarely did Port LaTour males marry Baccaro females, irrespective of the livelihood concerned. When they did, their wives came even more rarely from livelihood backgrounds similar to their own. These data also confirm that Port LaTour and Baccaro residents drew spouses from quite different locations when marrying someone not resident in their own communities.

While emphasizing that livelihood endogamy constitutes a key dimension in the formation of local culture, custom, and tradition, it would be erroneous, at the same time, to leave the impression that this would have translated into similar meanings and conditions for men and women. The most obvious observation is that the families represented in these data were, within their respective communities, thoroughly intermarried. If not directly intermarried with a particular family, families were related through marriages to other families that were married into the family in question.

The second observation is that, overall, women in these communities more commonly married "within" than did men. We suspect that this pattern has much to do with two factors. On the one hand, women were generally much less mobile than men. That is, they were excluded from many facets of life, particularly direct engagement in most of the era's occupations, that provided males with the opportunity to travel. Consequently, women simply had many fewer opportunities to meet men from communities other than their own. On the other hand, a woman's marriage to a person from outside the community usually meant a change of residence. Women moved to their husbands' communities. For many men the situation was exactly the opposite. They commonly brought wives from "away" to live in their community, often either with his family or virtually next door in a house built on land given by his family—an informal expression of patrilocality (Faris 1973). So, for women, marrying someone from outside frequently meant a move away from the natal family and community, as well as a sharp break in relationships that had largely defined social being to that point in life. Such a prospect would have moved many to prefer marriage with a man from "within."

Compounding this set of circumstances was the fact that women, as daughters and sisters, rarely received consideration respecting legal possession of and benefit from natal families' economically important property such as farms, nets, animals, and boats. Nor did marriage usually provide wives with much basis of a legal share in or claim to property. This is amply evident in the distributional decisions made in registered wills by Port LaTour and Baccaro husbands-fathers with respect to the designation of property for inheritance by sons and daughters as well as in the provisions made for wives. Additionally, the terms and conditions specified concerning the rights of wives in the event of their husbands' deaths are illuminating with respect to the roles and condition of women that prevailed at that time.[12]

Mainly men developed and registered last wills and testaments. Wills were rarely registered by women, meaning that men, not women, were the possessors of property and the social position arising from a relation to property. Therefore, the disposition of property was in the arena of male prerogatives and decisions. Typically, the lion's share of the key economically productive and livelihood-linked property, as well as the family house, were left to one or more sons. Personal property, such as household goods and occasionally some cash or cash equivalents, was distributed to daughters. Spinning wheels and sewing machines sometimes received special mention. These were also left to the family's female members. Daughters might also be provided with a house plot, as well as a domesticated animal or two. A milch cow and, less frequently, a sheep or two were often the specified animals; the former was associated with milk production and butter, while the latter were the source of wool. Male heirs received the property critical to livelihoods and the production of the key economic values; female heirs received goods centered on their household and domestic roles. But, having said this, these heirs at least received full and legal possession of whatever items were granted.

The situation for wives and mothers was considerably different. Married women commonly received very detailed mention in the wills. In fact, they were usually the first persons mentioned. But it is clear from the provisions made that married women were not considered either appropriate or legal heirs to their families' personal and productive property. Provisions made for them most frequently specified that they would be permitted to remain resident in the homestead and to receive full benefit from it as long as they lived or remained widowed. Privileges and benefits were specified as forfeited on death or remarriage, usually with the proviso that a son or sons would then receive full and clear legal title to the homestead and all its aspects. Occasionally, married women, as in the case of daughters, were given a milch cow, a few sheep, and cash. So married women were clearly dispossessed of any dispositional capacity with respect to the families' property, including the contents of the house and most personal effects. In this regard, they appear as if considered no more than special visitors for whom there had been incurred an obligation and responsibility to provide maintenance.

A few illustrations relate the flavor of typical mid-nineteenth- and early twentieth-century wills. One Port LaTour fisher specified, in his will of 1877, that "any money remaining shall be taken charge of by my wife . . . and applied to her own use and that of my youngest son. My wife may remain in the house as long as she does not remarry. If she remarries, she will forfeit all rights to any further maintenance as well as any money she has." Clearly, the wife's relation to the property was understood essentially as a maintenance obligation. This fully acknowledges her material dependency on her husband, and after the husband, on her sons. Even when providing approval for her to use cash specifically granted to her, the husband provides direction on how it is to be used. Additionally, this provision is not to be confused with full and clear rights to use or dispose. The cash is hers only so long as she satisfies the expectation of sustained widowhood. She is required to surrender any cash remaining in the event of a remarriage. With respect to sons, this will specified that "all land, property, and wood lots are to be divided equally among my three sons . . . as well as two sixty-fourths of [two schooners named]. Whichever of my sons marry and choose to occupy the homestead, he shall have a valuation set upon the house and half of such valuation he shall pay to my other sons to aid them in building elsewhere" (document 005).

In 1899, another Port LaTour fisher specified that his wife receive a couple of shares in a local business and the income from other shares, as well as "the right to occupy the house and use the furniture. [My wife] is also to receive one milch cow and the right to keep the cow on homestead lands [and] the right to take wood from the woodlands and $100.00." But, an additional provision and condition specified, "these last bequests are for and so long as she, my said wife, continues to occupy my said Dwelling House or remains in the state of widowhood but, and if my said wife shall again marry then in that case I will and bequest to her one feather bed and

bedding." Added at the end of this will, almost as an afterthought in recognition of their personal lives, the husband specifies, "In consideration of
the care and trouble I have been to my wife . . . I give and bequeath to her
$100.00 more than is mentioned in my will." One son is granted possession
of "all real estate in Port LaTour, all vessel property and boats, cattle,
horses, wagons, farming implements and all shares." And one granddaugh-
ter is to receive "one hardwood bureau and one high post bedstead together
with bed and bedding" (document 078).

In a final example of this type of will, another Port LaTour fisher, in
1918, bequeathed "everything I possess" to his wife "as long as she remains
a widow, and if she does not marry again to the end of her life." But it is
presumed that the wife will maintain all of these possessions. On the event
of her death, all property, boats, engine, household goods, and fish traps
are to be divided equally between two sons on the condition that they
"support, feed, clothe and maintain me and my wife as long as we shall
live" (document 092). So the woman in this case, as in the others, was
tacitly dispossessed of dispositional power. The family property was hers
to employ, to derive benefit from, and to be maintained by, but it was not
hers to sell. These examples illustrate that married women were treated, in
some key respects, as "outsiders" to the marriage family, and their material
dependence on family was acknowledged as an obligation, though an obligation defined solely by a woman's marital status. These practices under-
lined the material dependency of women on men and, further, maintained
that dependency.

In the very few instances in which wills were registered by women, their
provisions essentially reflect similar sorts of judgments and dispossessions
to those made by men. For instance, in a will of 1882, a Port LaTour
woman in legal possession of a house and property specified that "land
known as the homestead land . . . dwelling and buildings, also land known
as Pages Island" were bequeathed to a man. The man's relationship to the
woman is not stated. This woman specified provisions of land and lots for
a total of seven additional males, one of them identified as an infant. But,
when it came to the females, the five of those named were to receive household items such as a feather bed and bedspread, a parlor stove and room
stand, a set of china, and a large hardwood table. In a seeming reversal of
common gendered practices, yet another male was bequeathed "a milch
cow and four sheep," while the balance of "all remaining sheep, one bureau, sofa, rocking chair, feather bed and bedstead" were to be inherited
by a sixth named woman (document 010).

Here we see a continuance of the association between males and land;
females and the domestic sphere are represented in household goods. In
another woman's will, registered in 1902, the main inheritors are three
males, an adopted son and two nephews. They were to receive equal shares
in all land, meadows, and household goods other than a number of spec-

ified items that were bequeathed to another male. The only women mentioned are two nieces, and they were to receive "wearing apparel" (document 089). Among the wills of residents of Baccaro are the two remaining instances of wills registered by women from this period. In these wills, the women primarily bequeathed shares they had obtained in local businesses such as trading and telephone companies. In one, registered in 1897, the woman's son was given two shares, while her daughter received one. Additionally, the daughter's two sons were each given one share (document 076). The son and grandsons received a more favorable allocation from the mother and grandmother than did the daughter. In the final will, registered in 1901, the married woman bequeathed the three shares she owned in a local firm to her husband, with the stipulation that her three daughters were each to receive a share after his death. Here we have a reversal of the usual situation in that the husband, in this instance, is a designated caretaker under an assumption that the shares will be retained by him for eventual transferal to the daughters. Additionally, the woman bequeathed a woodlot, "along with a bureau and spring bottom bed," to another daughter. In a rather unique disposition, she also specified that a grandson was to receive a share, "1 feather bed, 2 quilts, 1 pair of sheets, 1 bolster bed and 2 pillows, and a bedstead" (document 080). Indeed, the characteristics of this particular will are such that it almost seems as if the woman was intentionally turning gendered inheritance practices on their head, perhaps expressing a form of resistance to the inherent inequity in these practices. Here the specifications attached to the husband's share read as those usually associated with wives, while the daughters are positioned as if sons with a grandson receiving household goods ordinarily bequeathed to daughters or granddaughters. But this particular will is a glaring exception among its "kin." Women, no less or more than men, were thoroughly enculturated with respect to the association of livelihood with male activities and domestic life with female roles. If material dependency and systemic limitation attended this arrangement, such was simply understood as the given life circumstances for women.

In the instances where women were specified in wills as the main inheritors, it appears as if they have benefited basically from the absence of any acceptable male candidates. There are a number of examples of wills wherein no mention is made of male heirs. In these circumstances, wives or daughters are the beneficiaries. For instance, one fisher specified, in 1889, that his wife was to receive all his personal and real property, but on her death it was to be passed on to his daughter (document 013). In 1915, a Port LaTour master mariner stipulated that his wife was to receive "½ of all household goods, 5 shares [in a named local company], all cash, . . . all farm and carpenter tools, and a home in the homestead during her lifetime." His daughter was specified as the primary heir, as she was bequeathed "all of my real estate, 1 cow, $100.00, ½ of all household goods

and 2 shares"(document 088). Again, there are no males named in this
will. In such circumstances, women may emerge as the primary or sole
beneficiaries, but they do so essentially through default rather than by design. In all likelihood, they, in turn, distributed their property in a manner
consistent with the prevailing inheritance practice of bequeathing economically productive property to sons, if available, and personal or household
goods to daughters.

These relations and conditions are emphatically evident in the different
considerations ordinarily given sons and daughters, that is, daughters receiving household goods, possibly a house plot and perhaps some cash,
while sons receive clear title to income- and livelihood-generating assets. A
few examples will illustrate this. In 1914, a Port LaTour master mariner
specified that his youngest daughter was to receive a piece of land for a
house site, but "if not used as a housesite it is to revert back to the general
estate," wherein his son was to inherit all property after the death of the
wife. The two other daughters named were bequeathed half of the household furniture each after the wife's death (document 093). In fact, the sheer
number of bequests made conditional on the remarriage or death of the
mother leaves one wondering if there was much impatience on the part of
sons and daughters for one of these eventualities. Consistent with this practice, a Baccaro fisher, in 1920, left his daughter household effects and a
small number of shares in a local firm, while two sons were bequeathed
the land, buildings, woodlots, pasture, nets, fishing gear, and access privileges to the shore and fish yard (document 094). In 1873, a father left his
daughter one plot of land while allocating all other personal and real property, fishing equipment, boats, and access rights to his sons (document 003).
Another father, in 1877, specified that each of his daughters were to receive
2 shillings and that the designated male heir (a son) was "to maintain my
daughters and wife as long as they remained unmarried or widowed." Failure to do so would mean that the son forfeited all property rights to his
mother (document 004). There are many other examples of a similar theme
to be found among the registered wills. In the main, daughters, like mothers, were to be taken care of and maintained until their fate was determined
through either marriage or death.

The social and material relations evidenced in these illustrations make
more understandable the qualities of and differences in conditions experienced by women and men within family and community settings. There is
no question that the labor and participation of women—as daughters, sisters, mothers, and wives—in the household economies of the time was
absolutely critical to the material well-being and success of the entire household, including its associated fishing, farming, and small business enterprises. Women did the vast majority of the domestic work, as well as much
of the work required outside the household on land and on the shore. For
example, women carried the brunt of the responsibility for gardens, milk-

ing, and care of domestic animals. In the fishing economy, they were a critical component in the organization of labor associated with the production of salt fish, the primary fish commodity of the time. In this arena, women were responsible for spreading, turning, tending, and kentching (stacking) salted fish as it dried in the sun.[13] Yet the dispositions contained in the vast majority of the registered wills clearly demonstrate that wife-mother and daughter-sister were conceptualized as dependent on father-son-brother-husband and entitled essentially to obligatory maintenance provisions, as well as some personal considerations.

These qualities and differences underscore the folly in treating local culture and custom as more or less homogeneous in organization and experience. Marriage and livelihood endogamy in these settings, at one and the same time, embody commonalities in background and condition, while also replicating a culture of differences, a culture of systemic and structured inequities.

Understanding the tensions and dynamics between commonality and structured inequalities is critical to understanding the character and topography of local culture and custom. Indeed, these very same qualities reside in the heart of "agency" within such community settings. The meaning of and the capacity for agency among and between women and men in such settings varied historically, as it varies to some extent today. Women were situated and maintained in a dependent and determined social position with respect to men. Consequently, their degrees of freedom and arenas of action were, at the same time, more constrained and necessarily different. Yet both women and men were "made" with reference to common and shared general backgrounds, sets of experiences, and personal histories. That is, the prevalence of livelihood succession and livelihood endogamy assured the interconnection of families within locality and region. They assured commonalties in gendered family histories and experiences. Additionally, they assured the forging of personal meanings, attachments, and identities, both gendered and otherwise, with respect to the ways of being and ways of living that arose from and were reproduced through livelihood succession and livelihood endogamy. "Agency," as the capacity and ability of humans to engage with intent in the expression and pursuit of things "meaningful," is sourced and made possible by the simple fact that these backgrounds, histories, and social relations are the stuff of attachments, loyalties, identities, and meanings. Consequently, they are the very basis of personal reference and of struggle, particularly against processes and forces threatening the viability of a way of life.

CONCLUSION

Our analyses have revealed essential qualities of organization and relations within and between communities that fully satisfy the conceptualization of "custom" as "habitual usages or ways of organizing and doing things" (Thompson 1991:4). Certainly, the documented practices of livelihood inheritance/succession, livelihood endogamy, intracommunity and intraregional marriage reflect "habitual" ways of doing things. More important, these practices focus our attention on the character and content of the particular local institutional and social relations that form dynamic and long-term linkages between people. In our view the substance and the historical depth of these relations are key to understanding attachment to and agency within such communities.

Likewise, local-level patterns of living, believing, and organization that embody the systemic exclusion of women (or "others" such as a marginalized ethnic community) from participation in livelihoods, possession of economically meaningful property, and a place of determination in social structures must neither be overlooked nor lionized simply because they are features of "local" ways of doing things, and therefore conceptualized as customary and presumed somewhat virtuous and defensible. The "local" features of systemic processes that exclude, discriminate, and otherwise limit are, regardless of their local flavor, nonetheless likely experienced in life as tyrannical by those subject to them. Indeed, the face-to-face immediacy and day-to-day intimacy of such conditions may, in fact, result in an experience of tyranny that is much sharper-edged and destructive than that sourced in broader structural, economic, and political relations of domination and exploitation.

In our view, approaches to local culture, custom, and tradition such as those found in Sider and Thompson are necessary but incomplete. The structures and relations of class, gender, and ethnicity within as well as between communities and families must be an essential component of any theorizing respecting local culture, custom, and tradition. We think this to be a critical dimension of understanding "agency." The history and context of coastal communities are frames wherein a political economy of relations of economic appropriation has been partnered with the institutions of patriarchal hegemony, particularly church and state. The formation and expression of local culture, custom, identity, and agency can no more be understood without systematic consideration of these forces than they could be understood through dismissive treatment of livelihood-referenced social relations.

NOTES

1. Lead authorship alternates with every study produced through our collaboration. The research reported herein has been supported by a research grant from the Social Sciences and Humanities Research Council of Canada (#410–92–0143).

2. While numerous, a few of the works speaking to satisfaction and survival include Brox (1972), Wadel (1973), Faris (1973), Matthews (1976), Apostle, Kasdan, and Hansen (1985), Sinclair (1988), and Thiessen and Davis (1988).

3. Communities included in this study are all sites of current and historical participation in household-based, small boat fisheries. Common to all is the economic importance in recent times of the lobster fishery. Each also reflects a particular profile of participation in a variety of other fisheries, for example, Cape George is associated with a herring gill net fishery, Port LaTour and Baccaro are sites of intensive hook and line fishing, Petit-de-Gras contains a notable groundfish gill net fishery, and a substantial small boat drag net fishery has developed in Little River. Communities also represent variations in settlement history, ethnicity, language, and institutional composition, for example, Little River and Woods Harbour, primarily English in ethnic origin and predominantly Anglican or Presbyterian in religion, Port LaTour and Baccaro, mostly Baptists or Methodists and English. In contrast, Petit-de-Gras is essentially Acadian French Catholic, while Cape George was Gaelic-speaking, Catholic Highland Scots.

4. The "marriage slips" are a rich and essential source of historical, sociological, and family information. They contain the following: specific date of marriage, brides' and grooms' names, ages, and marital status; the place names of the brides' and grooms' birth and of their residence at the time of marriage; the names of the brides' and grooms' parents; the grooms' occupation as well as those of the grooms' and the brides' fathers; and, finally, their religious denomination. The registration slips do not contain a single category allowing for the possibility that either brides or mothers might have had occupations and income-earning employment. Formal recognition of occupation and employment is solely associated with males, reflecting the presumption of the time that occupations and employment mark male roles, meanings, and identities. Specific marriage slips were included in the database on the condition that either the brides' or grooms' places of birth or of residence at the time of marriage corresponded with a list of the historic and contemporary community names associated with our study areas. In sum, a total of 1,734 registered marriages have been gleaned from the archived documents and included in the database. The marriages included occurred between 1851 and 1918, covering a period of sixty-seven years or slightly more than two generations in the selected communities' histories. The numbers of registered marriages are unevenly distributed across the selected communities.

5. Aside from a number of separate books on the various peoples and even more on the communities of Atlantic Canada, the back issues of the journal *Acadiensis* provide the single best source for recent scholarship on the settlement and social development of the various religious and ethnic groups who make up Atlantic Canada. Innis (1954) and Bates (1944) remain classic formulations on the early development of the fishery.

6. In this area, 39% of registered marriages were Roman Catholic, 52% were Anglican, 5% were Presbyterian, and 4% were Wesleyan Methodist.

7. There is an affinity between religion and ethnicity in Nova Scotia. Should both distinctive language and identity politics be additional criteria, the persistence of traditional ethnicity in Nova Scotia is limited to Acadians and a minority of Gaels among the European-origin populations. Long-standing communities of Germans, Irish, and recent groupings of rural Dutch are less socially visible. Racial discrimination continues to play a role in the generation of distinctive Afro-Nova Scotian and Mi'kmaq identities. Aside from the dynamic of North American assimilation, the effect of very low levels of emigration into Nova Scotia over the past

one hundred years has meant that very few new ethnic groupings (Eastern European, Mediterranean, Asian, and so on) have formed. At the same time, traditional communities have experienced relatively little challenge from incoming cultures.

8. The occupational categories employed by us were constructed through an assessment of the occupations recorded on the marriage slips with respect to qualities such as formal education, ownership of businesses, and the more standard sociological measures. There were more than 150 separate occupational categories listed in the original database. The fisher, seafarer (often referred to as mariner), and farmer categories are self-evident. Trades are an amalgam of livelihoods such as lighthouse keeper, sailmaker, blacksmith, barrel maker, carpenter, baker, and ferrier. Professions, aside from the standard teachers, lawyers, physicians, and such, were identified particularly with respect to indicators of business ownership such as fish merchant, fish buyer, dry goods merchant, and vessel owner.

9. By way of illustration, 79% of Woods Harbour wives' fisher fathers (N = 191), 78% of those in Canso-Little Dover (N = 255), 75% in Petit-de-Gras (N = 135), and 86.3% in Baccaro (N = 73), pursued the same livelihood as their husbands. In Cape George, 74% of those wives with farmer fathers married men who were also farmers (N = 83), while in Port LaTour, 41% of wives with professional fathers married men with professional livelihoods (N = 22). So men regularly married women whose fathers' livelihoods were common to their own.

10. The one notable exception is seen in the pattern associated with Roman Catholics. Very few marriages involving this denomination occurred during the months of March and December, reflecting religious discouragement of marriage during the Easter and Advent periods.

11. A brief explanation of the "Residence at Marriage" categories is in order before these tabular distributions. Recalling that this study concerns marriage patterns in nineteenth- and early twentieth-century Nova Scotian coastal communities, we thought it critical, first, to distinguish between intra- and intercommunity marriages. Then we thought it also important to draw distinctions between communities lying outside the study areas. These distinctions were drawn on the basis of geographical proximity to the communities under investigation and location within widely recognized physical, ethnic, linguistic, and religious denomination "regions." It was anticipated that the resulting categories would better enable us to determine and describe the character and density of intercommunity marriage patterns.

12. The information collected here is derived from the collection of last wills and testaments registered in the Municipal Deed Offices. The substance of these documents was transcribed, essentially in their entirety.

13. For more information on women's work in the fishery, see Nadel-Klien and Davis (1988), Antler and Faris (1979), McGrath, Neis, and Porter (1995), Binkley and Thiessen (1988), and Thiessen, Davis, and Jentoft (1992).

REFERENCES

Antler, E., and Faris, J. (1979). "Adaptations to Changes in Technology and Government Policy: A Newfoundland Example." In *North American Maritime Cultures*, ed. R. Andersen, The Hague: Mouton. 129–154.

Apostle, R., L. Kasdan, and A. Hanson. (1985). "Work Satisfaction and Community Attachment among Fishermen in Southwestern Nova Scotia." *Canadian Journal of Fisheries and Aquatic Sciences* 42:256–67.

Bates, S. (1944). *Report on the Canadian Atlantic Sea Fishery*. Province of Nova Scotia, Halifax: Department of Trade and Industry.

Binkley M., and V. Thiessen. (1988). "Ten Days a Grass Widow, Forty-Eight Hours a Wife: Sexual Division of Labor in Trawlermen's Household's." *Culture* 8: 39–50.

Brox, O. (1972). *Newfoundland Fishermen in the Age of Industry: A Sociology of Economic Dualism*. St. John's: Institute of Social and Economic Research, Memorial University of Newfoundland.

Davis, A. A. (1985). *You're Your Own Boss: An Economic Anthropology of Small Boat Fishing in Port Lameron Harbour, Southwest Nova Scotia*. Ph.D. dissertation, University of Toronto, Toronto, Canada.

Faris, J. C. (1973). *Cat Harbour: A Newfoundland Fishing Settlement*. St. John's: Institute of Social and Economic Research, Memorial University of Newfoundland.

Innis, H. A. (1954). *The Cod Fisheries: The History of an International Economy*. Toronto: University of Toronto Press.

Matthews, R. (1976). *There's No Better Place Than Here: Social Change in Three Newfoundland Communities*. Toronto: Peter Martin Associates.

McGrath, C., B. Neis, and M. Porter., eds. (1995). *Their Life and Times: Women of Newfoundland and Labrador: A Collage*. St. John's: Killick Press.

Nadel-Klien, J., and D. L. Davis., eds. (1988). *To Work and To Weep: Women in Fishing Economies*. St. John's: Institute of Social and Economic Research, Memorial University of Newfoundland.

Sider, G. M. (1986). *Culture and Class in Anthropology and History: A Newfoundland Illustration*. Cambridge: Cambridge University Press.

———. (1993). *Lumbee Indian Histories: Race, Ethnicity and Indian Identity in the Southern United States*. Cambridge: Cambridge University Press.

Sinclair, P. R., ed. (1988). *A Question of Survival: The Fisheries and Newfoundland Society*. St. John's: Institute of Social and Economic Research, Memorial University of Newfoundland.

Thiessen, V., and A. Davis. (1988). "Recruitment to Small Boat Fishing and Public Policy in the Atlantic Fisheries." *Canadian Review of Sociology and Anthropology* 25: 603–27.

Thiessen, V., A. Davis, and S. Jentoft. (1992). "The Veiled Crew: An Investigation of Wives' Contributions to Coastal Fishing Enterprises in North Norway and Nova Scotia." *Human Organization* 51 (4):342–52.

Thompson, E. P. (1991). *Customs in Common: Studies in Traditional Popular Culture*. New York: The New Press.

Wadel, C. (1973). *Now, Whose Fault Is That? The Struggle for Self Esteem in the Face of Chronic Unemployment*. St. John's: Institute of Social and Economic Research, Memorial University of Newfoundland.

10

Craft Production and Household Practices in the Upland Philippines

B. Lynne Milgram

My initial conversations with weavers in Banaue, Ifugao province, northern Philippines, emphasized to me the multifaceted nature of Banaue's rural, agrarian economy. Female artisans explain how they divide their time between agricultural and craft production and the roles each activity plays in their economic and cultural life. Weavers point out that the opportunity to earn additional cash by producing textiles specifically designed for sale to local and regional tourist markets not only makes their livelihood more secure but also facilitates their ability to move across spheres of activities both inside and outside the household. However, because the demand for crafts is subject to seasonal fluctuations in the tourist industry and because the Ifugao continue to invest not only economic but also cultural value in the ownership of irrigated rice land, artisans do not easily abandon their participation in agricultural production.

This chapter focuses on how female artisans draw on their culturally embedded association with weaving and rice cultivation to enhance their personal positions and those of their families. I suggest that, in Banaue, women are actively negotiating their gender roles by accessing new opportunities to produce textiles for the region's growing tourist market. Working within the context of the upland Philippines, where gender ideology accords a high degree of equality to women, some female artisans are shifting their skills from the production of "traditional-style" striped textiles, produced primarily for family and local community members, to the more lucrative sphere of commercially designed cloth production. Weavers, generally, are maneuvering to find new ways in which to combine their craft and agricultural practices to further their economic standing while protecting their cultural investment in their rice land. In Banaue's rapidly commoditizing economy, female artisans cross and recross borders between their varied activities—reproduction, agricultural and craft production, and sale—transforming their knowledge in one sphere for application in another. In so doing they have reconfigured the historical precedent of a high interchangeability of gender tasks to their economic and cultural advantage.

Much of the scholarship examining the commercialization of rural economies argues that modernizing forces such as expanding markets and tourism have dramatically restructured simple commodity enterprises at the household level such that women, particularly, have lost their access to the means of production and distribution (Etienne 1980; Ehlers 1990). In Banaue, however, independently based household producers remain the cornerstone of the municipality's handicraft industry. Artisans continue to weave on basic backstrap looms; they have ready access to locally available weaving materials and direct access to their buyers, the Banaue handicraft shopowners, as there is no intervening maze of middlepeople. The absence of "new" weaving technology and of foreign interlopers vying for control of craft production and distribution networks means that a "cottage industry" situation in which women are paid on a piecework basis, as documented in craft industries in other areas of the lowland Philippines (e.g., Aguilar and Miralao 1984), has not developed in the highlands of Ifugao. Rather, female artisans use Banaue's fluid economic system to continue to work as independent artisans, fashioning crafts for domestic use and for local market trade and, as cultivators, interweaving their craft activities with their agricultural responsibilities as farmers and landowners.

Income from handicraft production emerges as one source of earnings in a conscious mix of income-generating activities purposefully pursued by rural Banaue households. I suggest that female artisans engage in what Lambros Comitas (1973:157; cf. Illo and Polo 1990) terms "occupational multiplicity": a situation wherein an individual is engaged in a number of gainful activities that form for him or her an integrated economic and socially viable complex. Indeed, in Banaue, as documented in other agrarian communities, occupational multiplicity is not only a pattern of plurality in work, but it is representative of an economic and cultural system that is itself plural, oriented toward household autonomy, the maintenance of local institutions of social reproduction, and the earnings of participants in the wider market economy (Binford and Cook 1990; Rutten 1993; Lockwood 1993). I argue that Banaue's female artisans negotiate their current positions by blurring the arbitrary divisions between the productive and reproductive spheres; they weave textiles for export responding to global market tastes, while still producing cloth for local ritual use and still continuing to invest in "traditional" cultural institutions such as agrarian rites.

THE SETTING: BANAUE, IFUGAO PROVINCE, NORTHERN LUZON, PHILIPPINES

The Ifugao live on the western side of the Gran Cordillera Central mountain range that extends through the center of northern Luzon. This study focuses on three of the municipality of Banaue's seventeen villages that are known for their crafts. An average of 65 percent of each village's approximately 250 households have at least one member involved in handicraft production or trade. The main economic activity in Banaue, as throughout the Cordillera, is subsistence wet-rice cultivation, an extremely labor-intensive process carried out on narrow rice fields that terrace the region's steep mountain landscape. Women also grow vegetables for household needs and raise pigs and chickens.

Rice is the preferred subsistence crop in Ifugao as throughout the Philippines. However, Banaue's high elevation, 1,500 meters, and cool climate result in just one rice crop per year. This limitation of one yearly planting means that only the wealthiest Ifugaos can eat rice year round. The staple food for most people is *camote*, or sweet potato, grown in swiddens or slash-and-burn hillside gardens. Swidden farming, however, is not as prestigious as rice cultivation, and although *camote* is easier to grow, it is relegated to second place below that of rice. Early twentieth-century anthropologist Roy Barton (1919; cf. Conklin 1980) confirms that during his time in Ifugao the primary indicator of a family's wealth and prestige was their ownership of irrigated land and whether or not the family had enough "native" upland rice to serve at meals year round. Any surplus of upland rice is still never sold, but stored for later distribution to family and community members on special ritual occasions to enhance the cultural prestige of the giver.

Currently, however, wealth is also measured in the amount of cash one has been able to accumulate, often from successful businesses such as handicrafts or dry goods stores. Amassed capital may be transformed, in turn, into other traditional signs of Ifugao status such as moneylending[1] and sponsorship of community feasts. Although the newly rich are known as *bacnang* rather than as *kadangyan*, signifying the landed elite, *bacnang* can continue to earn prestige and respect within the community by following culturally prescribed customs such as the sponsorship of ritual feasts or *cañao*.

The region of the Gran Cordillera Central resisted Spanish domination for three hundred years (1565–1898). It became part of the Philippine state through negotiation, rather than conquest, during the American colonial period, 1898–1946. Early American policy in this region stressed local control over local economy and resources. Although this policy was later reversed, it set the precedent for the autonomy of the indigenous population

(Jenista 1987). This has meant that many of the community's cultural and economic elements have remained dynamic and provide the basis of unique local development. For example, as noted earlier, the production of crafts by independent artisans coexists with a commercial market economy introduced in the early 1900s that has accelerated after World War II, and particularly since the 1970s with growing tourism.

Similarly, traditional Ifugao animist beliefs in their ancestral cult coexist in a setting where, from 1900, but increasingly since the 1950s, most Ifugao have been baptized as Roman Catholic. In Banaue, the complex Ifugao cosmology includes an extensive pantheon of spirits, good and evil, who are assumed to be involved to varying degrees in the affairs of human beings (Barton 1946; Conklin 1980:12–13). As a means of propitiating the *anitos*, animals are sacrificed and upland rice and woven textiles are offered at *cañaos*, or spirit feasts (cf. Scott 1974:192–93). Sponsoring such feasts and redistributing part of one's wealth through gifts of rice, meat, and traditional objects such as textiles continues to be a major avenue through which influential individuals and families maintain or establish their status in Ifugao society. This provides an ongoing stimulus for the production of upland rice and traditionally designed textiles. The pluralism of Banaue's socioeconomic practices thus provides a provocative context within which to situate the dynamics of craft production and gender relations at the household level.

WOMEN'S CULTURAL ASSOCIATION WITH CLOTH PRODUCTION

The majority of the studies on regional (other-than-Western) cloth production demonstrate that weaving is often culturally defined as women's work. Why is weaving practiced primarily by women, particularly at the household level? Much of the scholarship on Southeast Asian textiles, for example, links cloth production to the female sphere on a symbolic level (e.g., Gittinger 1979; Hoskins 1989). Women's textile production symbolizes those qualities embodied by women, such as fertility and the power to give life. Indeed, Hoskins (1989) likens the practice of dyeing cloth in East Sumba to the process of women giving birth. Throughout Indonesia, the reciprocal exchange of gifts at rites of passage maintains both cosmic and earthly balance. In such symbolic exchanges, women's gifts of textiles are balanced by men's gifts of knives, money, and livestock, symbols of physical strength and endurance (Gittinger 1979:20).

Similarly, Messick, in her analysis of women's domestic weaving in North Africa, equates women's life cycles to the construction of cloth (1987:211–15; see also M'Closkey, this volume). She argues that weaving constitutes a "subordinate discourse" for women that empowers them within an Islamic system that supports a patriarchal ideology. In her work with weavers in Nepal, March (1983:729) agrees that men and women define each other and negotiate their positions in society through the interaction of their separate (writing versus weaving), but intertwined and symbolically grounded activities.

There is very little documentation discussing women's symbolic association with cloth production in the Philippines. Lambrecht's (1932) early twentieth-century account of Ifugao rice-planting rites, provides one of the few examples linking women, textiles, cultivation, and fertility. He explains that, during planting, the first deities invoked are described as those who cover themselves completely with blankets. The gods of reproduction are then summoned to ripen the rice plants: "wrap the rice in a leaf-sheath fabric . . . and let it hasten and turn pink [ripen]" (1932:52, 113; cf. Conklin 1980:14). Similarly, Barton establishes the symbolic role of textiles by illustrating that the entire weaving process is deified; different gods are responsible for different aspects of cloth production (1946:15–30). Filipino scholar Pastor-Roces briefly touches on this topic in her historic overview of Philippine textiles. She maintains that the complementary dichotomy of male (weapons) and female (textiles) goods has been most highly defined in the garments worn at marriage rituals throughout the Philippines (1991: 219–20). She argues, however, that the volume of such exchanges were "clearly limited, relative to that documented in many Indonesian societies," and that such "engendering of material culture elements did not appear to be an overt theme of birth and death ceremonies in the Philippines" (1991: 220). It is important to note then, that although women in the upland Philippines take great pride in being the major cloth producers, and that although textiles embody symbolic significance, both men and women give textiles as gifts in ceremonial exchanges. The type of textile one gives is based on one's kinship relation to the celebrant of the ceremony, not necessarily on whether the giver is female or male or on whether the giver has produced the cloth. This differs quite dramatically from the symbolic circumstances of gift exchange in neighboring areas of Southeast Asia such as Indonesia.

Weavers in Banaue, indeed, confirm the ongoing link between women and cloth production as they explain that "this is our *ugali* (tradition) here; we have been making cloth through the generations, and our daughters will continue to weave." Two weavers in their late sixties insist that the production of Ifugao's "traditionally striped" textiles required for special occasions will not die out. They explain that young women in the village, such as high school students, have asked the weavers to teach them the special stripe arrangements. Both emphasize that they "voluntarily and intentionally instruct the younger women in this type of weaving and tell them about the significance of these cloths to Ifugao customs." They continue that "now, there is even more local interest in wearing and using Banaue's traditional, striped textiles in many public celebrations." Although cloth production in Ifugao today does not always display the explicit symbolism typical of Indonesian textiles, there is no doubt that female artisans in Banaue regard weaving as a practice requiring particular skills and knowledge and assert that they are proud to reproduce their tradition of cloth production.

In Ifugao, cloth production is also firmly rooted in economic transactions that impart exchange value to producers as well as symbolic value (Milgram 1992). Roy Barton points out, for example, that in the early 1900s the Ifugao commonly paid their fines in weavings. He also records the trading stories of a weaver that transpired in the 1880s. She tells of how she traveled to neighboring villages to sell her cloth for vegetables, salt, and livestock: "[I] turned to my loom as a means of acquiring other goods and made trips to neighboring regions in order to exchange the products of my work" (1963:48, 204–10). Similarly, Banaue weavers in their fifties and sixties explained to me that they often traveled to neighboring municipalities, two to five hours away by truck, to trade their weavings for livestock and vegetables not locally available. Still others relate stories of how they have been traveling on their own, since the 1960s, to sell their textiles to specific textile and craft dealers in Manila. Indeed, my conversations with one of the most noted craft businessmen in Manila confirm that weavers we both know have been bringing their weavings to him since the mid-1960s when he started his business. Thus women in Banaue have always been associated with cloth production on both a cultural and economic level and are currently using this association as a springboard from which to mount their commercial weaving initiatives.

BANAUE HOUSEHOLDS, GENDER RELATIONS, AND THE ORGANIZATION OF LABOR

As both cloth and agricultural production occur at the household level, it is necessary to identify how the household is understood. A growing literature has increasingly challenged the conception of the household as a unitary, bounded, and independent unit (e.g., Wilk 1991; Eder 1993). These studies have emphasized that households, as social units, must not be reified if we are to understand how they generate and respond to wider patterns of social and economic change. Acheson quoting Wilson (1991) suggests that households are best understood in terms of the "co-operative conflict model" in which the "complex behavior" evident in some households is understood as a concern for the common good, mixed with "self-interested behavior" (1996:345). In this chapter, households are regarded as activity groups whose members are usually co-resident (cook and eat together) and who usually share activities such as production, consumption, reproduction, and transmission of property (Eder 1993:649).

In Ifugao, as throughout the Cordillera, women retain a high degree of gender equality. This is usually attributed to the region's bilateral kinship system, to the tradition of ambilocal residence, and to the fact that there are few restrictions on women's participation in economic opportunities within and outside the household. In addition, in the upland Philippines, the positions of men and women are construed in terms of an ideology of "nonhierarchial complementarity" and balance rather than an unequal valuing of gendered roles (Atkinson and Errington 1990:viii).[2] Differences in work patterns are viewed simply as complementary differences in gender roles, as many of men's and women's tasks are interchangeable (Bacdayan 1977:277–81). Consistent with the Cordillera custom of primogeniture, inheritance is bilateral. Women and men inherit land equally from their parents at marriage, with seniority being the deciding factor. The oldest child, female or male, inherits the largest rice field, while the second child receives the second largest, and so on. In marriage, wife and husband retain personal ownership over their inherited land, whereas land they buy together with their collective earnings is considered conjugal property.

In Banaue, consistent with other studies of domestic organization in the Philippines (Illo and Polo 1990; Rutten 1993; Illo 1995), women are prominent in the management of households. Women exercise authority through their control of household finances, their allocation of the household's cash resources, and their major role in decisions on work. Married women collect most or all of the earnings of their husbands and children. The family's pooled income is collectively used first to meet daily subsistence needs. The majority of Banaue families state that decisions on the allocation of income for major purchases such as land are usually made collectively by husband and wife. In those instances where decisions come from one individual, it is commonly the women who assume this responsibility.[3] While some tasks within the household unit are assigned by age and gender, many are highly interchangeable, as noted earlier. Generally, women assume the bulk of child care responsibilities, wash clothes, and prepare food, while men gather and collect firewood, carry water, and build and repair houses and livestock enclosures. As children grow older they assume an increasing responsibility for household tasks.

Women are also identified with and valued for their productive labor outside the household. Women decide equally with men how to divide their time between self-employed and wage labor, both of which often combine crafts and agricultural production. Men and women both work as cultivators in their rice fields, but women assume the major roles in this production. Women work continuously in rice cultivation, controlling planting, weeding, and harvesting, while men repair the rice terrace walls and clean the fields before planting and then, later in the season, carry the bundles of harvested rice from the fields to the storage area. Women also work cooperatively in reciprocal labor groups, or *ubfu*, typically consisting of relatives and neighbors.

Hence the contemporary construction of womanhood in Ifugao simultaneously involves the expectation that women fulfill the role of mother, manage the household, and engage in ongoing productive and paid work both inside and outside the home. Each activity is valued equally by the Ifugao as significant roles for women (Kwiatkowski 1994). Yet men are equally active in domestic work. It is usually a question of who is home at the time a job needs doing. When women's craft businesses are successful, men often assume responsibility for more domestic tasks. Respondents consistently confirm that "it depends on who comes home first" or "who had the time."[4] Women generally, then, do not take on craft production as a "double burden," as they increasingly delegate domestic tasks to their older children or husband when the demand for crafts is high (cf. Rutten 1993: 93; Tice 1995:36). As Heyzer (1986:14) points out for Southeast Asia generally, women of poor households do appear to have longer working days than men, but she cautions that generalizations can be misleading due to the great variety in household compositions.

The contradictory character of gender relations in Banaue's egalitarian system becomes evident, however, when one transforms this accepted universal into context-dependent particulars (Errington 1990:9). Inequalities between men's and women's social prestige and power emerge in men's general predominance as community leaders and as religious and spiritual leaders. Although there are specific rituals in which female priests preside, the majority of public religious celebrations are presided over by men. In addition, agricultural wage labor displays the major discrepancy between men's and women's rates of pay. Men's daily pay is twice that of women (100 pesos or $5.00 versus 50 pesos or $2.50), ostensibly for doing the more physically demanding labor that women cannot manage. Formerly, men also had more opportunity to migrate out of the province to secure long-term wage labor in the mines and lumber industries in provinces to the south. This opportunity to travel, however, is becoming increasingly open for women through their production and trade in commercial crafts.

It is also important to consider the differences among Ifugao women themselves, rather than seeing them as one homogeneous group equal to a similarly homogeneous group of men. Depending on factors such as their social class (landed elite, tenant, or landless), age, and their education, some female artisans may have more of an advantage than others to gain prestige through their involvement in the handicraft industry.

Women, moreover, work equally as hard as men in both reproductive and productive activities and may, in many cases, earn the majority of household income. Ortner (1990) contextualizes such contradictions in gender relations with her concept of "gender hegemonies." She suggests that prevailing ideologies, whether egalitarian or hierarchical in content, coexist with and are contradicted by alternative, sometimes less pervasive ideologies of gender. My intent here is not to argue the extent to which Ifugao society is egalitarian, but simply to point out that within a framework of cultural and economic "equal opportunity" (Lepowsky 1993:174), women in Banaue have been able to renegotiate their positions through their commercial weaving practices.

ARTISAN HOUSEHOLDS: CASE STUDIES

The following three case studies of weaver households explore the cultural and economic opportunities in and constraints on female artisans' engagement in agricultural and craft production within the household operation. These cases examine why and when artisans move between craft and agricultural production and among different craft and wage work situations and how they utilize their ability to cross and recross such borders to negotiate their positions both within and outside the household. The households featured vary according to their access to land (owners, tenant, or landless), type of nonfarm work, and demographic compositions.

Weavers in Banaue engage in two spheres of cloth production. Many weavers, particularly new, younger artisans who have started to weave since the mid-1970s to take advantage of Banaue's growing number of tourists, produce the market-driven, woven cotton table runners (150 by 30 centimeters) that are sold to local Banaue shopowners for resale to tourists. The vitality of Ifugao's ongoing indigenous religion, however, means that there is also a need for traditionally striped textiles that are given as gifts at rites of passage. Those women involved in this sphere of production work on a sporadic basis responding primarily to orders from their village neighbors, and occasionally selling some pieces to selected Banaue shops. These spheres of production are not mutually exclusive, as commercial weavers may also produce traditional-striped textiles when there is a demand within their families. It is interesting to note, then, that traditional-style weaving has not caved in to commercial demand, but rather, new consumer markets have spawned a second sphere of production targeted strictly to tourist tastes. Moreover, as not all women weave, traditional-style textiles, although destined for the ritual sphere, find themselves in a commodity situation when sold in Banaue craft shops that stock weavings for local nonweavers or when sold in informal transactions between a local maker and buyer (Appadurai 1986). In either situation, as outlined in one of the case studies, the production of traditional textiles, like commercial weavings, imparts exchange value and economic gain to the maker as well as respect for her weaving skills.

The Angeles Household

The Angeles household does not own rice land. Cornelia and her husband, Peter, both in their mid-forties, live with five of their eight children plus their fourteen-month-old grandson. The Angeles family illustrates how a landless household divides its labor between agricultural and craft production, and among different crafts in order to meet daily subsistence needs. Cornelia, forty-six, provides the family's main source of income through her weaving of commercial table runners. She earns 49 percent of the total household income, cash and in-kind earnings. Her fourteen-year-old daughter Sarah weaves part-time, and Annie, twenty, who always wove on weekends and after school, now weaves full-time since finishing high school in 1994. In the summer of 1995, to increase her income, Annie started to sew her and her mother's runners into functional bags that she sells to local traders. Without factoring in her labor time, Annie sells her sewn items for twice the amount she receives for her single runners.

During the planting season, January to February, Cornelia feels she can earn more money by weaving, and thus in 1995 she spent only two days planting and none weeding. During the harvest time, June and July, however, when demand for runners is low, Cornelia took advantage of the opportunity to harvest to earn, not only cash, but also upland rice, working for thirty days in the fields of her relatives and neighbors who needed assistance. Cornelia's husband, Peter, who is often unemployed, secured only one small construction contract in 1995 for paving part of the local village road. He spends most of his time playing cards, and this is a constant source of tension within the family. Cornelia gives Peter only small amounts of money with which to gamble, and the amount he has borrowed and lost is the main source of the family's 2,100 peso debt. In 1994 he tried to find work in either construction or gold prospecting in Benguet province to the south, but returned after three months without having secured a job.

In August 1995, Cornelia decided not to return to weaving but to learn how to apply the basketry edge to carvings, a new craft technique being developed to meet tourist demands. As a way to ensure cash income when the demand for weavings is low, Cornelia began to work for her neighbor, a trader who had just received a large order and needed workers. Cornelia also saw this craft as a source of work for her husband who could do the preparatory scraping and cleaning of the rattan. Although Peter was reticent when presented with this proposal, by mid-August he was busy preparing the rattan for Cornelia to use. By the end of September, Cornelia's skill had increased, enabling her to earn 45 to 60 pesos a day, more than the daily agricultural wage of 50 pesos. She plans to alternate between the two crafts as the demand dictates.

The Tayad Household

Dora and David Tayad, both in their mid-sixties, are large landowners. As their children are still single and have moved to urban centres, Dora and David retain ownership of their fields. They support themselves through their farming, weaving, and the remittances from one of their three children. In addition, Dora obtains vegetables for almost ten months of the year from her garden and keeps chickens. Dora produces traditionally striped textiles in response to special orders from her neighbors as well as some table runners for commercial sale. As the market for the former is erratic, her sales fluctuate, making her more dependent on the produce from her garden and rice fields. To increase her sales, she has encouraged her son to sell her commercial work in Manila. Between January and September 1995, he sold six pieces to Manila handicraft stores. Formerly, David did construction work but currently participates in farming and sells at Banaue's Saturday market the bananas and mangoes that grow on the family's land.

To pay for the education of two of their children, the Tayads mortgaged their two rice fields and currently farm the fields in a tenant arrangement with the moneylender. Sharing half of the harvest, however, still gives them almost enough rice to last the year. Dora proudly assumes the majority of the agricultural work and hires laborers to help her plant and harvest the fields. By paying laborers in rice, not cash, Dora is regarded within the community as a generous benefactor, earning cultural prestige for herself and her family. Dora's personal pride in maintaining her rice fields has often taken precedence over her commercial craft production. She has refused to fill weaving orders when her fields needed cleaning and planting despite pleas from traders. In addition, Dora obtains extra contract work in harvesting for which she is paid in cash. Dora has a loan of 2,000 pesos from a trader which she is repaying in weavings.

Because of their long-standing status as part of the landowning elite, Dora and David feel compelled to make substantial contributions of cash and food at village rituals, and this is a constant strain on their resources. Over the long term, however, these contributions seem to be reciprocated, in part, in the continuous gifts of meat and vegetables they receive from their neighbors' gardens and from ceremonial distributions of food.

The Balog Household

The Balog household owns large irrigated rice fields that they have purchased with their new income from craft production, rather than inherited. The family includes Fermina and her husband, James, both in their mid-thirties, and their four young children. Fermina has made commercial cloth production the household's primary income-generating activity, and through this initiative they have moved from being a landless household to one that owns irrigated rice fields that supply them with rice for approximately eight months of the year. Fermina Balog's achievement illustrates that in particular circumstances artisans can accumulate enough capital from their craft production to effect such a transition. The Balog family's savings from their sales of weavings have been invested in the visible signs of Ifugao prestige: land, livestock, and moneylending.

With the whole family involved in each aspect of cloth production, Fermina can complete ten to twelve table runners per week, double that of most other weavers working on their own. When Fermina's thirteen-year-old daughter Carol is not in school, she weaves the warps Fermina has prepared while her eleven-year-old daughter Gemma helps set up the looms. Her son James and her husband always help with the time-consuming process of winding the yarn into balls. In 1995, as a laborer, James received only one four-month contract to repair the eroded walls along the National Highway. He spent most of his time at home helping with domestic tasks and cloth production, grazing their *carabao* (water buffalo), and expanding their two-room house.

In 1994, the Balog family lent their savings of 24,000 pesos to some of their relatives. This loan is being repaid in a share of the latter's rice harvest. Because Fermina can earn more from weaving than from cultivation and because she has this additional source of rice, she has decided to hire other women to plant, weed, and harvest the family's fields and not to maintain a garden. However, the cultural value the Ifugao place on villagers maintaining some personal connection to upland fields means that Fermina always participates in the harvest by cooking the generous midday meal for her workers, and she regularly participates in ritual planting and harvesting activities. In July 1995, for example, she helped harvest the fields of her newlywed cousin in a custom known as *bayanihan*. This Ifugao tradition prescribes that all available family members assume responsibility for gathering a new couple's first rice harvest.

Fermina sells her weavings to two traders who buy all the runners she weaves during the busy season, December to May. This gives her some financial security from June through November when the demand for weavings is low. From June to August, Fermina deliberately accumulates her finished weavings, refusing to sell them when traders commonly try to bargain down the prices they pay. She explains that selling in volume allows her "to see her money when they are sold." Even with her reserve of rice, however, Fermina explains that she still had to purchase rice in June 1995, just before the harvest. The demands of family expectations mean that she is obligated to distribute part of her rice surplus to her less fortunate relatives throughout the year. Her family also made a substantial contribution of rice to the funeral ceremonies for her uncle who died in April 1995. The earnings from cloth production, moreover, have enabled the Balog family to diversify their sources of income and establish a secure source of their own rice.

CRAFT PRODUCTION IN THE CONTEXT OF OTHER WORK

These case studies reveal that income from handicrafts cannot be thought of as providing "pin" money for women (Tice 1995:84; Rutten 1993:97). Although income from crafts is most essential to poorer households who have little or no access to land and only irregular wage work, such as the Angeles family (cf. Rutten 1993:97; Binford and Cook 1990:35), in each instance women's earnings from crafts are used to buy, not only household necessities, but also additional materials for craft production. In the latter case, this enables some women, like Fermina Balog, to expand their businesses. Those households like the Balogs', who are able to accumulate capital on the basis of craft production, jointly invest their money in the education of their children and in rice fields, visual statements of their new wealth and prestige as *bacnang*. The demands of contributing to the traditional Ifugao *cañao*, or ritual, moreover, constrain artisan families' resources. Families continually make cash contributions to relatives or neighbors sponsoring rituals in their village. Even the poorest households, like that of the Angeles, donate some money, if only 35 or 50 pesos when the occasion demands, to fulfill their cultural commitment to the community.

As female artisans are also the primary agricultural producers, what criteria do they use to decide whether to devote their time to weaving or to cultivation? The earlier scholarship examining the interdependence of agriculture and crafts at the household level postulates that artisan-cultivators balance the time devoted to each of these activities in order to maximize their economic returns (Chayanov 1966; Binford and Cook 1990). This approach, however, does not account for how cultural determinants, such as the prestige value of upland rice or the expectation to maintain one's association with one's rice land, may, at times, determine one's choice of labor regardless of its economic gain. Artisans in Banaue thus divide their labor between craft production and cultivation not only to meet subsistence needs but also to gain cultural capital.

The seasonal variation in local and regional tourism, the primary market for commercial weavings, determines, in part, whether artisans work in their rice fields or engage in craft production. The times of high tourist demand, however, may or may not coincide with times of low agricultural demand, and this contributes to artisans' decisions about where to work. In planting season, for example, January to February, although it is cool and often wet, tourists still visit Banaue to create a small but steady demand for local handicrafts. At this time a weaver's choice of activity, weaving or cultivation, varies. Most landless weavers indicate that during this time they can earn almost the same income whether they remain at home to weave or earn wages by planting rice. Many of these women decide to weave at this time instead of engaging in the physically demanding work of planting.

Given this option, if artisans with land have sufficient money to pay laborers, some choose to weave and hire other women to plant their fields. Still, other weavers like Dora Tayad, who takes personal pride in her fields, choose to cultivate even as their favorite buyers beseech them for weavings.

Harvest season presents quite a different situation. Rice is harvested from June through mid-August. As this is the rainy season, the number of tourists, and hence the demand for handicrafts, are at their lowest. Artisans actively look for work harvesting to earn both cash and upland rice and to participate in harvesting festivities that are integral to reproducing communal relationships. Weavers explain that during harvest season they are often able to earn more than the 50 peso a day agricultural wage. Because landlords have a small window of time within which to harvest their rice before the rains, they often pay 60 or 70 pesos a day to have the rice cut when it is at its peak. In addition, if the landlord is a relative or a close neighbor, he or she often pays laborers in harvested rice. As a bundle of harvested rice contains 1 ½ kilos of edible rice, worth 110 pesos for the five bundles earned by women, both the monetary value and the cultural prestige of receiving upland rice outweighs that of being paid in cash. Harvesters also have the opportunity to gather some of the unripened rice, which they subsequently roast and pound into a sweet snack called *ballu*. Families seek opportunities to earn this seasonal treat, which is available only at this time of the year, as a sign of their participation in the harvest and as a commodity they can share with other community and kin members. In contrast to planting season, during the harvest when it is difficult to sell weavings, women who have access to rice land prefer to do *ubfu*. They organize reciprocal labor exchanges in order to accumulate credit in labor that they can then draw on when they have to harvest their own fields. Indeed, when artisans need help to fill large weaving orders, they often draw on the skills of the women in their *ubfu* groups. Thus the organization of agricultural production designed to fulfill reproductive needs (food) may provide the foundation for the commercial production of crafts (cf. Stephen 1991).

Weavers, like Cornelia Angeles, however, are particularly vulnerable to traders' efforts to reduce the prices for their products during the harvest season. If artisans like Cornelia can obtain enough rice to sustain their families during this time, whether through access to their rice land or through wage labor, they are less likely to have to sell their weavings at discounted prices, as evidenced in Fermina Balog's accumulated stock of table runners.

It is interesting to note, moreover, that even in those households with large land holdings or where another family member periodically increases his or her income from noncraft sources, artisans do not stop making crafts. They continue to weave, not only because the noncraft income, usually from contract wage labor, is sporadic and often unreliable, but also because women's weaving is culturally embedded in what women do as well as being economically important. Like Dora Tayad, Lilian Tuklin, another weaver who owns extensive rice land and runs a successful tourist hotel with her husband, can always be seen weaving on her front porch and personally attending to her fields. Rutten's findings in the lowland Philippines (Aklan province) show that hat and mat weavers in fact decrease their production when household income from other noncraft sources increases, demonstrating the importance of local-level contexts for understanding the cultural importance of craft production for specific households (1993:103). In the Philippine lowlands, the increased potential for producing an agricultural surplus, the wider availability of wage work, and women's changing attitudes toward their craft diminish the economic and cultural roles of craft production in Aklan households.

Women in Banaue, then, decrease their involvement in craft production only when another type of work, particularly rice cultivation, yields needed income in cash or in kind or fulfills cultural expectations. In each instance, female artisans exercise their agency to decide in which activity to participate. As Roseberry (1988:171) notes, it is "knowing subjects" that create new situations, not reifying processes such as "tradition" or "capitalism."

CONCLUSION

The dynamics of artisan households illustrate the heterogeneity of female artisans' involvement and investment in both agricultural and craft production. The multiplicity of women's activities at the household level dispels the picture of female artisans as a bounded category of producers who are "stoic, unenterprising creatures of circumstance . . . persist[ing] in traditional and unrewarding work for want of innovativeness" (Binford and Cook 1990:58–59). Artisans such as Cornelia, for example, are exercising their option to shift their skills from weaving to basketry to bring variety and added income into their work. Other artisans, like Fermina, with support from their husbands, have been able to respond to the increased demand for commercial weavings by working within the Ifugao gender ideology that supports a high interchangeability of men's and women's tasks. Most artisans, both those in good financial positions and those wanting to strengthen their community standing, develop active social support networks by participating in cooperative labor exchanges that, in turn, blur the boundaries between the productive and reproductive spheres.

With more weavers turning toward commercial cloth production, the most visible gendered cleavage to emerge is not that between men and women but that among women themselves. Female artisans' positions depend on the extent of their control over the means of production and distribution of their products, the latter of which is dependent on a good relationship with traders. Those artisans who have been able to meet their basic subsistence needs, and additionally accumulate enough capital to buy land, identify themselves as an emerging "better-off" class of artisan or as *bacnang*. Fermina Balog's comments to me crystallized this transition when she explained: "With my earnings from weaving, my family no longer has to eat *camote* (sweet potato); everyone will see that we have our own rice to last us all year."

Producing commercial weavings for sale to tourists has also changed how women spend their time and has altered the organization of women's work between generations. Formerly, women alternated between agriculture, their household responsibilities, and weaving, if they were also artisans. Currently, some younger female weavers are spending less time than their mothers and grandmothers working in the rice fields and more time in craft production; others like Cornelia, instead of alternating between agriculture and weaving in their productive work, may divide their labor between weaving and basketry. One craft is not necessarily more prestigious than the other, as the basketry materials are still woven, but the seasonal fluctuation in the demand for different crafts means that artisans can move between these two practices to match their labor to demand.

Resistance to this shift in activities has emerged, not from men, but from other women. Older women in their sixties and seventies accuse these younger artisans of being "lazy" in not wanting to spend the bulk of their time "working in the fields." They explain that cultivation is skilled work encompassing its own body of knowledge: "in transplanting, you have to separate the seedlings and correctly align them; in weeding, you have to know what grasses to pull and what ones to leave; in harvesting you must be able to choose the best seed stalks for the following year's planting." Such attitudes reveal a local transformation among women in how different groups value and identify themselves with their different spheres of work. The husbands of the artisans involved in commercial craft production support their wives' new occupations. They explain that "women can do any craft they like, as long as they are physically able to do it; the important thing is that they are earning money for our family." Most female artisans involved in producing commercial weavings confirm that even though they may not be spending as much time in the fields as their older female family members, they respect their cultural obligation to regularly renew their association with their land holdings and redistribute a share of their rice surplus.

Thus, rather than being marginalized by capitalist market forces, female artisans in Banaue paradoxically function as "commodity-producing peasants" (Cook 1982:392). They have successfully turned their skills to commercial production by building on their long-standing economic and cultural engagement in cloth production. At the same time, constrained by the cultural value the community places on irrigated rice land, artisans have developed different solutions to maintain their cultural connection to rice cultivation. The multifaceted nature of their involvement in and combination of different craft and noncraft work points to the heterogeneity within and among artisan household economies and how women as innovative and productive social agents play an integral role in manifesting this plural texture and in weaving it into their community's cultural networks.

ACKNOWLEDGMENTS

The fieldwork for this paper was conducted from December 1994 to September 1995. The author acknowledges the financial support for this research provided by the Social Sciences and Humanities Research Council of Canada, doctoral fellowship, and by the Canada-ASEAN Centre, Academic Support Program.

NOTES

1. Accessibility to informal credit continues to be particularly important in rural areas such as Banaue, where the requirements to obtain loans through formal banking and cooperative institutions restrict most local people's access to such channels of credit. Anyone with sufficient funds to lend can become a moneylender. The Ifugao have had a long-standing practice of advancing informal, personal loans to one another, usually relatives and close neighbors, and of taking pride in their astute business dealings as outlined by Barton (1919; cf. Scott 1974:85–186). Success in moneylending continues to be regarded as a prestige activity. Indeed, a number of successful handicraft artisans and traders have reinvested their capital into this activity, although they may lend as little as 500 to 1,000 pesos. Interest charges of 10 percent per month, common in 1995, reflect the potential earning capacity of successful moneylenders.

2. In such a "complementary" system, Errington (1990:54–55) explains, there is an ideology of "unity . . . men and women [are regarded] as very much the same sort of creature, descended from a common ancestral source." In such systems, if women tend to be repeatedly disadvantaged in their efforts to achieve prestige, the reasons offered emphasize practice rather than stated rules; women are not prohibited from assuming certain roles, but the reality of their everyday tasks are such that they are disadvantaged in this pursuit (Errington 1990:55).

3. In her study of a lowland Philippine fishing village, Illo (1995:217) similarly notes that the building up of human and other resources is generally undertaken jointly by women and their spouses. "The jointness lay, not only in the process of decision-making, but also in the work involved in the acquisition of resources."

4. Illo's (1995:218–219) work in the lowland Philippines identifies the differences in the way work is valued in upland and lowland contexts. She notes that lowland cultural ideals define female work as destined to be done in the home, while male work covers tasks performed outside the home. Even this norm, however, is being diluted as male adolescents continue to stay home to perform domestic chores while girls are being increasingly drawn into commercial fishing activities.

REFERENCES

Acheson, J. M. (1996). "Household Organization and Budget Structures in a Pur-epecha Pueblo." *American Ethnologist* 23 (2):331–51.

Aguilar, F. V., and V. A. Miralao. (1984). *Handicrafts, Development and Dilemmas over Definition (The Philippines as a Case in Point)*. Handicraft Project Paper Series 1. Manila: Ramon Magsaysay Award Foundation.

Appadurai, A., ed. (1986). *The Social Life of Things: Commodities in Cultural Perspective*. Cambridge: Cambridge University Press.

Atkinson, J. M., and S. Errington, eds. (1990). "Preface." In *Power and Difference: Gender in Island Southeast Asia*, ed. J. M. Atkinson and S. Errington, vi–xii. Stanford, Calif.: Stanford University Press.

Bacdayan, A. (1977). "Mechanistic Co-operation and Sexual Equality among the Western Bontoc." In *Sexual Stratification: A Cross-Cultural View*, ed. Alice Schlegel, 271–91. New York: Columbia University Press.

Barton, R. F. (1919). "Ifugao Economics." *University of California Publications in American Archaeology and Ethnology* 15 (1):385–446.

———. (1946). *The Religion of the Ifugaos*. Menasha, Wisc.: American Anthropological Association, Memoir Series 65.

———. (1963). *Philippine Pagans: The Autobiographies of Three Ifugaos*. London: George Routledge and Sons Ltd. (Originally published 1938.)

Binford, L., and S. Cook. (1990). *Obliging Need: Rural Petty Industry in Mexican Capitalism*. Austin: University of Texas Press.

Chayanov, A. V. (1966). *The Theory of Peasant Economy*, ed. D. Thorner, B. Kerblay, and R. E. F. Smith. Homewood, Ill.: Richard D. Irwin.

Comitas, L. (1973). "Occupational Multiplicity in Rural Jamica." In *Work and Family Life: West Indian Perspectives*, ed. L. Comitas and D. Lowenthal, 157–73. Garden City, N.Y.: Anchor Books.

Conklin, H. C. (1980). *Ethnographic Atlas of Ifugao: A Study of Environment, Culture and Society in North Luzon*. New York: American Geographical Society of New York.

Cook, S. (1982). *Zapotec Stoneworkers: The Dynamics of Rural Simple Commodity Production in Modern Mexican Capitalism*. New York: University Press of America.

Eder, J. F. (1993). "Family Farming and Household Enterprise in a Phillipine Community, 1971–1988: Persistence or Proletarianization?" *Journal of Asian Studies* 52 (3):647–71.

Ehlers, T. (1990). *Silent Looms*. Boulder, Colo.: Westview Press.

Errington, S. (1990). "Recasting Sex, Gender, and Power: A Theoretical and Regional Overview." In *Power and Difference: Gender in Island Southeast Asia*, ed. J. M. Atkinson and S. Errington, 1–58. Stanford, Calif.: Stanford University Press.

Etienne, M. (1980). "Women and Men, Cloth and Colonization: The Transformation of Production-Distribution Relations among the Baule (Ivory Coast)." In *Women and Colonization*, ed. M. Etienne and E. Leacock, 214–39. New York: J. F. Bergin.

Gittinger, M. (1979). *Splendid Symbols: Textiles and Tradition in Indonesia*. Washington, D.C.: The Textile Museum.

Heyzer, N. (1986). *Working Women in South-East Asia: Development, Subordination and Emancipation.* London and Philadelphia: Milton Keynes and Open University Press.

Hoskins, J. (1989). "Why Do Ladies Sing the Blues? Indigo Dyeing, Cloth Production, and Gender Symbolism in Kodi." In *Cloth and Human Experience*, ed. A. B. Weiner and J. Schneider, 142–73. Washington, D.C., and London: Smithsonian Institution Press.

Illo, J. F. (1995). "Redefining the *Maybahay* or Housewife: Reflections on the Nature of Women's Work in the Philippines." In *"Male" and "Female" in Developing Southeast Asia*, ed. W. J. Karim, 209–25. Oxford and Washington, D.C.: Berg Publishers.

Illo, J. F., and J. B. Polo. (1990). *Fishers, Traders, Farmers, Wives: The Life Stories of Ten Women in a Fishing Village.* Quezon City, Philippines: Ateneo de Manila University.

Jenista, F. L. (1987). *The White Apos: American Governors on the Cordillera Central.* Quezon City, Philippines: New Day Publishers.

Kwiatkowski, L. M. (1994). "Malnutrition, Gender and Development in Ifugao, an Upland Community in the Philippines." Ph.D. dissertation, University of California, Berkeley, California, U.S.A.

Lambrecht, F. (1932). "The Mayawyaw Ritual: Rice Culture and Rice Ritual." *Publications of the Catholic Anthropological Conference, Washington, D.C.* 4 (1):1–167.

Lepowsky, M. (1993). *Fruit of the Motherland: Gender in an Egalitarian Society.* New York: Columbia University Press.

Lockwood, V. S. (1993). *Tahitian Transformation: Gender and Capitalist Development in a Rural Society.* Boulder, Colo.: Lynne Rienner Publishers.

March, K. S. (1983). "Weaving, Writing and Gender." *Man* (n.s.) 18:729–44.

Messick, B. (1987). "Subordinate Discourse: Women, Weaving, and Gender Relations in North Africa." *American Ethnologist* 14:210–25.

Milgram, L. (1992). "The Textiles of Highland Luzon, Philippines: The Artifact as Cultural Performer." In *The Quality of Life in Southeast Asia*, ed. B. Matthews, 137–46. Montreal: Canadian Asian Studies Association.

Ortner, S. B. (1990). "Gender Hegemonies." *Cultural Critique* 15:35–80.

Pastor-Roces, M. (1991). *Sinaunang Habi: Philippine Ancestral Weave.* Manila: Nikki Coseteng Filipiniana Series.

Roseberry, W. (1988). "Political Economy." *Annual Review in Anthropology* 17: 161–85.

Rutten, R. (1993). *Artisans and Entrepreneurs in the Rural Philippines: Making a Living and Gaining Wealth in Two Commercialized Crafts.* Quezon City, Philippines: New Day Publishers.

Scott, W. H. (1974). *The Discovery of the Igorots: Spanish Contacts with the Pagans of Northern Luzon.* Quezon City, Philippines: New Day Publishers.

Stephen, L. (1991). "Culture as a Resource: Four Cases of Self-Managed Indigenous Craft Production in Latin America." *Economic Development and Cultural Change* 40 (1):101–30.

Tice, K. E. (1995). *Kuna Crafts, Gender and the Global Economy.* Austin: University of Texas Press.

Wilk, R. R. (1991). "The Household in Anthropology: Panacea or Problem?" *Reviews in Anthropology* 20:1–12.

Wilson, G. (1991). "Thoughts on the Cooperative Conflict Model." *International Development Studies Bulletin* 22 (1):31–36.

11

Rural Women Face Capitalism: Women's Response as "Guardians" of the Household

Parvin Ghorayshi

The growing interest in Iran, after the Islamic Revolution, has mainly focused on the urban population, in particular, on the interplay between Islam and politics.[1] Likewise, the scholarship on women's issues has been concerned with urban women (Neshat 1980; Afshar 1985, 1988; Tabari and Yeganeh 1982) and, as such, neglects those rural women who comprise 42.5 percent of the total 27 million population of women.[2]

A review of the literature on rural agricultural Iran (Hooglund 1981; Najmabadi 1987; Keddie 1972; Khosravi 1993) makes it clear that until recently very little has been written on women in rural farming villages there. However, during the past decade we observe a move away from a genderless discussion of the agricultural sector and rural areas to studies that focus on rural women (Mir-Hosseini 1987; Sarhaddi et al. 1989; Sarhaddi and Motiee 1995; Shaditalab 1995; Motiee 1993). The most important contribution from this body of literature comes from individual case studies that demonstrate, depending on the type of production, unit size, and other factors, women's high levels of contributions to agricultural production, ranging from 50 percent to 90 percent (Motiee and Sarhaddi 1994). These studies make it very clear that national census data, which documented only 8.8 percent of rural women as active labor force participants in 1991 (Iran 1993b), are both inaccurate and grossly underestimated.

No doubt, writings on rural women have enhanced our knowledge of women's contribution to farming. However, these studies have major conceptual and methodological shortcomings that impede our ability to grasp the dynamics of social relations in the rural communities. These studies rely on structured interviews that not only isolate women by focusing on their economic role but, above all, speak for them (Ghorayshi 1997).

In this chapter, I try to understand the combined impact of market relations and gender relations of power on rural women in the households located in the village of Rostamkola in Iran.[3] I am interested in grasping how women, within their own cultural, economic, and political parameters, set their priorities, fulfill their interests, and work for change. My concern is to understand women's points of view and to recognize that they have diverse interests and specific social characteristics. Specifically, I focus on women's experiences and their everyday lives to arrive at concepts, rather than imposing external categories to identify their realities and interests. What women regard as being important, and the strategies they use to fulfill their interests, have to be understood within the structuring differences that "come from complex choices in the construction of reality and the meaning given to it" (Couillard 1995:63).[4] My challenge in this research is to understand how women, in this rural community, define their realities while placing them in a wider context.

In my attempt to understand women's everyday lives, I give primary importance to women's experience as subject-knowers-actors. By adopting this method I attempt to lay bare the "world-taken-for-granted" of women—their assumptions and what it is they find problematic about their lives (Smith 1987). By focusing on everyday life I found that there are differences between gender norms and practices and between the situation that culture prescribes and where women find themselves living out their lives. This comparative focus forced me to confront the universal notion of Iranian women living under the oppression of Islamic rules. My analysis reveals, instead, that women, as individuals, are competent social agents (Giddens 1991) who actively build their universe, are aware of the structural constraints within which they operate, and have agendas. Women as subject-agents make choices and have a critical perspective on their situations.

In understanding women's lives, I came to appreciate the complexity and diversity of their experiences. From the beginning it became very clear that social relations in this village are complex and multilayered: it is patriarchal, class based, and affected by other dimensions of hierarchies (Labrecque 1994; Dumont 1992).[5] The notion of "complex strategies" (Couillard 1995), rather than a focus on the binary opposition between those who have power (men) and those who do not (women), is very appropriate in this village. In this community one cannot escape masculine domination, but all hierarchical relations are not masculine. Men and women are in relation with each other, and gender relations are tied to other relations of power. Market relations, class position, age structure, the life cycle of the household, the cultural and political environment of the village, all affect how women define themselves and how they develop their tactics and strategies for change.

It is within such a perspective that I present the following discussion. I argue that women are central to the daily life of the farms, households, and the village. A growing number of women are left to manage their multiple tasks on the farm, in the house, and in the village, but hierarchical relations of power deny them equal access to resources. This reality has shaped how, why, when, and what women do. Women, as "guardians of the households," in various degrees, use different tactics and strategies to challenge the existing power relations, create spaces for themselves, and promote their own interests.

THE VILLAGE OF ROSTAMKOLA AND THE MARKET ECONOMY

The village of Rostamkola is located in the mountainous northern region of Iran. After the Revolution of 1979, the old semifeudal land tenure system was replaced by small individual ownership. The Islamic Revolution's presence has also introduced a new level of control and supervision in the community. New political and administrative levels with ties to the central government were introduced. A mosque[6] was founded, and the school curriculum was revised to reflect religious ideology. In addition, the state-imposed religion has prescribed moral beliefs and dress codes that greatly affect the way men and women act and relate to each other.

It must be noted that this village is tied to the central regional and political structures but has its own administration and political leadership. It has its own separate institutions, such as a school, health unit, and a mosque. Villagers have their own religious ceremonies and social, cultural, and political events. Their life revolves around cycles of agricultural production. Individual households, farm units, and the community are three distinct but interrelated parts of village life.

In this agricultural community, activities are organized on a household basis. Households in this village have unique characteristics that affect women's work and their identity. Agricultural products are produced for sale and for the daily consumption of household members. Therefore, labor requirements for subsistence and commodity production cannot be easily distinguished. Similarly, household activities are not limited to what is known in the literature as domestic work, but include many tasks that are essential for the reproduction of farm and village. Farm household members, for instance, produce tomatoes that they consume in preparing their daily food, and they also sell these in the market as well as process the seeds to grow more tomatoes. The preparation of seeds for the next production cycle, the cleaning of products for sale, and so on, take place in the house. In general, most activities performed in the individual households underscore different aspects of farm, village, and household work.

Rostamkola, with a population of over two hundred households, is what
Cole (1991), in her study of a Portuguese fishing community, refers to as
a face-to-face society in which people know one another in multiple capacities as neighbors, relatives, work companions, and friends. Extended
household organization, usually containing three generations, is the most
prevalent type of household. Household members are related through kinship and marriage and have rights and obligations based on age and gender.
In general, households rely on the labor and expertise of their family members to satisfy their needs. As pointed out earlier, the activities in this village
include commodity and subsistence production as well as wage work in the
service sector.

There is a sexual division of labor in the household and on the farm.
Certain tasks are seen as delicate and feminine, others are regarded as masculine. For instance, preparing the land, plowing, and working with machines are seen to be a man's job, whereas planting, weeding in the rice
field, and working on the vegetable garden are activities that are thought
to require "feminine" delicacy, patience, and attention. While there is no
question that work and space are divided along gender lines, this division
is not always rigid. This has to do with the nature of the agricultural households, as discussed earlier, and the increasing impact of market relations.
Many of the tasks performed in the households are often essential for agricultural production, and these involve the labor of men, women, and
children. As well, when the family faces crises, such as when household
labor is in short supply during the peak season or when men work out of
the village, women and men cross and recross gender lines. For instance,
the expansion of market relations has intensified women's work, but, at
the same time, women, by performing various tasks, have started to claim
spaces in the market that traditionally belonged to men. Moreover, the
younger generation of women is increasingly using the discourse of "modernity" received through the media, education, and other sources, to question the rigid sexual division of labor.[7]

Households rely on three primary sources of income: agricultural production, orchard and garden produce, and service and wage work. They
also depend on money earned through the sale of citrus fruits, tomatoes,
and garden vegetables. On the one hand, village households have many of
the characteristics of small-scale subsistence producers, that is, they produce
some of the agricultural products they need. On the other hand, they depend on the capitalist market for selling their products and satisfying their
growing consumption needs.

Increasingly, household activities are constrained by what happens in the
larger economy. Despite the official anti-West and anti-capitalist discourse
of the government, this village is deeply integrated into different levels of
the capitalist economy (see also Katouzian 1981; Limbert 1987; Goodell
1986; Moghadam 1992). Market relations are extremely important to the

households in Rostamkola. Some agricultural products, such as rice and citrus fruits, are sold in various parts of Iran and in neighboring countries. As well, villagers are consumers of products that are produced either in Iran or other countries. Moreover, Western and urban products are becoming part of everyday life in this village. The radio or the television set in the room could be Japanese, the carpet in the house could be from another province of Iran, and some seeds and chemicals used on farms and soaps used for washing clothes are imported from outside the village.

Over the years, the villagers have become more dependent on imported products. They rely on the market to satisfy their needs both at home and on the farm. In general, the trend has been toward the expansion of the market economy and the erosion of the "natural economy." As one woman noted, "in the past you needed a piece of land, one cow for milk, and a few chickens for eggs and meat. But today wherever you go you need money."

Not only is there an increased reliance on purchased commodities, but access to such services such as health care, education, and the like are beyond local control. As well, the economic difficulties that Iran has been facing (see Amuzegar 1993) affects the value of the currency. As Iranian currency falls, prices rise dramatically. This situation touches all households. The devaluation of the currency has resulted in an increase in the cost of living. Many of the things farmers buy, both consumer goods and production inputs, are imported and dependant on fluctuations in the exchange rate. Expansion and contraction in the national and international economy quickly translate into fluctuations in the prices of what the villagers consume and sell. This village is experiencing what has been referred to as the "dollarization" of the economy in the Latin American literature (Nash 1988). In fact, the American dollar is the "hot" money in Iran, and its fluctuating rate affects the daily prices of goods there. Commodities produced and purchased in this village are at the mercy of the market. Therefore, what goes on at the national and international levels directly affects villagers' daily lives.

The pressure of the market is compounded by an expansion in population size.[8] The demand for farmland, which is a limited commodity, has gone up. In addition, with the rise in the cost of living, households require more land to maintain their living standard and to survive as an agricultural unit. The result has been that household members have been forced to look for nonagricultural sources of cash income. At present, a growing number of households complement their farm income with wage work. It must be stressed that these changes have affected men and women differently. Overall, the expansion of market relations resulted in outmigration of males. The hegemonic moral codes do not approve of women's movement outside the village. Women's mobility is constrained by both patriarchal and religious ideologies. Additionally, women have low levels of education and have limited contact with different levels of the capitalist market.[9] Therefore, men, especially the younger generation, leave the village in search of paid work. However, working off the farm, by and large, is associated with low-wage employment that does not guarantee a survival income for the household. This means that households struggle, as long as they can, to combine farming with other sources of earnings. They hold onto their agricultural farmland as a means of survival and security. With the growing outmigration of men, the result has been that more and more women are expected, and are left, to run the farm household. In fact, we are witnessing what is known in the literature as the "feminization" of farms.[10] Women are restricted in the village, but are, as "guardians" of the household, setting their own priorities, claiming new spaces, and challenging the existing relations of hierarchies in and outside the village.

THE HOUSEHOLD: WOMEN AS PROVIDERS

The household as a unit of production and consumption is socially and culturally constructed at different levels. The hegemonic discourse defines a household as a unit headed by a male provider where family members live under one roof in harmony, share resources, and protect and support each other. At the state level, male domination is legislated. However, in Iran, and elsewhere (Morris 1990; Phillips 1989; Hedley 1995; Ilcan 1996a), there is a major gap between household ideologies and everyday household relations and practices. According to the Islamic ideal of the family, the male, that is, the father, is considered to be the provider, to protect women and children, and to raise a respectable family. This image of a sole breadwinner is "ideological" and represents a view of social relations that does not correspond to everyday life in this village. In fact, in this community, men, with few exceptions, cannot afford to be the sole provider of their household members. To be a man or a woman in this village is to be a hard worker. Both men and women, old and young, work in different ways to sustain a viable household unit. The experience of women in this village speaks to these issues.

The expansion of market relations has given rise to new relationships both in the village and in the households. At present, we can identify three types of households: (1) those households that have sufficient land, capital, and resources to enable their members to live off the land and remain as agricultural participants; (2) those households that permit their members to combine farming and nonagricultural activities; and (3) those households that have members who rely on nonagricultural sources of income. The following examples shed light on the different situations that women have in these three types of households.

Batool belongs to one of a small number of households whose members are regarded as well-off and have enough land to support their families.

She is forty-eight years old, and her husband is fifty. She has five sons; one is married and has a two-year-old child. They all live in a four-room dwelling made of brick. Their rooms are furnished with carpets. They have a refrigerator, a color television set, one radio, a simple gas stove, and a separate kitchen. This household is among the few fortunate ones in the village who own a small "tractor."[11] They also have two cows and a number of chicken. Before the Revolution, Batool's father-in-law was one of the large landowners. At that time, they did not work on the land. As she put it: "Life has changed. Working on the land was beneath us, but now we have to work. There is no choice. . . . You know, at first, I did not know anything about weeding, planting . . . but life forces you to learn. . . . When I was my children's age we had peasant-servants, but now my children work as hard as my husband and I."

Goli belongs to one of a growing number of households whose male members have nonagricultural jobs in order to complement the family's income. Men are holding other jobs as drivers, wage workers, civil servants, or as workers in the so-called informal sector. Women in these households bear the major brunt of unpaid work. Goli's husband has a truck and transports goods from the village to other parts of the country. He is absent and on the road most of the time. Goli's father-in-law is ill, lives with them, and requires care. She works on their small farm and is the manager of the household. They also keep one cow and have a number of chickens for their own household consumption. Her kitchen is on the veranda; she has an old refrigerator and a limited number of plastic dishes. They also have a black and white television set and a radio. She has a young family, two daughters and two boys. The oldest child is thirteen; the youngest is eight years old, and they all go to school. She says: "I am the man most of the year. My children help. During peak season, my sons skip school to help. . . . I wash the rice in the morning, before going to the field, and my father-in-law has the rice ready when we come back. . . . My neighbors and my in-laws are around and give me a hand." She adds that "my husband helps when he is in the village. . . . But I have to plant rice in a particular time of the year. . . . Rice-cycle has an exact calendar. . . . We give dinner on Ashura.[12] I cannot wait for him; work has to be done on time. . . . Our work depends on the weather and the time of the year. When the time is right I have to plant or dry the seed."

Maryam is the head of her household. She is forty-five years old, and her husband died many years ago. She raised her family all by herself. Her three sons are married and have children. They all live in two separate, two-room dwellings, beside each other, in one yard with one entrance door. They have a very small plot of land, and, based on village standards, they are poor. They do not have a kitchen. She does not have a refrigerator or own a cow. During the hot summer days she borrows ice from her neighbors. She cooks on a small kerosene stove. They do not have a television set but go to their neighbor's house to watch soap operas and other programs. Her sons are mainly wage workers, and her daughter-in-law and Maryam are both *karegar*, or paid workers. They work on other people's land during the peak season. Maryam also helps other households in a variety of tasks whenever she is needed. Maryam's mother, who is eighty-five and receives a small amount of assistance from the government, helps her financially and in farm work. Money enters this household in a number of different forms, mainly as wages and salaries, social assistant payments, gifts, and money from the sale of a small amount of agricultural commodities. This family relies mainly on wage work, and, like other poor families in this village, struggles to survive.

In these households, the relationships between women can be hierarchical. Poor women, like Maryam, are at the call of rich households for various services as needed. This kind of work includes housecleaning, preparing special food, and cooking at feasts. For some of these services there is no immediate return; for others they receive some of the food they process or prepare. The relationship between rich and poor women is more feudal than commercial. Batool, Goli, and Maryam come from different economic classes, but in all cases their work is indispensable to their households. In general, women, regardless of their household income, are providers (though in different ways), and without them their households cannot survive. Women work in agricultural production, are responsible for domestic work, and contribute to work in the community. In fact, the combined impact of the Revolution and the expansion of market relations has intensified the necessity for women's work in all types of households.

Women's work in agriculture is central. Women start working on the farm at a young age, and by the time they are in their mid-teens they hold major responsibilities. After marriage, they continue their work on the farm. It is common to see women having their babies with them while they labor in the fields. When they get older, they may have shorter working days, but continue being active in agricultural work. The overwhelming majority of women carry out their various agricultural work in trying conditions. The technology employed, for the most part, is rudimentary. Only a few families, like Batool's household, have a small, old "tractor." It must be noted that modern technology is gendered, and women depend on men when they need to use the tractor. These traditional instruments are used because the modern tools are either too expensive or unavailable. Here, again, the high rate of inflation and the devaluation of the Iranian currency have influenced the high price of farm machines. In general, agricultural production remains labor-intensive. Household members' personal fields are relatively small, and because they are not intensively prepared for planting, they are often full of roots and stumps. Moreover, they are scattered and far from the village. Because of the lack of transportation and the fact that women do not drive, they walk long distances with heavy loads on their heads. Limited availability of motor vehicles coupled with gender ideology, inaccessible roads, and the long distance of farm sites from homes make women's work very difficult.

Households often experience the severity of labor shortage during peak agricultural activity (weeding, harvesting, drying, and storing of produce). This is particularly acute when such agricultural requirements coincide with illness (personal or in the family), death, social visits, the recovery period after childbirth, and other domestic commitments. At such times households like Goli's face major problems. In contrast, Batool's family can afford to hire other women and men from those poor households. However, Goli cannot afford to hire wage workers. In general, most households offset labor and time shortages by emphasizing among themselves the principle of collective work and mutual obligation and cooperation. Agricultural work, in this region of Iran,[13] has traditionally been based on labor exchanges between group members, mainly groups of women. If a "member" is unable to participate, she may send a substitute or the money to hire a substitute for the time that she cannot be present.

When it comes to domestic work, in a narrow sense,[14] all women, regardless of their economic class, are responsible for seeing that their household members are fed, clothed, and cared for. In these rural households, domestic work, as mentioned earlier, include many tasks related to agricultural production. Women, in general, are responsible for the subsistence production, especially when they keep hens for eggs, chickens for meat, cows for dairy products, and vegetable gardens. As well, when times are hard, it is woman's responsibility to borrow goods, such as rice and flour, from their neighbors. Women are generally closely associated with the "collective" aspects of household consumption, and their obligations to meet their children's needs are regarded to be stronger than men. Household members turn to wife/mother/daughter for solutions to household problems. When any member of the family becomes sick, women, in particular the older unmarried daughters, take care of them. They provide rudimentary health care in accordance with their knowledge and experience.

Basic housework in rural households is not as important as the labor directly related to farming. Household members spend relatively little time on meal preparation, laundry, and housecleaning. These tasks are comparatively simple chores and are not time-consuming because they are usually shared with other children or the elderly women in the household. A woman tends to direct her daughters to prepare basic meals.

Village life revolves around a number of religious and social events in which women are essential participants. For instance, there are special days in the month of Moha-ram and Safar[15] when household members, depending on their social and economic status, individually and as a group, distribute special meals in the community. At such times, what distinguishes households is how elaborate the meals are and how many times during the year they participate in these events. These activities in the village serve a number of purposes: they solidify, in different ways, the households' status, representing their occupants as good farmers, committed villagers, and so on, in the community. Participation in religious events indicates that they are "committed Muslims," which can help to improve their relationships with the religious officials in the village. Social, cultural, and religious events require a good deal of advanced preparation and organization. While men, in general, are in charge of purchasing goods, women cook, clean, and serve the food. Women work in groups; neighbors and relatives, old and young, join together to make these events happen. Of course, when it is the turn of "well-off" households to participate, they hire women from the poor households to help them out. There are a few women in this village who are known as being "good" cooks; two are single women who supplement their family income by cooking during special events in the village.

These varied tasks are not perceived by women as falling into separate categories; instead, they are seen as intrinsically related to the nature of village households. All activities, at different levels, contribute to the survival of the household as an agricultural unit. Within this context, women as the "guardians" of these households, by and large, see themselves as *zare'e*, people who work on the land. Their identity is based on their involvement in agricultural production and their status as a *dehghan* (rural person involved in agriculture). In this regard, they do not see themselves as "housewives." In fact, the concept of housewife, in comparision to the way it is used in urban settings, does not exist in the village. Those women who stay at home are either ill or unable to work on the land because of old age. A few women who are connected to the religious male leadership are kept at home, but they continue to perform much of the work related to the farm from the confines of their houses. They cook meals for the household members, including the agricultural workers, prepare seeds for the next year's planting, process and preserve food, keep vegetable gardens, and take care of the domestic livestock and poultry. Women, as well as men, realize that their contributions are indispensable to the viability of their household and the village. However, this realization has not resulted in the equal distribution of resources.

"WOMEN DO NOT NEED MONEY"

Relations within the households parallel those of the larger society. In the household, and in the village at large, there are hierarchies of power relations. The assumption that a household is a unit based on consensus and harmony has been widely questioned (Phillips 1989; Sparr 1994; Morris 1990). In this village, the household is not a monolithic unit, but contains differentiated structures that allocate resources according to various criteria, among which age and gender are preeminent. Individuals within the household do not always have shared interests, but may have separate or even opposed interests.

While the role of women in production is critical, and they are responsible for the survival of the family in a large number of households, property ownership and inheritance laws are gendered.[16] In general, in this village, men own land and property. Land is a commodity, sold and bought, with few exceptions, by men. The life stories of women make it clear that their husbands or their brothers have economic ownership over their property. However, women, especially the younger generation, are slowly learning to claim their rights. One woman used the official discourse of the Islamic government to support the weak and the poor, and consequently made one of the officials intervene in her case and take her small plot of land from her brother. Another woman, the daughter of an ex-landlord, took advantage of her husband's absence and arranged to sell the products of her farmland herself. In this case, she gained the support of the villagers by emphasizing the fact that her husband was not responsible and did not provide for her and her young children.

Marketing is another instance where gender relations of power are at work. Marketing, especially the wholesale market, is in the hands of men. Women do not market the products of their labor. The increase in market relations has intensified the divisions between the male head of the household and his other dependents. The man is the only family member who has access to credit and to technical, and other, information necessary for dealing with the growing capitalist market. In households where the father is absent or dead, older sons take over financial affairs. Daughters do not have access to external wage and commercial markets. Women, for the most part, depend on men to satisfy their financial needs. They do not receive a fixed allowance but instead receive money as needs arise.

Typically the husband decides the overall allocation of financial resources, especially when it involves large sums of money. Women make the decisions about expenses that relate to the day-to-day finances of the household. In the great majority of cases, women do not know how much their husbands make. In this context, Morris' distinction between household income and domestic income is very useful (1990). She makes it clear that there is a major gap between the total income of the household and the money made available to women for domestic expenditure. In this village, men's income does not necessarily translate into income that is at the disposal of their "dependents" (women and children). In pointing out that some men do not tell their wives how much they make, one woman said, "we just picked fifty boxes of tomatoes, he [husband] took them to the market, came back two days later, did not give me any money for the children and for the house. . . . He says prices were too low, the tire had to be changed . . . always something is happening. . . . He tells me he will give me some money when he sells the next load."

It must be added that, in the face of growing economic pressure, an increasing number of women are entering petty trading inside the village. Many of the women in the households who have domestic livestock or vegetable gardens, sell milk, eggs, and seasonal vegetables. A number of women use their sewing and hairdressing skills to make money on the side. These women tend to spend the money on the immediate needs of their children and family members. Young unmarried women save their money for their future dowry, trying to lessen the economic stress on the household. In many cases, women do not reveal to men the exact amount of their earnings. They use secrecy to protect themselves and promote their own interests. As one woman put it, "If I tell my husband I have money, he will take it from me . . . he believes women do not need money." Older women may receive money from their children, mainly their sons. This provides them with some financial freedom, as they share this money with their household members and may also use some of it to pay a visit to holy places.

In general, women who engage in petty trade on the side, or are the head of their households, tend to have more access to cash and more flexibility when spending their money. By and large, women find themselves in a difficult situation. On the one hand, they are managers of their households and are responsible for satisfying the day-to-day needs of their families. On the other hand, as managers, they do not have equal access to the resources needed to manage their household and perform the expected tasks. As a result, women have become the major actors in the drama of daily survival.

WORKING FOR CHANGE: INDIVIDUAL TACTICS[17] AND GROUP STRATEGIES

Women and men have expanded the scope of strategies to which they had traditionally resorted. Men have attempted to find nonagricultural occupations and work in the cities; households have intensified commodity production; and women and men have expanded petty trade in both the village and the household. However, in the households, within the present socioeconomic and cultural context, women operate under increasing pressure. Women as a group struggle against two powerful forces: capitalism and gender hierarchy.

The majority of women have to maintain the household on reduced resources. They must devise ways to cope with inflation, cost and price fluctuations, unpredictable variations in weather, and illness and injury that at any moment may threaten their livelihood. Women carefully organize the family's budget and establish priorities. In fact, many women have been forced to cut basic consumption to the minimum. As one woman states: "Prices go up every day. . . . Now, in the market no one deals with small bills, everything is in 100s. . . . The cheapest sweater is 400 Toman,[18] running shoes for my boy cost me 1,500 Toman. . . . I bought a package of salt for 30 Toman . . . and one soap for 20 Toman . . . and yet my husband sold a full box of tomatoes for 50 Toman. . . . I cannot even tell my husband how much I need for the month since prices vary so much. . . . Plus, everything is in short supply. . . . We are eating less and less. . . . We are not destitute, but we have a nagging worry." Most households have postponed purchasing basic household items, or they simply cannot afford to buy them. For instance, they either do not have a refrigerator or their refrigerator is too old and is not functioning properly. In general, their household belongings are limited and kept very simple.

In Goli's household, when her husband is on the road, the family dinner is simple; they eat whatever is available in the house and in the garden. They may have rice with tomatoes or eggs and bread for dinner. Meat and more elaborate food are cooked when her husband is home or when they have guests. A similar pattern exists when it comes to health care. The most common response to health care is no response. They visit the doctor in town when they have to, that is, when an emergency arises. There are only a number of cases, involving accidents and heart problems, that may be regarded as urgent. In most cases, they try to rely on their knowledge and experience in order to save money.

Women stretch their limited funds by using cheaper items and setting up informal exchanges with neighbors and kin. When times are hard, households are dependent on the retention of strong family ties, which are the primary responsibility of women. The resources women employ in cultivating these ties include time, information, and social networks to detect opportunities in situations of a limited economy. Households rely on each other in satisfying their daily needs; they share labor and barter some products. Even when they purchase products from each other, neither the price nor the amount is fixed. There are always exceptions made for relatives, friends, and neighbors. Family ties are also important, and women are instrumental in seeing the family through economic crises. In one case, a civil servant son, in the face of the inflationary economy, is unable to support his family with his fixed income. He lives in town but counts on his parents to provide him with his annual consumption of rice and other products. In another household, the older brother gives money to his sister who cannot solely rely on her small plot of land for survival. They also borrow money from family, friends, and relatives.

Women use their social networks to promote their own interests and those of their families. In this village, going to the mosque in the evening is a legitimate way of leaving the private dwelling and the continued demands of family members. This does not necessarily indicate that women are religious, but women use religion to socialize, gain information, and keep in touch with the latest news. From these meetings they bring firsthand information on the prices of commodities, what kind of government assistance is available, and which farmer is facing difficulties. Women use this knowledge to receive help for themselves or to assist others who are in need. For instance, women, as a group, collected money and other items to assist a family with a daughter's marriage expenses; the family could not handle this added economic strain on its own.

The pressure to survive is, of course, greatest on those women who are poor or have to manage the household mainly by themselves. Poor families rely on the sustenance and support given to them in the form of food distributed during religious and other occasions, such as marriage ceremonies and death anniversaries. The rich may provide small loans, distribute old clothing, lend pots, pans, and even ornaments, or give other assistance for which the labor of the poor woman, man, and children are "payment."

Women, in their everyday discourse, are aware that they face common problems that have deep social, political, and ideological roots. Within their limits and boundaries, they attempt to change their situation. They use individual tactics and group strategies to protect themselves and alter their situation. They use religion and the official discourse of equality to demand justice. In this village, women played a central role in taking possession of the farmlands and distributing them among households during the Islamic Revolution. Women have organized and established women's committees to enhance their access to credit, education, and other resources. They have taken advantage of the increasing pressure of the market economy and claimed a space for themselves in the market. Women stress their position as mothers to reverse the power relationships vis-à-vis their husbands. They have mastered the knowledge of their sociocultural environment and subtly used the available means to invert power relations. The ideals of gender are not fixed in this village; they are a matter of debate. Women do not exist as some essentially gendered, passive, ahistorical group. Their identity is worked out and is constantly under negotiation and review. Women continue to create their lives out of the possibilities they see.

CONCLUSION

My study of this small agricultural village shows that, despite government rhetoric, the Iranian economy, under the banner of "Islamization," remains tied to global capitalism. This agricultural village is integrated into the larger economy through the sale and purchase of products and services (agricultural and nonagricultural) in nearby towns, large cities, and other countries. What goes on at the national and international levels has an impact on this village but affects men and women differently. The "dollarization" of the economy, increasing economic pressure, and the corresponding rise in the cost of living have forced households to augment their sources of cash income. Outmigration, in search of employment, mainly available to men, has been a growing response to the penetration of market relations. Men, in rising numbers, try to find employment outside the village, leaving women behind to take care of the farms.

The expansion of market relations, combined with the patriarchal, Islamic ideology, has fostered the "feminization" of farms. Increasingly, women are becoming managers of their households. Women are central in the three separate but interconnected parts of this community: household, farm, and village. Women manage and are providers of the households, run the farms, and do work in the community, but they do not have equal access to resources. The hierarchical relations of power both in the household and in the larger society have prevented women from being equal partners with men. However, women, as "guardians" of the household, are using various tactics and strategies to challenge the existing relations of power.

Women as a group realize that they face common and complex problems. In their own ways, within their possibilities and limits, they use different strategies to reverse their situations. They have used the official discourse, the increasing pressure of the market, their obligations as mothers, the absence of their men from their households, and so on, to claim a space in the market economy, to gain some financial independence, and to achieve greater gender equality. They constantly fight against the negative effects of relations of domination, as they see it, and they continue to try to widen their spheres of influence and achieve a certain degree of autonomy. No matter what the extent and forms of these efforts are, they demonstrate relations of struggle and power.

AKNOWLEDGMENTS

I would like to thank Suzan Ilcan and Lynne Phillips for their comments on an earlier version of this chapter. I am grateful to the Social Sciences and Humanities Research Council of Canada for its financial support.

NOTES

1. For more on this, see: Keddie 1980; Amirahmadi and Parvin 1988; Bakhash 1985; Bina and Zanganeh 1992.

2. According to the Iranian Census, 42% of the total population of Iran is rural (Iran 1993a).

3. I base my findings here on more than two years of fieldwork in an agricultural village that I call Rostamkola, which contains over 200 households. In this study, I relied on qualitative methods: participant observation, informal guided

interviews, case studies, focus group discussions, biographies, life stories, and visual methods, often combining these. I speak both Persian and the dialect of this village. I took part in both formal and informal gatherings, weddings, religious ceremonies, women's get-togethers, family reunions, and special occasions.

4. For instance, Couillard (1995) shows that the notion of housewife among rural Malay women is different from what we commonly understand in the West.

5. In a study of gender and power relations in rural Turkey, Ilcan (1996b) goes beyond centralist notions of power by conceptualizing the numerous effects of power relations in micropolitical terms and contexts.

6. Before the Revolution, Tak-kiyeh was a small public place where villagers gathered for social and religious events. They used Tak-kiyeh for preparing community dinners and other ceremonies, both religious and social. However, after the Revolution, Tak-kiyeh was reestablished and acquired a religious character. An elaborate new mosque has been added to the village with the help of the state. In increasing numbers, villagers are encouraged to use the mosque for their daily prayers and religious ceremonies.

7. Population growth, urbanization, and the increase in market relations have influenced relations between men and women. Urban lifestyles and television programs also shape men's and women's views of the household and gender relations in ideal terms. However, younger, educated women are increasingly aware of their individual rights and are asking their male partners to take part in some of the housework.

8. The Islamic government's stress on the importance of the family, as a reproductive unit, contributed to the state's abandoning family planning projects. The result was that Iran experienced a dramatic increase (3.7%) in the rate of population growth (Nazari 1989).

9. Women do not have access to different levels of the capitalist market, such as credit, banking, and large-scale trading. While they have knowledge of the daily prices, they do not have the chance to enhance their knowledge of the capitalist market.

10. Crucial changes are also occurring within households, between men and women, parents and children, young and old. Women's tasks are changing. The younger genderations are not satisfied with village life, and even children are questioning their parents' authority.

11. This vehicle has a small engine and looks like a tractor.

12. Ashura is the tenth day of the month of Moha-ram and is a religious holy day.

13. Methods of agricultural production vary by region (see Khosravi 1993).

14. As discussed at the beginning of this chapter, the nature of the household in this village is such that we cannot easily distinguish domestic work from other tasks performed in the household.

15. Moha-ram and Safar are the two months of mourning in Iran. Many special events take place during these periods.

16. According to Islamic law, women, as daughters, are entitled to receive half of a son's share when it comes to inheriting the parental property. Women, as wives, receive, after the death of their husbands, only a small fraction of the household property. However, the law exists, in the overwhelming majority of cases, only on paper. The official discourse centers on the assumption that the man is the

head of the household and has authority over family holdings. Arguments are advanced that daughters marry and leave the paternal household, and therefore it is the son who will keep the family name and property alive.

17. I define "strategy" and "tactic" as all the elements women use (in the social, cultural, and economic context of this village) to gain control over their lives and to work toward greater equality.

18. As of 31 March 1997, 400 Toman was equal to one U.S. dollar.

REFERENCES

Afshar, H. (1985). "The Legal, Social and Political Position of Women in Iran." *International Journal of the Sociology of Law* 13 (1):47–60.

———. (1988). "Behind the Veil: The Public and Private Faces of Khomeini's Policies on Iranian Women." In *Structure of Patriarchy: State, Community and Household in Modernizing Asia*, ed. B. Agarwal, 228–47. London: Zed Books.

Amirahmadi, H., and M. Parvin. (1988). *The Dynamics of Islamic Revolution.* Albany: SUNY Press.

Amuzegar, J. (1993). *Iran's Economy under the Islamic Republic.* London: I. B. Tauris.

Bakhash, H. E. (1985). *The Reign of the Ayatollahs.* London: I. B. Tauris.

Bina, C., and H. Zanganeh. (1992). *Modern Capitalism and Islamic Ideology in Iran.* New York: St. Martin's Press.

Cole, S. (1991). *Women of the Praia: Work and Lives in a Portuguese Coastal Community.* Princeton, N.J.: Princeton University Press.

Couillard, M. A. (1995). "From Women's Point of View: Practicing Feminist Anthropology in a World of Differences." In *Ethnographic Feminisms: Essays in Anthropology*, ed. S. Cole and L. Phillips, 53–73. Ottawa: Carleton University Press.

Dumont, L. (1992). "Anthropologie, totalité et hiérarchie." *Philosophie et Anthropologie* 11–24. Paris: Edition du Centre Pompidou.

Ghorayshi, P. (1997). "Women and Social Change: Towards Understanding Gender Relations in Rural Iran." *Canadian Journal of Development Studies* Vol. 18, No. 1.

Giddens, A. (1991). "Structuration Theory: Past, Present and Future." In *Giddens' Theory of Structuration: A Critical Appreciation*, ed. C. Bryant and D. Jary, 201–21. London: Routledge.

Goodell, G. (1986). *The Elementary Structure of Political Life: Rural Development in Pahlavi Iran.* New York: Oxford University Press.

Hedley, M. (1995). " 'A Little Free Time on Sunday': Women and Domestic Commodity Production." In *Ethnographic Feminisms: Essays in Anthropology*, ed. S. Cole and L. Phillips, 119–37. Ottawa: Carleton University Press.

Hooglund, E. (1981). "Iran's Agricultural Inheritance." *Middle East Research and Information Project* (MERIP) 99:15–19.

Ilcan, S. (1996a). "Fragmentary Encounters in a Moral World: Household Power Relations and Gender Politics." *Ethnology* 35 (1):33–49.

———. (1996b). "Moral Regulation and Microlevel Politics: Implications for

Women's Work and Struggles." In *Women, Work and Gender Relations in Developing Countries*, ed. P. Ghorayshi and C. Belanger, 115–32. Westport, Conn.: Greenwood Press.

Iran. (1993a). *Salnameh-e amai-ye keshvar*. Tehran: Markaz-e amar-e Iran (*National Annual Statistics*).

———. (1993b). *Sar Shomar-i Keshavarz-i Iran* (Census of Iranian Agriculture). Tehran: Markaz-e Amar-e Iran.

Katouzian, H. (1981). *The Political Economy of Modern Iran: Despotism and Pseudo-Modernism, 1926–1979*. New York: New York University Press.

Keddie, N. (1972). "Stratification, Social Control, and Capitalism in Iranian Villages: Before and after Land Reform." In *Rural Politics and Social Change in the Middle East*, ed. R. Antoun and I. Harik, 364–402. Bloomington: Indiana University Press.

———. (1980). "Iran: Change in Islam; Islam and Change." *International Journal of Middle East Studies* 10: 225–40.

Khosravi, K. (1993). *Jame'eh shena-si Deh dar Iran*. (Sociology of the Village in Iran). Tehran: Nashr-i Daneshgahi-i Tehran.

Labrecque, M. F. (1994). "Pour l'étude des hiérarchies de genre et de génération: aspects méthodologique." *Communication dans le cadre du XXIe congrès annuel de la société Canadien d'anthropologie*. Vancouver.

Limbert, J. (1987). *Iran: At War with History*. Boulder, Colo.: Westview Press.

Mir-Hosseini, Z. (1987). "Impact of Wage Labour on Household Fission in Rural Iran." *Journal of Comparative Family Studies* 18 (3):445–61.

Moghadam, V. (1992). "Patriarchy and the Politics of Gender in Modernizing Societies: Iran, Pakistan and Afghanistan." *International Sociology* 7 (1):35–53.

Morris, L. (1990). *The Working of the Household*. Cambridge: Polity Press.

Motiee, N. (1993). "Naghsh-i Zanan-I Roost-I Iran dar Fa'aliyat-ha-I Zera-I" (Rural Women's Role in Farming). *Zanan* 14.

Motiee, N., and F. Sarhaddi. (1994). *Moghaye-seh Fa'ali-yat-ha-I Tawli-di Zanan-I Roosta-I dar Seh Mantagh-I Motefavet az yek Eghlim* (A Comparison of Rural Women's Activities in Production in Three Different Places in One Country). Tehran: "Faslnameh-I Olum-I Ejtema'i."

Najmabadi, A. (1987). *Land Reform and Social Change in Iran*. Salt Lake City: University of Utah Press.

Nash, J. (1988). "The Mobilization of Women in the Bolivian Debt Crisis." In *Women and Work: An Annual Review*, ed. B. A. Gutek, A. H. Stommberg, and L. Larwood, 3:67–86. Newbury Park, CA: Sage Publication.

Nazari, A. (1989). *Population Geography of Iran*. Tehran: Karoon Publishing.

Neshat, G. (1980). "Women in the Islamic Republic of Iran." *Iranian Studies* 13 (1–4):165–94.

Phillips, L. (1989). "Gender Dynamics and Rural Household Strategies." *Canadian Review of Sociology and Anthropology* 26 (2):294–310.

Sarhaddi, F., and N. Motiee. (1995). "Yafte-ha-I Moghadamati Kar-I Zanan Dar Gorgan" (The Preliminary Findings on Women's Work in Gorgan). Unpublished.

Sarhaddi, F., et al. (1989). *Bar-rasi-I Ejtema'i, Eqtesadi dar Roosta-I Ahandan* (A

2

Socioeconomic Study of the Village of Ahandan). Ministry of Agriculture, Tehran: Center for Rural and Agricultural Research.

Shaditalab, Zh. (1995). "Zana-I Keshavarz Irani Dar Barnameh-ha-I Tawsi'ah" (Development Plans and Women Farmers in Iran). *Iqtisad-I Keshavarzi va Tawsi'ah: Vizheh Nameh-I Naghsh-I Zanan Dar Keshavarzi.* (A special issue on Women's Role in Agriculture). Tehran. Vol. 3.

Smith, D. (1987). *The Everyday World as Problematic: A Feminist Sociology.* Boston: Northwestern Press.

Sparr, P., ed. (1994). *Mortgaging Women's Lives: Feminist Critique of Structural Adjustment.* London: Zed Books.

Tabari, A., and N. Yeganeh, ed. (1982). *In the Shadow of Islam: The Women's Movement in Iran.* London: Zed Press.

12

Sustainable Agriculture: Implications for Gender and the Family Farm

Alan Hall

Over the last two decades, studies of the gender division of labor in modern agriculture have revealed the important and often ignored contributions of women to farm production (Reimer 1983; Buttell and Gillespie 1984; Rosenfeld 1985; Harper Simpson, Wilson, and Young 1988). At the same time, researchers have documented the historical impact of increasing capitalization, mechanization, and specialization on women's involvement in farming. These studies suggest that women have been separated from the "business" of farming as their farm production labor and decision-making powers have been supplanted by the use of sophisticated machines and chemical inputs. Given the profitability crises in farming, more and more women have been pushed into off-farm employment (Reimer 1984; Wilson, Harper Simpson, and Landerman 1994). Consequently, the household has become less integrated with the farm, while productive and reproductive labor have become more segregated by gender (Meares 1997).

Within this historical context, however, a sustainable agricultural model has emerged that suggests some potential for altering the structure of the household and gender relations in farming. If we are to understand sustainable agriculture as a distinct production and social paradigm that challenges many of the central principles of modern conventional agriculture (see Beus and Dunlap 1994), then there may be a basis for arguing that sustainable agriculture will feminize control and desegregate labor within the farm labor process. Even though some scholarly literature claims that sustainable agriculture will strengthen women's position in the farm production process (Feldman and Welsh 1995; Kloppenburg 1991), it is only in the past few years that researchers have examined the relationship between the adoption of alternative methods and gender relations within the North American context (Meares 1997).

In broad theoretical terms, there are two main reasons why we might expect a relationship between sustainable agriculture and gender relations on the farm. First of all, sustainable agriculture is generally thought to encourage smaller low-capital production units and technology, reduce the reliance on external sources of energy, inputs, and credits, and thereby increase the dependence on personal and local farm knowledge, skills, and labor (Beus 1995). Whether in neoclassical or political economic terms, this should create a greater demand for female labor, skills, and knowledge. This is especially the case as families seek rationally to meet the greater labor and skill requirements of organic farming, together with the lower levels of capitalization and small farm sizes, making wage labor problematic (Lobao and Meyer 1995:579). The likely impact of this not only makes female decision-making power more problematic, but some evidence suggests that increased involvement in production activities necessarily leads to the lesser marginalization of women in farm decision making (Sachs 1983; Lobao and Meyer 1995).

Second, although the underlying ideology of sustainable agriculture does not directly address gender segregation in farm production, there is a strong social justice component that advocates putting people, families, and communities before individual competition and large corporate enterprises (Beus 1995). Specific ideas of sustainable agriculture have also been advanced around its harmony with nature, community cooperation, self-reliance, way of life, and nonmaterialism that suggest a distinctive and more progressive view of social relations (Beus and Dunlap 1991, 1993, 1994). The emphasis that many proponents of sustainable agriculture place on the traditional family farm and rural values could also mean a move toward conventional conceptions of segregated female and male roles in household and farm production. In a more progressive social justice orientation, however, there is the suggestion that sustainable farmers may be less rigid in their gender ideologies and may even be attracted to organic farming in part because it implies a more active family involvement in the farm.

There is room for some skepticism regarding the progressive impact of sustainable agriculture. To begin with, the ideological framework underlying sustainable agriculture does not directly deal with gender relations and indeed largely ignores them (Meares 1997:22). Moreover, the substantial feminist literature on farming suggests that the asymmetrical gendered nature of labor and power in farming is very resistant to change (Whatmore 1991; Wilson, Harper Simpson, and Landerman 1994). For example, within the context of the 1980s farm crisis, many analysts suggest that the threat to farm survival can engender a major increase in women's involvement in farm labor and new farm survival initiatives. However, with the exception of increased off-farm employment, women, whether in small or large operations, have not expanded their roles in farm production or management as a result of the farm crisis (Lobao and Meyer 1995). In fact, recent studies have increasingly questioned the claim that women are more involved in farm labor and decision making in smaller less-commercialized operations (Lobao and Meyer 1995; Wilson, Harper Simpson, and Landerman 1994).

To complicate matters further, there is the increasing recognition by analysts that sustainable agriculture is characterized by various distinct forms of practice, ranging from the adoption of soil conservation measures or the use of integrated pest management techniques to mixed organic farms (Saltiel, Bauder, and Palakovich 1994). Along with these varying practices, numerous studies have already shown that there are substantial differences in ideological orientation that bear directly on the prediction that sustainable farmers will be oriented to gender equity in farm labor and decision making (Beus and Dunlap 1991, 1994; Allen and Bernhardt 1995).

While a full examination of these opposing predictions requires a large-scale study of farm households, this chapter uses data from an exploratory research effort conducted in southwestern Ontario to provide some initial qualitative insights into the relationship between the adoption of sustainable agriculture and the gender structure of household and farm production. Relying largely on the case studies of twelve family farm households, a comparison of gender relations is made between two types of "sustainable" farmers operating in the same area, namely, mixed organic farmers and conservation tillage grain and oilseed farmers.[1] The analysis that follows cautions against a broad prediction of substantial improvements in women's farm labor position within the context of the current shift to sustainable agriculture as it is presently developing. Nevertheless, I suggest that there are elements within sustainable agriculture that reflect and encourage less rigidity in the gender division of labor and control of production.

SUSTAINABLE AGRICULTURE: WHAT KIND OF "ALTERNATIVE" ARE WE TALKING ABOUT?

In an attempt to understand the impact of sustainable agriculture, an important starting point begins with the recognition that the desegregation potential of farming practices depends substantially on what we mean by sustainable agriculture. In the rural studies literature, important efforts have been made to identify the core principles or beliefs of sustainable agriculture as a distinct production paradigm that challenges conventional agriculture (Beus 1995; Beus and Dunlap 1994). In fact, a considerable variety of farming practices and orientations are now called "sustainable agriculture" (Allen et al. 1991; Gale and Cordray 1994). Some analysts view this development as a positive one (Saltiel, Bauder, and Palakovich 1994). Others, however, argue that the concept of sustainable agriculture has been appropriated by agribusiness and the state to mean something very different from its original formulations (Gale and Cordray 1994; Hall, forthcoming; MacRae, Henning, and Hill 1993). In particular, certain technologies and methods, such as conservation tillage farming, have been heavily promoted by the state, by the more "established" farmer organizations, and by agribusiness as "sustainable methods." Although these methods can potentially reduce soil erosion and groundwater contamination, they also retain a heavy reliance on chemical inputs and, at the same time, maintain an emphasis on high levels of production and capitalization (Hinkle 1983; Lighthall 1995). In recent years, some low-input sustainable agricultural methods, such as integrated pest management (IPM) farming, have been promoted to a greater extent than others. Organic farming, however, has received relatively little official attention and support (MacRae, Henning, and Hill 1993; Crouch 1991).[2] Consequently, the adoption of conservation tillage and IPM is now quite widespread, while organic farming remains marginalized in most farming communities in both the United States and Canada (Hill and MacRae 1992).

CONSERVATION TILLAGE: A SUSTAINABLE METHOD?

There are marked differences between organic farming and conservation tillage farming methods, most of which bear directly on the expected impact of sustainable agriculture on the gender division of labor. Conservation tillage, especially the widely promoted method called no-till, is often presented and understood as a more efficient technology. In its ability to eliminate certain steps in the labor process (plowing and leveling),[3] this form of farming is believed to save labor time and reduce equipment and energy costs. Consistent with the conventional emphasis on productivity improvements through new technology, conservation tillage depends on access to expensive new planting technology and continued high use of chemical inputs and increasingly on specially designed chemical resistant bioengineered seeds (Hinkle 1983). Thus, in adopting conservation tillage, no additional room or demand for women's labor is being created. If anything, it further reduces direct farm labor requirements and intensifies the management requirements.

This latter point is evident in both my four case studies and thirty-two interviews where conservation tillage farmers reported that they used these labor savings either to expand their production base by taking on more land or to reduce their costs. None reported an increase in their direct farm labor as a result of the shift, and most reported a substantial decrease in their overall field time. A large number of farmers using conservation tillage also stated that there was some additional management time required for planning, crop and soil monitoring, and record keeping. However, neither the husband nor the wife farm operators in my case studies described any increase in the wives' involvement in direct farm labor or management activities following the adoption of no-till or other forms of conservation tillage. As well, neither the males nor the females in the case studies recited any change in female participation in farm decisions. There was also no report of changes in female participation among the additional thirty-two male farmers interviewed who were using conservation tillage. However, with a few exceptions, the wives' level of involvement in day-to-day farm production was quite negligible before the adoption of no-till or other types of conservation tillage.

Particularly interesting was the observation by two women in my case studies who believed that their involvement in both farm labor and decision making had declined over the period in which no-till had been adopted. While one was uncertain that no-till was related to her declining involvement and influence, they both observed that the demands of the modern farm were such that they no longer felt they had the knowledge to participate actively in important farm decisions. As one woman stated: "As we got more land, I was more involved initially, and we talked a lot more about the decisions [then]. Now I don't do as much anymore—our son is working with him now and they talk a lot . . . it just kind of happened that way. I don't know that I know enough now to say much." From her perspective, however, she made it very clear that no-till had further eroded her direct involvement in farm production. As she put it, "without the plowing he just doesn't seem to need me as much." It is also worth pointing out here that in the course of several interviews and conversations, it was evident that this woman welcomed her reduced role in farm labor, which in her view had always been limited to occasional supportive roles that she found "physically uncomfortable," "stressful," or simply "boring." Although she never stated so directly, she did seem less content with her reduced input into decisions and discussions regarding the farm.

R: We don't talk as much as we used to [shrugs].

Q: Are you happy with that?

R: [Hesitates] Well sure, I'm happy that [their son] is getting involved. . . . I miss it but that's okay. He still talks to me about some things, especially in the winter.

On the other hand, there were two other women who observed that the adoption of no-till had freed up their husbands to spend more time with them and the rest of the family. Indeed, it is important to point out that some farmers adopted no-till in part because they were looking for ways to reduce their labor load in the fields. As one put it, "I'm getting now to the point where I want to take it a little easy. Plowing was never much fun, and I don't miss it."

Many of the male no-till farmers also recognized the need to pay more attention to the careful planning and monitoring required within the no-till system, a system that demands more intensive knowledge of fertilizers and pesticides and assessments of pest and fertility conditions. While many farmers stated that they still "talked things over" with their wives, their comments suggested that this greater attention to administration and management may have further reduced their view of their wives' input into decisions as important. The adoption of no-till was only one of a number of factors leading to this conclusion. As one farmer put it when asked about his wife's involvement in the farm decisions: "It's a business, and it better be run as a business. Obviously if you don't run it as a business, then eventually you are going to get caught up—everybody else you're dealing with [is a business]—you're dealing with banks, suppliers . . . they are all in business . . . ya, it's a family farm—it's a family that lives on a farm, and chances are they are all involved in it to some degree, but it's a business . . . it's not like it used to be . . . those days are gone."

In light of the argument made at the outset regarding the ideological orientation of sustainable agriculture, it is also important to recognize that, with a few exceptions, most of the conservation tillage farmers in this study expressed very conventional views about farming and the environment. Consistent with the statement just quoted, their farms are seen clearly as business enterprises distinct from the household and family. Additionally, higher levels of production are viewed as important economically and morally ("to feed the world"), and new technologies are generally seen as the major solutions to problems of economic prosperity and environmental damage. Thus, in terms of my case studies at least, the no-till farmers are more conventional in their production ideologies than the farmers who had made more modest changes or no changes in their tillage practices. This finding is supported in part by the literature that suggests that the larger-scale family farm operators, that is, those with the stronger business orientations emphasizing economies of scale and expansion as their major routes to profitability, have been the earliest and strongest supporters of no-till (Lighthall 1995). Moreover, regardless of the size of the farm, almost all the no-till farmers in my study reported that they made the shift to no-till primarily for economic reasons. Environmental concerns were reported as important considerations for some farmers, but they were still secondary (see also Nowak and Kirsching 1985; Milham 1994; Napier and Camboni 1993).

While the participants in the case studies were not asked specifically about their beliefs regarding the gender segregation of labor on the farm and the household, interview questions about sharing household and child care duties, along with informal discussions and observations in the household, reveal fairly conventional views and practices: they segregate male and female roles in rigid terms. Compared to the conventional farm operations, there is no evidence of systematic differences in gender relations, and indeed the no-till farmers in particular seem to have very rigid divisions by gender. And, in those cases where there was some expansion in production and workload, the male farmers consistently looked to their sons, not their wives or daughters, for increased involvement, a finding supported by other studies of farmers more generally in the United States and Canada (Wilson, Harper Simpson, and Landerman 1994).[4]

In the current context, then, the evidence suggests that if sustainable agriculture largely means the adoption of conservation tillage, then there will be relatively little gender desegregation in farm labor as a result of this shift. This is largely because the shift to conservation tillage is not much of a change from conventional agriculture, either ideologically or in practice. In this study, the farmers who had moved to conservation tillage did not reflect the kinds of practices or the ideas of sustainable agriculture that can be seen as challenging the assumptions underlying conventional agriculture. Instead, this version may be best understood as a conventional form of sustainable agriculture that simply extends and thus reproduces the logic, ideas, and interests of conventional farming practices and ideologies. And it does so with little or no positive prospects for women's involvement in farm labor and decision making.

ORGANIC FARMING AND GENDER: THE TRULY SUSTAINABLE METHOD?

Sustainable agriculture has another face: it is usually understood in practice as the adoption of organic farming. Organic farming is not developing at the pace of conservation tillage methods. However, low-input farming programs (such as Low-Input Sustainable Agriculture [LISA] in the United States) and the persistent public demand for organic produce suggest that organic farming, if the demand for low-input farming remains, is a viable force in North American and world agriculture (Lighthall 1995; Crosson 1991). Whether organic farming will develop further prominence remains to be seen, but the central research question posed here is: is there evidence of greater equity in female participation in and control over production in this kind of sustainable farming operation?

In looking at the four case studies of organic farms, I find some support for the argument that these kinds of operations involve greater female participation and control, but the evidence also suggests considerable variability among organic farmers both in how they farm and how they distribute the work.[5] To begin with, three of the four organic case studies revealed much more female involvement in the farm production labor process and in decision making than was evident in all but one of the other conservation tillage case studies. The male farmer in the fourth organic case study, who was only beginning to farm his own land organically on a small scale while at the same time farming the bulk of his father's large operation using conservation tillage, expressed a willingness and a preference for a greater involvement by his wife in the farm operation. However, she expressed relatively little interest in doing so, given her preferred off-farm career. In the other three cases, a strong interest was expressed by both spouses in "farming together" as an important motive for or benefit from organic farming.

One case study is particularly interesting in that it fits the "ideal" sustainable model as outlined by Beus and Dunlap (1994), that is, a mixed livestock/grain farm operation with small acreage (150 acres) serving local markets with low levels of capitalization, mechanization, and debt. On this farm, there exists ample evidence of substantial sharing, cooperation, and collaboration concerning farm labor and substantial joint involvement in major farm production and management decisions. When asked about farm-related decisions in this context, the female spouse said: "we talk about it, we'll discuss it and come to an agreement—like there is hardly a time where we don't ask each other well what do you think." What is also interesting is the extent to which both spouses perceive the household and farm decisions as interrelated or linked. For example, when asked about who was involved in household decisions versus farm-related decisions, both responded by saying they did not make a distinction, because any household decision had to be weighed against farm needs and vice versa for household needs. Likewise, both spouses viewed the allocation and organization of farm and household labor and decision making as closely linked. The woman on this farm, however, articulates the division of labor by gender.

I have to organize the day to make sure I have time to get out [to the farm yard]. I do the laundry at night, have meals planned for the next day. In the morning I would probably be in the house one and a half hours, then we [husband and wife] would stay out till noon, an hour at lunch and a nap for the kids, then out later. It's really something that fluctuates too because in really busy times, planting, I'll spend a lot more hours taking over some of the regular chores that [her husband] does. On average, I'd say I spend five hours outside and three hours inside during the day.

It is worth pointing out that, in my observations during the growing season, it appeared that she had underestimated considerably the amount of time and labor spent in the household. Nevertheless, this woman's labor "on the farm" was valued by the couple as a critical contribution in much the same way that their older children's farm input was considered important. Also, both partners envisioned the greater household demands as a temporary situation that would change as their children get older. In terms of farming, both clearly saw their model of organic farming, that is, a mixed livestock/horticultural farm focusing on local markets, as an alternative practice that permits her participation.

In the two other organic cases, both characterized by a substantial female involvement in the farm, it is apparent, in comparison to the vast majority of the conservation tillage and conventional tillage farmers studied (both in interviews and case studies), that the women in these farm operations are also viewed and treated as major partners in the farm enterprise. Further, these farms contain mixed livestock/grain farming, and they vary in important ways from the "ideal case." Although one of the operations is also well established as a functioning organic farm, this farm is different in that it is a larger, more heavily capitalized farm operation that contains a more export-market emphasis. Relative to many of the no-till case studies, this farming operation is still smaller (500 acres versus 2,000 acres); it has much lower levels of capitalization and a very high level of local innovations. While the female spouse joined the household after the male farmer had already adopted organic farming, it is difficult to say whether or not her involvement in the farm was a function of the labor demands of organic farming. However, during the course of the year when she became involved and showed an interest in being active in the operation, it was clearly observed that her participation facilitated the further expansion of organic farm production plans.

A third case study operation is only moving to organic farming in a very limited way, largely due to the owners' lack of control over much of the land in which they work. Since farming livestock is, in itself, quite demanding in terms of labor, it seems likely that in this case the female spouse's increased involvement reflects these and other demands, rather than the demands associated with organic farming. The couples' engagement in organic farming was, at this point in time, minimal. Nevertheless, there are indications in all three cases that the couple's willingness and interest in "farming together" remain important aspects of their commitment to organic farming.

In light of these case studies, while there is some support for making a general argument that a correspondence exists between organic farming and more equitable gender relations, this does not mean that gender inequities in farm labor and decision making are absent in these family operations and households. Even in the "ideal" case cited above, the female farmer did acknowledge that all decisions were made jointly, but she also qualified this claim in an important way: "I have to trust him because I feel he has more experience and background knowledge." She also acknowledged that while there was some sharing of domestic household duties, most of those duties, including child care, were "hers." Because of the priority of domestic duties, she was often unable to do as much on the farm as she would have liked. She considered these limitations on her day-to-day involvement in the farm as a valid reason for continuing to rely on her husband to make certain farm decisions, though this also made her feel less competent about making such decisions. Her goal is to become more involved, and, with this involvement, she expects to have a more active control over farm decisions. Nevertheless, she accepts the household constraints as both natural and unavoidable and as necessitating a delay in achieving greater involvement.

Women in the other households express similar sentiments. Some, however, recognize additional constraints on their involvement in farming (see also Evans and Ilbery 1996). In one case study, the degree of female decision making is very high. In this particular case, the female spouse works on the farm and also supports the household through a part-time off-farm job, and the husband works full time on the farm. At the time of the study, the couple had just begun to make the shift to organic farming and did so in a conventional manner.[6] Even though most of the day-to-day production is the male's, it is conceivable that with the shift to organic farming the couple will move to a more equitable distribution of farm production work. In fact, both spouses expressed a desire for the farm operation to support the family without the need for off-farm income. They also insisted that they would perform equally the different roles in farm production and decision making without reference to gender. Certainly, their farm decisions were largely made jointly, but they did not see a fully equitable situation as being viable at this time because of the land ownership and the financial need for off-farm income. Yet this situation still raises the question as to why it is the woman who gets selected as the one to work off the farm (see Lobao and Meyer 1995). The farm couple in this case expressed the view that the selection of the female for the off-farm employment reflected the availability of particular part-time jobs, especially those in the office and retail sectors. There is an important point to their argument since we know that much of the paid labor market is gender-segregated and that men cannot readily obtain traditional female jobs even if they try (Krahn and Lowe 1997). Yet their readiness to see certain jobs as "female" suggests, at minimum, the systemic influence of patriarchy on farm families, even when they may have feminist ideas about work. And indeed, in this case, the subtle influences of sexist hegemony do creep in despite a general awareness of these issues. In talking with them over extended periods of time, there was never serious consideration given to the husband working off-farm; it was largely just understood that the wife would have to engage in the off-farm work.

It is worth pointing out that in the situation of the "ideal" organic case study, the male did take on seasonal off-farm employment in the local canning industry in an effort to ease some financial problems. His employment during this period, however, warranted more farm work by his spouse. Ultimately, their decision to select the male for off-farm work was heavily informed by the fact that they had preschool-aged children. From their point of view, this prohibited the female from working outside the home. Again, of course, the implicit assumption that child care was primarily the female's responsibility, rather than something the husband could take on, implies the persistence of gendered conceptions of work roles that were operative, notwithstanding the many positive signs of greater equity in decision making and duties. Indeed, this woman emphasized that "[her husband] isn't one to do much housework."

Despite these limitations on women's farm participation, it is interesting to note that in two of the four cases the women remain as the key sources of knowledge about organic farming and its underlying philosophy. Women, in fact, do much of the outside research required to develop greater knowledge of organic farming techniques: they attend local or provincial meetings or seminars on organic farming and subscribe to and read organic farming magazines or journals. Interestingly enough, in one of the organic farming cases, the male farmer appeared to be the consumer of the wife's knowledge that she gained largely in an abstract text form. This form of consumption potentially permitted him to integrate, develop, and apply her information into his own personal knowledge of the farm and of farming. In this context, he felt less comfortable with the abstract "book" knowledge and the social contexts within which this knowledge could be obtained. He also knew nothing about organic farming until she began attending meetings and subscribing to a journal and an organic association newsletter. In contrast, the men in the two other organic farm case studies were the primary sources of the initiative to shift to organic farming, and they directly developed their own knowledge around organic methods and principles. In one situation, in particular, the woman was active in the farm operation and increasingly took the role of the "researcher" together with her husband.[7]

This gender division in organic farming knowledge is in direct contrast with the vast majority of the conservation tillage farmers. Based on my case studies and farmer interviews, the males were the ones who took the initiative to gain access to this information and, with perhaps one notable exception (see note 7), to conduct the self-education and research on and off the farm. During an eighteen-month period, in one county I attended several major demonstrations, seminars, and meetings on conservation tillage farming. While attendance at some of these events reached one hundred farmers, I met only two women during this period. In only one of these cases did it appear, judging from the level of participation and questions, and repeat attendance at multiple events, that women were a key force in collecting new information.

One final observation regarding the ideological orientation of organic farmers in this study suggests a further need for caution when predicting a substantial shift in gender relations within these farming households. In contrast to the case study, which was referred to as representing the "ideal" model, there were important variations found among the small number of case studies in this research that deviate from the ideal. While two of the other case studies were consistent with the ideal model in the sense that they were concerned with addressing both environmental and social issues through their farming practices, they were also at the very early stages of the shift to organic farming and were, for the most part, still farming conventionally. However, as noted earlier, in one of my other cases where the shift to organic farming was well developed, the farmer viewed the adoption of organic farming in more conventional economic or business terms centered around growth, export markets, value-added and large-scale production, and achieving higher efficiency levels through the use of local and scientifically developed technologies and knowledge.

Whether these kinds of variations between organic farmers will make a difference in gender relations is not immediately evident from the limited data available from this study. There were, in fact, no indications of a major difference between this and the other organic households as far as gender relations were concerned. Nevertheless, this different orientation does translate into different management strategies and labor processes that may approximate the conventional model in key areas relating to the wife's participation in farming. For example, the greater use of paid labor on the larger-scale farm, which was the longer-term goal of this farmer, may eventually discourage the female spouse's participation. This emphasis on paid labor, growth, and competition suggests an ideological orientation that, although still different from the conservation tillage farmers, may translate into a less progressive social justice orientation in gender relations. Indeed, as Buck, Getz, and Guthman (1997) point out in their study of organic farmers in northern California, large agribusiness firms and family farms emulating agribusiness practices are penetrating the most dynamic and profitable segments of organic markets. If this pattern persists, then there is the potential for the "conventionalization" of organic farming, a process more broadly found in sustainable agriculture (as in the case of conservation farming).

There are, nevertheless, potentially important differences among organic farmers in ideology, labor processes, and marketing practices that, in part, bring us full circle to the initial starting point of this chapter. When studying and analyzing the relationship between sustainable agriculture and gender relations, we need to be very clear about what we, as researchers, mean by sustainable agriculturalists; or, to put it another way, we need to recognize that there are different, and to some extent quite contradictory, forms of sustainable agriculture that need to be defined and identified as part of the research process. Moreover, it is also important to bear in mind that different kinds of people and families may adopt and adapt an "organic model" in ways that will not necessarily reflect or lead to a deseg-regated division of labor and decision making.

CONCLUSION

I have attempted to show that as we move more closely to farming op-erations that fit the "ideal" model of sustainable agriculture, as outlined by Beus and Dunlap (1994), gender relations become more equitable in terms of farm production activities and decision making. There is also some evidence to suggest that both of the theoretical explanations for this rela-tionship, as outlined at the beginning of this chapter, may have some va-lidity in understanding why this is the situation. That is, in comparison to the conservation tillage farmers, organic farmers (along with their more progressive ideas concerning production, the environment, and social re-lations more generally) are more liberal in their ideological views of gender and more interested in having an active male/female partnership on the farm. In three of the cases, these views formed part of the attraction of organic farming. In all four cases, an understanding of gender relations was clearly developed prior to shifting to organic farming, suggesting that the ideologies that played a role in the adoption of organic farming may also be accompanied by more liberal views of gender relations. These views in turn become important in shaping the organization of organic production and decision making in more equitable terms. At the same time, there is evidence to suggest that the organization of the organic farming labor proc-ess, given its demand for more human labor power and local innovations, provides women with important avenues for participating in and influenc-ing farm production. By comparison, the organization of the conservation tillage labor process, with its continued emphasis on mechanization, chem-ical inputs, productivity increases, and efficiency improvements through technological innovations, seems to reinforce the exclusion of women from most of these operations. Women, in most of these households, were al-ready marginalized as far as the farm operation was concerned.

There are two important cautionary notes to derive from this analysis. First, the study has revealed that important differences in farmer ideology and in practices prevail among organic farmers (Buck, Getz, and Guthman 1997). These differences may translate into continued segregation for women farmers even if organic farming becomes more dominant. Again, as in the case of sustainable agriculture more generally, we need to recog-nize the capacity of capital to transform production methods and social ideas to meet the requirements of accumulation and regulation (Gramsci 1971). We should assume, in other words, that the development of organic farming will take a form that reflects capital's interests in centralization, market and expert dependencies, efficiency, and competition. This point further substantiates the main thrust of this study: as researchers and activists, we need to define clearly what we mean by alternative or sustainable agriculture. We cannot simply assume that the adoption of any new method or technology brings with it a necessary challenge to the social relations of production and reproduction in a capitalist society.

Second, the study has shown that even when the "ideal" sustainable model is in place, and indeed even when there is a progressive ideology evident within the family concerning the participation of women, the woman's capacity to be an equal partner is still constrained. In line with the central concern of this study, sustainable agriculture may reflect and support over time the breakdown of gender segregation in farm labor. This may be a process that will be confirmed over time, but we need more detailed and extensive research to determine what varying patterns hold in the population as a whole and to what extent these patterns are characterized by particular types of farmers from different countries and regions.

In terms of gender relations, the key implication to draw from this study is that the adoption of sustainable organic farming will not in itself lead to the equal participation of women at the individual family level or at the broader societal level (Meares 1997). Gender inequalities do exist, and are not readily dismantled or weakened as a simple function of shifting technologies, production ideologies, or class relations. As such, we should not expect individual families to overcome the constraints of sexist ideologies or relations simply because they adopt a different way of working their farms. Nor should we be predicting any substantial generalized shifts that supposedly result from large-scale changes in farm production systems without a sustained gender-based politics aimed at achieving this kind of change. I remain convinced, however, that there is progressive potential in the development of sustainable organic farming, both in terms of gender and class relations. This potential must be consciously recognized by those who not only participate in social movements but who are interested in linking the issues of gender with environmental and class concerns.

NOTES

1. An additional forty family farm operators were interviewed prior to the case studies. These were selected purposively according to their involvement in various local farm organizations (e.g., Essex Soil and Crop Improvement Association) in the county and their use of alternative farming methods. The interviews lasted from 90 to 120 minutes with open-ended questions on the characteristics of their farms, their farming methods, and their views and concerns regarding farm economic and environmental issues.

2. IPM refers to methods of pest control that combine and integrate biological and chemical controls to ensure appropriate and specifically targeted uses of pesticides that do not kill beneficial plants and insects.

3. Conservation tillage refers broadly to changes in conventional tillage techniques that can range from modification of the plowing equipment used to less

frequent plowing to no plowing at all. No-till is a method that involves planting in untilled soil using a special no-till drill leaving the full residue from the previous harvest on the field; that is, there is no plowing before planting nor after harvest.

4. In one case, for example, the male farmer brought the son fully into the operation at the same time that he made the shift to no-till farming. Also important here is that in this case the expansion of the farm was motivated by an interest in creating room for the son to participate in farming.

5. It should be noted that two of the four case studies were only in the initial stages of moving to organic farming. In both cases, their ability to move more quickly was also hampered by the fact that their parents owned much of the land they were farming and were refusing to endorse the move to organic farming.

6. They were having difficulties because of parental ownership of much of the land, and the father was resisting a more significant shift to organic methods.

7. What is also perhaps worth recognizing from the point of view of future research is a possible class influence that may explain the different roles of women in conveying and translating externally produced knowledge into a household and local context. In particular, the two case studies in which the males were the major initiators and researchers were university educated, and they felt comfortable in obtaining and converting the abstract knowledge into local and personal practices. In the other organic case study, the male had a working-class background with a more limited formal education. A similar situation was also evident in one of my other conservation tillage case studies involving a working-class background where again it was clear that, compared to the other conservation tillage cases, the female was more involved in making contacts and in collecting information on new technologies than was the case in the other farm operations, which were generally on a larger-scale.

REFERENCES

Allen, J., and K. Bernhardt. (1995). "Farming Practices and Adherence to an Alternative Conventional Agricultural Paradigm." *Rural Sociology* 60 (2): 297–309.

Allen, P., D. Van Dusen, J. Lundy, and S. Gliessman. (1991). "Integrating Social, Environmental, and Economic Issues in Sustainable Agriculture." *American Journal of Sustainable Agriculture* 6 (1):34–49.

Beus, C. (1995). "Competing Paradigms: An Overview and Analysis of the Alternative-Conventional Agriculture Debate." *Research in Rural Sociology and Development* 6:23–50.

Beus, C., and R. Dunlap. (1991). "Measuring Adherence to Alternative vs. Conventional Agricultural Paradigms." *Rural Sociology* 56 (3):432–60.

———. (1993). "Agricultural Policy Debates: Examining the Alternative and Conventional Perspectives." *American Journal of Alternative Agriculture* 8 (3): 98–106.

———. (1994). "Agricultural Paradigms and the Practice of Agriculture." *Rural Sociology* 59 (4):620–35.

Buck, D., C. Getz, and J. Guthman. (1997). "From the Farm to the Table: The Organic Vegetable Commodity Chain of Northern California." *Sociologia Ruralis* 37 (1):3–20.

Buttell, F., and G. Gillespie. (1984). "The Sexual Division of Farm Household Labor Allocation among Farm Men and Women." *Rural Sociology* 49 (2): 183–209.

Crosson, P. (1991). "Sustainable Agriculture in North America: Issues and Challenges." *Canadian Journal of Agricultural Economics* 39:553–65.

Crouch, M. (1991). "The Very Structure of Scientific Research Mitigates against Developing Production to Help the Environment, Poor and Hungry." *Journal of Agricultural and Environmental Ethics* 4 (2):151–58.

Evans, N., and B. Ilbery. (1996). "Exploring the Influence of Farm-Based Pluriactivity on Gender Relations in Capitalist Agriculture." *Sociologia Ruralis* 36 (1):74–92.

Feldman, S., and R. Welsh. (1995). "Feminist Knowledge Claims, Local Knowledge, and Gender Divisions of Agricultural Labor: Constructing a Successor Science." *Rural Sociology* 60 (1):23–43.

Gale, R., and S. Cordray. (1994). "Making Sense of Sustainability: Nine Answers to 'What Should Be Sustained?' " *Rural Sociology* 59 (2):311–32.

Gramsci, A. (1971). *Selections from Prison Notebooks*. New York: International Publishers.

Hall, A. (forthcoming). "Sustainable Agriculture and Conservation Tillage: Managing the Contradictions." *Canadian Review of Sociology and Anthropology*.

Harper Simpson, I., J. Wilson, and K. Young. (1988). "The Sexual Division of Farm Household Labour: A Replication and Extension." *Rural Sociology* 53 (2):145–65.

Hill, S., and R. MacRae. (1992). Organic Farming in Canada. *Agriculture, Ecosystems and the Environment* 39 (1):71–84.

Hinkle, M. (1983). "Problems with Conservation Tillage." *Journal of Soil and Water Conservation* 38 (3):201–7.

Kloppenburg, J. (1991). "Social Theory and the De/reconstruction of Agricultural Science: Local Knowledge for an Alternative Agriculture." *Rural Sociology* 56 (4):519–48.

Krahn, H., and G. Lowe. (1997). "Women's Employment." In *The Sociology of Labour Markets: Efficiency, Equity and Security*, ed. A. Van Der Berg and J. Smucker, 451–70. Scarborough, Ontario: Prentice-Hall and Bacon Canada.

Lighthall, D. (1995). "Farm Structure and Chemical Use in the Corn Belt." *Rural Sociology* 60 (3):505–20.

Lobao, L., and K. Meyer. (1995). "Economic Decline, Gender, and Labor Flexibility in Family-Based Enterprises: Midwestern Farming in the 1980s." *Social Forces* 74 (2):575–608.

MacRae, R., J. Henning, and S. Hill. (1993). "Strategies to Overcome the Barriers to Development of Sustainable Agriculture in Canada: The Role of Agibusiness." *Journal of Agricultural and Environmental Ethics* 6 (1):21–51.

Meares, A. (1997). "Making the Transition from Conventional to Sustainable Agriculture: Gender, Social Movement Participation and Quality of Life on the Family Farm." *Rural Sociology* 62 (1):21–47.

Milham, N. (1994). "An Analysis of Farmers' Incentives to Degrade the Land." *Journal of Environmental Management* 40 (1):51–64.

Napier, T., and S. Camboni. (1993). "Use of Conventional and Conservation Practices among Farmers in the Scioto River Basin of Ohio." *Journal of Soil and Water Conservation* 48 (3):231–37.

Nowak, P., and P. Korsching. (1985). "Conservation Tillage: Revolution or Evolution." *Journal of Soil and Water Conservation* 40 (3):199–201.

Reimer, B. (1983). "Sources of Farm Labour in Contemporary Quebec." *Canadian Review of Sociology and Anthropology* 20 (3):290–301.

———. (1984). "Farm Mechanization: The Impact on Labour at the Level of the Farm Household." *Canadian Journal of Sociology* 9 (4):429–43.

Rosenfeld, R. (1985). *Farm Women: Work, Farm and Family in the United States*. Chapel Hill: University of North Carolina Press.

Sachs, C. (1983). *The Invisible Farmers: Women in Agricultural Production*. Totowa, N.J.: Rowman and Allanheld.

Saltiel, J., J. Bauder, and S. Palakovich. (1994). "Adoptions of Sustainable Agricultural Practices: Diffusion, Farm Structure, and Profitability." *Rural Sociology* 59 (2):333–49.

Whatmore, S. (1991). *Farming Women*. Basingstoke, U.K.: Macmillan.

Wilson, J., I. Harper Simpson, and R. Landerman. (1994). "Status Variations on Family Farms: Effects of Crop, Machinery and Off-Farm Work." *Rural Sociology* 59 (1):136–53.

13

Economic Restructuring and Unpaid Work

Anne Forrest

Studies of economic restructuring often marginalize women by focusing on work traditionally performed by men. Typically, researchers investigate how the cutbacks and downsizing that are the hallmarks of restructuring in the 1990s have narrowed job opportunities and intensified the work process in the manufacturing sector. Studies such as Bakker (1996) that seek to identify the particular impact of restructuring on women and traditional women's work are few and far between, and even those studies have tended to overlook women's unpaid work or treat it as an afterthought.[1]

In this chapter, I have reversed the investigative lens to demonstrate that an analysis of unpaid work is central to the project of understanding economic restructuring. Indeed, I argue that an analysis of unpaid work provides a framework for understanding the organization and value of women's paid work and the implications of restructuring. Women routinely spend significant portions of their days performing unpaid work in the forms of personal, home, and family care, but much of this work is invisible as such because it goes to the essence of who women are in North American society. Seymour (1992:188) argues that "women carry out domestic tasks because it is part of the definition of what they are not what they do." Similarly, other activities such as keeping up one's appearance or facilitating social interaction, though often mislabeled as personal attributes, are work because they are required of women both on and off the job. Women only appear to perform these tasks "naturally" because these forms of work are mistakenly assumed to be part of gender identity rather than gender activity (Fishman 1978).

My analysis begins with unpaid work on the job in a variety of occupations and workplaces located in North America. I show that tasks performed in conjunction with jobs traditionally held by men are more likely to be conceptualized as work and more likely to be paid than similar tasks performed in conjunction with jobs traditionally held by women. Next, I explore how the division of unpaid work in the household underpins job segregation by sex—the process by which women are matched with a limited number of cleaning, caring, and serving occupations[2]—and low pay for "women's work" outside the home. I argue that the nature of women's unpaid work and its time demands define women as unreliable employees legitimately confined to a narrow range of low-skilled, poorly paid jobs. Thus the division of labor by sex in the workplace appears natural or inevitable because personal upkeep and unpaid work in the household are the quintessential forms of "women's work." Furthermore, because women perform these services for free, the skill and effort involved have little intrinsic value in the labor market, at least when performed by women.

I also demonstrate that economic restructuring is multiplying the demands on women's time and energy. Cutbacks and downsizing have significantly expanded the amount and varied the forms of unpaid work expected of women (and men) on the job, while sharp cuts in government spending increase their domestic workloads by transferring a variety of health care and educational responsibilities to the household. Finally, I conclude by offering some suggestions for change.

UNPAID WORK ON THE JOB

Although there are many pockets of job-related tasks routinely performed by employees without pay, the likelihood that these activities will be recognized as work depends largely on their association with jobs traditionally performed by men. Changing into work clothes, washing up after shift, working outside one's formal job description, job training, and even some forms of union business (e.g., processing grievances) are all examples of job-related activities recognized as work in industries in which men predominate.[3]

What men do in conjunction with their employment is more likely to be labeled job-related than what women do. Because unpaid work has been a relatively minor feature of men's lives, employers and employees alike have less difficulty identifying as work a wide range of activities performed by men in conjunction with their jobs. Male workers have traditionally sought to draw a sharp distinction between work and home—that is, between time spent on the employer's behalf (work) and their own time—and whenever possible have pressed to be paid for the former. Despite employer opposition, many workers have been successful; however, the outcome often depends on the workers' bargaining power. Thus we find that workers represented by the Canadian Auto Workers Union at CAMI Automotive in Ontario[4] are paid for time spent doing the warmup exercises required by the company, whereas workers in similar nonunion plants in Canada and the United States are not. But whether time spent performing these tasks is paid or not, the claim for pay is considered legitimate because male workers have made it so.

As a rule, similar tasks associated with jobs traditionally performed by women have not been conceptualized as work and have not been paid. Examples of unpaid work performed by women on the job everyday include tasks such as getting coffee, tidying the lunchroom, and listening to the problems of customers and clients. Secretaries (and women faculty) in my university routinely listen to the personal problems of students, as do waitresses, hairdressers, bank tellers, and any other woman who deals with customers and clients in her job. Similarly, hospital and nursing home cleaners perform unpaid work when they attend to patients' needs by fetching a drink of water or helping a wobbly patient in the bathroom when nursing staff are not available. Yet this work and the skills associated with it are typically unrecognized and uncompensated. When noticed at all, women's extra effort is dismissed as trivial or construed as the exercise of the worker's personal choice, not a job necessity, even in workplaces where "teamwork" and "customer service" are part of the managerial philosophy.

The difference is not the nature of the activity, but the gender of the worker performing it. Getting dressed is a particularly good example of work attached to women's jobs that is generally dismissed as personal choice—even evidence of vanity—when, in fact, a "feminine" appearance is an implicit job requirement in many women's occupations. Being pretty—or at least making the effort—is assumed of women in the workplace, particularly when the job involves contact with the public. In occupations ranging from receptionist to air flight attendant to waitress, women employees' appearance is thought to be critically important to the success of the business. Receptionists are required to adhere to a dress code (formal or informal) that stresses an appealing, but not too suggestive self-presentation; air flight attendants are required to maintain their weight within certain bounds and may have their makeup inspected by their supervisors; and waitresses in bars and restaurants are frequently required to wear sexually suggestive uniforms that mark them as "available" to customers. For many more women, maintaining a "look" that involves the careful application of makeup, the styling of hair, and close attention to the choice of clothes is an implicit job requirement and a vital component of workers' job performance.[5] Yet the considerable knowledge, skill, and effort that women apply to their appearance is not conceptualized as work. Accordingly, it has no apparent value even though equivalent tasks associated with men's work, such as changing into work clothes or washing up after shift, are commonly recognized as job-related.

Men in the workplace are assumed to be workers/breadwinners whatever their actual circumstances. When asked to define the meaning of masculinity, the majority of American women and men still say "good provider for his family" (Faludi 1991:65);[6] hence what men do on the job is implicitly defined as work until proven otherwise. But the same cannot be said of women. Women carry into the workplace their (lower) status as women. By virtue of their gender, they are expected to perform certain caretaker and beauty functions whatever else they are doing, which explains why employers and employees alike can understand male workers' demand for paid washup time but have no comprehension of putting on makeup or fixing hair as job-related activities.

On the job, women's status as workers is always qualified by their gender, as evidenced by identifiers such as "the blonde accountant" and "the girl bus driver." (My friend's mother calls me "the lady professor.") Consequently, when the tasks involved are those associated with women only or with jobs traditionally performed by women, they are not readily identified either as work or as job-related, that is, until the work is not performed to the employer's satisfaction. Caldwell (1991) describes the lengths to which airlines in the United States go to enforce their dress and beauty codes. In her view, the industry has attempted to maintain a chorus line image by excluding women, most notably black women, because their height or weight or choice of hairstyle or makeup does not conform to industry standards.

Because so much of what women do on the job is associated with their femininity or replicates their domestic responsibilities, the skill and effort entailed in the work women do because they are women is often invisible. It is precisely because women are expected to attend to their appearance, facilitate social interaction, and perform cleaning and caring services in their capacities as women that they find it difficult to assert their right to be paid for this work, even when it is performed on the job. One suspects that if there were a tradition of men packing their own lunches for work or washing their own work clothes, unions would try to negotiate premium pay for these activities and employers would take the demand seriously.

UNPAID WORK IN THE HOUSEHOLD

Whereas thirty years ago we might have argued that employers paid indirectly for women's work in the household by paying men a family wage, today this is no longer the case. As a result of economic restructuring, the prevalence of the "breadwinner wage" sufficient to support a family has fallen dramatically, especially for working-class men. Downsizing and cutbacks have wiped out many of the "men's jobs" in resource extraction, manufacturing, and construction that, in the past, were relied on to support a family. Today the average male worker earns just over half of the family income,[7] and most families need two earners to make ends meet.[8]

But the fact that most women now work for pay does not mean that their household labor is no longer required. In most families, the division of unpaid labor has changed little (Jackson 1996; Chandler 1993). Although younger men are more likely to perform housework on a regular basis than older men, women retain primary responsibility for housework and child care.[9] Women employed outside the home devote half as many hours to these tasks as their at-home counterparts; however, the difference is only partly made up by men's contributions. As a rule, women are expected to take responsibility for organizing and planning family life, and men participate as "helpers" even when they perform a significant share of the chores. Livingstone and Asner (1996:86) found that among male steelworkers and former steelworkers in Ontario "there were fewer differences among married men generally, the most notable being the above-average housework times of men with spouses employed full-time. But, even in the most extreme case of dependent men with full-time employed wives, the woman was still doing about five hours [per week] more housework than the man."

Yet the effort expended by women with family responsibilities to accommodate the needs of others is not always conceptualized as work, but as activities undertaken out of love or commitment. Typically, home and family are associated with rest and relaxation, whereas, for women, home is also a workplace. Women cannot rest when they come home from their jobs, but face multiple demands from family members for emotional and physical care. For this reason, women's jobs can be exhausting even though they are generally classified as "light work." One thinks of grocery store clerks and child care workers who are required to lift relatively small weights throughout the day, or bank tellers and retail clerks who stand for long periods of time, or cleaners who spend much of their day bending or crouching. When combined with women's unpaid work, these jobs are more taxing than has generally been thought.[10]

Counterbalancing these effects, however, is the possibility that the satisfaction women derive from their family roles may offset the trials and tribulations of the workplace. In a study of nurses and nursing assistants, Walters et al. (1995) reported that, for women, family ties and responsibilities were more likely to act as a buffer against the demands and frustrations encountered in their paid work than for men, despite the fact that the women in their survey reported less personal time.

The widely held assumption that domestic work is "women's work" underpins job segregation by sex in the labor market. Defined as wives and mothers first, women are expected to take family life as their central responsibility around which all other commitments must be organized. Such an understanding constructs women as family- rather than job-oriented. One result is that women are labeled "unreliable" or "secondary" workers, justifiably confined to a narrow range of low-skilled, poorly paid jobs with few opportunities for advancement. Employers often believe that they need not offer "good jobs" to attract women workers who, by definition, are unwilling or unable to put their obligations as employees ahead of their family commitments.

The construction of women as "temporary" workers is so pervasive that women as well as men often assume that women do not get ahead at work because they are less committed to their jobs and likely to leave paid work while their children are young.[11] Recently a union organizer described to me her frustration with women who say they are not interested in joining the union because they are only working temporarily ("until my daughter gets married" or "until we pay off our debts" are common responses) when, in fact, they have been employed by the same firm for many years. The organizer then laughed and said that she, herself, started work twelve years ago thinking she would stay only long enough to buy a dishwasher.

The idea that women are not permanently or fully attached to the labor force may reflect women's preferences[12] but does not match the reality of most women's lives. Given the difficulties of combining paid and unpaid work, it is hardly surprising that many women find the ideology of the wife-mother role appealing. Nonetheless, most women in North America who are employed outside the home hold full-time jobs, even when they have young children. Only one woman in four works part-time, and fewer than half report doing so out of personal preference or because of personal and family responsibilities.[13] Today the majority of Canadian and U.S. women can expect to work for pay until retirement, apart from short periods of time out for childbirth.[14] Phillips and Phillips (1993:35) argue that "female participation patterns are more and more approaching male labour participation patterns," even though the gender division of labor in the home retains its 1960s character.

The easy assumption that women perform "women's work" by choice is problematic. Despite the fact that women are often willing to trade money[15] or ambition for part-time or flexible hours, there is no evidence to suggest that women are less committed to their jobs than men. Even with their lower pay and poorer fringe benefits, women consistently report themselves to be as satisfied with and committed to their jobs (Krahn and Lowe 1988:162). Rather than choosing family over paid work, women may simply feel they have no choice. Whatever their personal preferences, women are socialized to accept responsibility for family members' well-being, a responsibility that feels particularly inescapable in the absence of affordable alternatives. When asked why they spent so much time attending to the needs of their elderly mothers, women teachers saw it as unavoidable both because it was expected of daughters (but not of sons) and because there was no one else to do it (Aronson 1992).

It is difficult for women to leave behind their role as family caretaker. On average, they miss three times as many workdays as men (Canada, Ministry of Industry 1995b:82) and are more likely to structure their jobs to accommodate family responsibilities. In their study of professional couples in the United States, Karambayya and Reilly (1992) found that the women were more likely than men to adjust their hours of arrival and departure or limit the amount of work for pay done at night or on the weekend to meet the needs of children, even though they were less well established in their careers than their male partners. Especially prized is the "understanding" employer that offers flexible starting and finishing times whether formally or informally: that fifteen minutes at the beginning or end of the work day appears to ease the tension between work and home.[16]

Women's work in the home also limits the earning potential of those employed in jobs traditionally performed by women. When job duties commonly mirror the tasks entailed in unpaid domestic work, the value of the skills and effort required to perform this work is undermined. The pay equity/comparable worth exercise[17] revealed that employers in North America systematically undervalue "women's work" and get away with it, in part, because women routinely provide cleaning and caring services without remuneration in the home. The high degree of skill entailed in caring for others and effort required to cook and clean are concealed by the belief that women are endowed with the appropriate "feminine" talents by nature. Looking after home and family are so much a part of being a woman that the work involved is inseparable from the person. Housework and child care are part of who women are, not just what they do (Seymour 1992).

The construction of women as "secondary" workers is reinforced by the view that their wages are supplementary, not essential. On average, women in Canada and the United States earn almost a third of family income, a contribution that, while smaller than men's, could not readily be done without. Yet women's earnings and their effect on the family's standard of living are often minimized by women as well as men. Only one in six of the women co-breadwinners interviewed by Potuchek (1992) had completely redefined breadwinning as a shared, nongendered activity. Not long ago, a woman auto worker explained to me that she earns more than 60 percent of her family's income but would never press the point at home. She does not wish to embarrass her spouse, who maintains his position as breadwinner by paying the mortgage and house bills out of his wages. Or consider the contribution of the woman whose income was described as supplementary because, in her husband's words, her wages were used "just" to pay the mortgage (Hood 1986:355). From his study of middle-aged professional men in New England, Weiss (1987:114) concluded that "insofar as the income from their wives' work is helpful to the family, [husbands] see it as a matter of their wives helping out—analogous to their own contributions to home maintenance."

The social construction of women as domestic workers has its parallel construction of men as reliable workers/breadwinners for whom employment takes precedence over family. However, much of what is taken for granted about the demands of traditional men's work is open for inquiry once we make unpaid household labor visible as work. The assumption that unpaid domestic work belongs to women "frees" men for paid work. Reexamined in this light, industrial norms such as long hours, unpredictable overtime, and around-the-clock shift work are not dictates of the market in any simple sense but what employers can get away with because men are assumed not to have responsibility for the day-to-day physical and emotional needs of family members. Men's work patterns vary little over the life cycle of the family, whereas women's schedules are affected by the number and ages of children in the home (Lero and Johnson 1994:13). Without women at home, it is unlikely that employers could require men to be so unavailable to their families.

Hannah Papanek's concept of the "two-person career" is helpful here. Papanek (1972:853) observed that "women often find the demands of their husbands' jobs to be a factor in their own reluctance or inability to develop independent careers at levels for which their education has prepared them." Although she was examining the lives of women married to professionals, a similar dynamic can be found in many working-class households. Particularly when men work rotating shifts,[18] women often seek jobs that permit them to accommodate his (and their children's) comings and goings. Part-time work and irregular hours are options for women needing to balance off the demands of "greedy" employers. Telephone operators who reported choosing their jobs because of the flexible hours are a case in point. Starting times could vary from day to day within a six-hour block period; yet the women were reluctant to have their schedules fixed more than two weeks in advance, citing the need to be available to drive children here and there, visit the school, and so forth and flexible enough to be able to coordinate their child care needs with their husbands' and other family members' schedules (Messing 1997).

The ideology of the wife as "secondary" worker has been highly profitable for corporations. The idea that women choose to work to supplement the family income legitimizes their overrepresentation in temporary and low-paying jobs, so much so that we commonly believe that part-time and other forms of "nonstandard" work arrangements exist to accommodate women's needs, whereas, in fact, more men than women have access to so-called family-friendly work arrangements (Fast and Frederick 1996).[19] Jensen (1996) argues that, increasingly, part-time work is the choice of employers, not because women prefer it in any simple sense but because it is more profitable. The rapid growth in part-time and seasonal jobs, particularly in private-sector services where most of the growth in women's employment has been concentrated, has resulted from employer-initiated changes in the organization of work designed to increase productivity and profitability (Smith 1984). Part-time workers are preferred both because their flexibility allows employers to cover daily and seasonal fluctuations in demand and because they almost always earn less per hour than their full-time counterparts. The fact that women are available and willing to take these low-paying jobs may be more indicative of the lack of alternatives for women in the labor market and the shortage of affordable child care than their personal preferences (Smith 1984; Jensen 1996).

RESTRUCTURING PAID WORK AS UNPAID

New forms of unpaid work are being created in employment and in the household as employers in both the private and public sectors downsize and reorganize. On the job, restructuring coupled with managerial systems such as Total Quality Management (TQM) and lean production require workers to be even more available to their employers and to perform more and different forms of work than in the past; indeed, the press for greater "flexibility" of labor typifies restructuring in the 1990s. In the context of static or declining real wages, this means that more and more work on the job is unpaid. And there is a similar expansion of unpaid work off the job. Government downsizing coupled with cutbacks in spending have greatly narrowed the range of services provided by publicly funded institutions. The off-loading of educational and health services to the private sector has greatly expanded the amount and sophistication of unpaid work required of women in the household.

Managerial systems such as TQM and lean production are designed to increase profits "by completely eliminating waste such as excessive stocks or workforce" (Robertson et al. 1992:83). Gone are the stockpiles of parts and the buffer of the labor pool. Work has been redesigned around the "just in time" principle that demands clockwork precision of workers and constant attention to the production process. At CAMI, where work is organized along these principles, time keeping is strictly enforced and workers are expected to fill in for absent or injured team members. They are also expected to offer ideas for tightening the production process by reducing the time or materials required to complete a task (Rinehart et al. 1994).

The stress of additional job duties is particularly acute for team leaders who have been given responsibility for supervisory functions that would normally be part of middle management's job. Under TQM, team leaders may be held responsible for organizing work schedules, ordering supplies, and ensuring that team members complete their assigned duties—a volume of work that often requires them to work beyond their scheduled hours without additional pay. Confusion and ill-feeling among workers over the team leader's role—are they management or labor?—has also added to their burdens.

TQM and lean production in traditional men's work are substantial barriers to the hiring of women. Although corporations no longer bar women on the basis of their sex, most are effectively precluded by the demands of the job. What women need most—flexibility in starting times and the occasional day off to look after sick children, meet with teachers, or take an aging parent to the doctor—are not tolerated by employers or co-workers who must cover for absent team members. With restructuring the incidence of shift-work and overtime, both scheduled and unscheduled, has increased the length and eroded the predictability of the work day (Cohen 1992; Sunter and Morissette 1994). Workers in production jobs are also more likely to be tied to the workplace during their shifts, making it impossible for them to run errands on their breaks, and are generally inaccessible by telephone except in an emergency. Typically these are working conditions that few women can tolerate, given their family responsibilities. For men, they are the price of the coveted "good job" that is harder and harder to find.

Increasingly, these managerial systems are being adopted in the public sector as well. Armstrong et al. (1997) offer many examples of the ways in which teamwork, as practiced under TQM, has increased the volume of work and expanded the number of tasks performed by hospital employees as part of the Ontario government's plan to restructure health care. Under the TQM model, team members are obliged to cover all of the duties of all of the members of the team, even when some are absent from work. Hospital workers also report that they are routinely expected to work outside their formal job descriptions. Multiskilling, a central expectation under TQM, means that employees never have a moment free: as soon as their work is completed they are expected to assist someone else (Armstrong et al. 1997:57). Yet workers are not always fully trained to perform the tasks expected of them. Not infrequently, working outside one's job description entails specialized functions that require particular training in order to maintain standards, as in the case of a carpenter expected to clean up after him- or herself without knowing how to reestablish a sterile environment (Armstrong et al. 1997:58).

Restructuring and downsizing in the public sector have led to new forms of unpaid labor off the job as well. The curtailment of social services provided by all levels of government has led to an unprecedented shift of work from paid to unpaid by relocating responsibility for certain educational and health care functions from government-funded institutions to the home. Examples include cutbacks in the number of affordable child care spaces, the elimination of junior (and in some places) senior kindergarten, sharp reductions in the amount of hospital care deemed medically necessary, and the systematic reduction of services provided by staff in institutions such as hospitals and nursing homes.

The collective effect of these "reforms" has been to increase dramatically the unpaid work expected of women in the home. Armstrong et al. (1997) argue that both the amount of work and the skill level required of home-based caregivers to look after the ill have exploded. They have documented the experiences of family members and friends (the vast majority of whom were women) trying to provide for the needs of people too ill to be left untended or requiring procedures well beyond the competence of the caregivers. The in-home support services that have been promised to fill the gap remain inadequate. To reduce significantly the unpaid labor required of them, family members are forced to purchase medical services that, not long ago, were provided by government-funded institutions.

Person after person also reported that staff shortages required them to feed and bathe patients in hospitals and nursing homes. Some said they found it necessary to change bedding and monitor equipment because staff were so overworked. In one case, family members administered their own version of "physiotherapy" to their elderly mother who was too far down the list to receive professional attention (Armstrong et al. 1997:69–126).

Restructuring is relocating responsibility for a growing number of health care and educational services to the home when most women are no longer there on an hour-to-hour basis. Thus we can expect that, for women, these increasing demands on their limited time and energy are likely to provoke stress and anxiety. Many of the women whose experiences are reported by Armstrong et al. (1997) noted that they would not have been able to do what was necessary had they been employed outside the home. Others reported missing work or experiencing extreme forms of guilt when they could no longer stay away.

The unprecedented expansion of unpaid work on the job and in the home resulting from restructuring greatly increases the likelihood of labor-management conflict. In the workplace, employees are likely to grow resentful of restructuring strategies motivated by management's desire to cut costs in ways that undermine job security and increase workloads without comparable increases in compensation. For women workers, the added pressures on the job are augmented by new responsibilities in the home. To understand fully the implications of these changes for women, we must reach beyond our traditional analysis of work that begins and ends with paid work in the workplace.

CONCLUSION

Women, like men, are employed because they need the money. For this reason, we can expect that women's labor force participation will continue despite the overly busy lives that result. Juggling the demands of employers and families stretches the work day to the physical limit and leaves women with little time for themselves. Not surprisingly, a variety of Canadian and U.S. studies suggest that work-family stress is widespread, ranging from 25 percent among general populations of employees to as high as 68 percent among parents with preschool-age children. Along every dimension, women are more acutely affected than men (Lero and Johnson 1994).

We should not assume, however, that women would abandon the workplace if given the chance. Counterbalancing the wear and tear of conflicting home and work obligations are the satisfactions typically associated with employment. In North American society, a person's sense of self is tied up with his or her job. Women as well as men value the self-confidence and sense of accomplishment that come from paid work. For many, wage earning is a marker of maturity and tangible evidence of contribution to family and community. Unpaid "women's work," by itself, offers few of these rewards. "Good women" who take proper care of themselves and their families may be honored for conforming to the conventional definition of femininity yet find themselves labeled "lazy" or "dependent" because they do not "work."

Study after study indicates that work-family stress should not be viewed as an individual employee's problem or even as a women's issue. Reviewing the literature, Lero and Johnson (1994:23) conclude that "significant change will occur only with the adoption of enlightened approaches to work-family conflict that view the harmonization of paid work and family life as a systemic issue involving wellness and productivity." But we are far from this place. At present, each woman is left to make her accommodation as she will, weighing the particular needs and expectations of her family against the demands of paid work—an equation that often requires her to sacrifice financial independence or personal ambition before it will balance. Alternatively, when women come together to provoke change in employer, union, or government policies, they frequently find their demands marginalized because they are defined as the needs of a "special interest" group.

What women need, first and foremost, are policies that support their choice to work full- or part-time, full-year or part-year, as their needs dictate without suffering unduly harsh financial penalties or blocked opportunities. Without doubt, the cornerstone of such policies is a program of universally available, government-funded maternity and parental leaves designed to protect the right of employees to return to their jobs without loss of pay or seniority. Almost as critical, and far more controversial, is the institutionalization of equal pay for work of equal value across all industries and all jobs. There is every reason to believe that benchmarking jobs traditionally performed by women against "men's jobs" will make visible the skills, effort, and responsibilities entailed in "women's work" and increase wages substantially. Women employed part-time would be affected even more dramatically: equal pay for work of equal value applied to all jobs will ensure that the worth of the job, not the status of the employee, determines the wage. Access to affordable day care completes the circle.

None of this is new. Women's groups have been organizing and lobbying for these changes for years. What may be new, however, is the urgency of the need as economic restructuring increases the demands on women to provide unpaid work both on the job and in the home.

NOTES

1. See Armstrong et al. (1997) and Leach (1996) for analyses of restructuring that integrate unpaid work in the home.

2. In 1994, 70% of employed women in Canada were working in teaching, health care, clerical positions, sales, or service occupations (Canada, Ministry of Industry 1995a: 67). In the United States, these occupations accounted for 65% of employed women in 1995 (U.S. Bureau of the Census 1996:405–7).

3. Pay for these activities is common in the auto, steel, rubber, mining, and oil and gas industries in Canada and the United States.

4. CAMI is a joint venture between General Motors and Suzuki. Of the dozen or so "transplants" in Canada and the United States, only five are unionized (Robertson et al. 1992).

5. Recently I learned that women employees of a trust company are not permitted to wear socks at work, even when they wear pants, but must always wear hose.

6. This definition may be somewhat less salient for African-American men, for whom racism has limited earning opportunities (Hunter and Davis 1992).

7. Among heterosexual couples in Canada, men on average contributed 46% and women 30% of family income in 1994 (Canada, Ministry of Industry 1995a: 47). In the United States, women in couples contributed an average of 29% of family income in 1993 (U.S. Bureau of the Census 1996:471).

8. In Canada, both spouses were employed in 61% of all husband-wife families in 1992 (Canada, Ministry of Industry 1995a:87). The proportion of married couples with two earners was 48% in the United States in 1993 for white and black families and 37% for Hispanic families (U.S. Bureau of the Census 1996:427).

9. Chandler (1993) estimated that Canadian women performed 66% of work in the household, and Marshall (1993) reported that women have primary responsibility for housework more than three-quarters of the time. For every hour contributed by men in two-earner households, women perform almost two (Canada, Ministry of Industry 1995a:83). For the United States, Coltrane (1996:163–64) found that women's household labor time exceeded men's by a wide margin (1.7: 1) and tended to be concentrated in repetitive and time-consuming indoor tasks, whereas men's time was concentrated in less frequently performed outdoor tasks. He also found that marriage had little effect on the amount of housework performed by men; for women, marriage was associated with an additional ten hours per week, so that married women, on average, perform twice as much housework as married men. Household labor time increased for both women and men when children were present, again, in the ratio of 2:1.

10. The extent to which the synergistic effects of paid and unpaid work undermine women's (and men's) overall health was investigated by Hall (1994).

11. See, for example, Bank of Montreal (1991). Running against employees' beliefs was the fact that, despite having children, women had longer service records than men at every level except senior management (and that because middle and senior managers were commonly hired from outside).

12. The National Child Care Survey asked employed parents what working arrangements they would prefer. The majority (53%) of those with primary responsibility for child care said they would prefer to work part-time, and 13% said they would prefer not to work at all while children are small (Fast and Frederick 1996).

13. In Canada, 26% of employed women worked part-time in 1994. Of these, 12.3% chose part-time employment because of personal or family responsibilities; 30.3% because they did not want full-time work; and 30.4% because they could not find full-time jobs (Canada, Ministry of Industry 1995a:73–74). Note, however, that among women in the primary ages for child rearing (25–44) more than one-quarter cited personal and family responsibilities for working part-time (Stone 1994:65). In the United States, 27% of women were employed part-time in 1996. Approximately 22% of women working part-time do so for noneconomic reasons, that is, for reasons other than the unavailability of full-time work. (U.S. Department of Labor 1997:10, 29).

14. Six out of ten women are in the labor force in both Canada (Phillips and Phillips 1993:34) and the United States (U.S. Bureau of the Census 1996:393); moreover, participation rates no longer decline during childbearing years or when children are young (Canada, Ministry of Industry 1995a:72; U.S. Bureau of the Census 1996:400).

15. Shelton and Firestone (1989:111) calculated that 8.2% of the earnings gap between American men and women employed at least twenty hours per week was directly attributable to women's greater participation in household labor; women's fewer hours worked per week and fewer years of experience accounted for 21.3%. Jacobsen and Levin (1995) concluded that women in the United States who withdraw from the labor force for a period of time to rear children suffer an economic penalty. They estimated that a seven-year break from paid work cost women the equivalent of ten years of income over their working lives.

16. Fast and Frederick (1996:17) concluded that, for women, flextime is a stress reliever.

17. The principle of pay equity requires that female and male workers performing jobs of equivalent skill, effort, responsibility, and working conditions be paid equivalent amounts, even if the jobs are dissimilar. Legislation to this effect has been enacted in Ontario, Manitoba, and the federal jurisdiction in Canada and in Minnesota, New York, Oregon, and several cities in the United States (where it is called comparable worth). For the most part, pay equity/comparable worth legislation affects public sector employees; only in Ontario are employees in the private sector affected (Ames 1995).

18. Rotating shifts require workers to move from day to afternoon to night shift, commonly on a one-or two-week rotation and possibly with different days off each rotation.

19. These include paid maternity leave, job sharing, flextime, and flexplace.

REFERENCES

Ames, L. J. (1995). "The Effectiveness of Comparable Worth Policies." *Industrial and Labor Relations Review* 48 (4):709–25.

Armstrong, P., et al. (1997). *Medical Alert: New Work Organizations in Health Care*. Toronto: Garamond Press.

Aronson, J. (1992). "Women's Sense of Responsibility for the Care of Old People: 'But Who Else Is Going to Do It?' " *Gender and Society* 6 (1):8–29.

Bakker, I., ed. (1996). *Rethinking Restructuring: Gender and Change in Canada*. Toronto: University of Toronto Press.

Bank of Montreal. (1991). "The Task Force on the Advancement of Women in the Bank." Unknown: Bank of Montreal.

Caldwell, P. M. (1991). "A Hair Piece: Perspectives on the Intersection of Race and Gender." *Duke Law Journal*, 365–96.

Canada, Ministry of Industry. (1995b). *Earnings of Men and Women, 1994*. Ottawa: Statistics Canada.

———. (1995a). *Women in Canada: A Statistical Report*, 3rd ed., Ottawa: Statistics Canada.

Chandler, W. (1993). "The Value of Household Work in Canada, 1992." *National Income and Expenditure Accounts* 41 (4). Ottawa: Statistics Canada, xxxv–xlviii.

Cohen, G. L. (1992). "Hard at Work." *Perspectives on Labour and Income* 4 (1):8–14.

Coltrane, S. (1996). *Family Man: Fatherhood, Housework, and Gender Equity*. New York: Oxford University Press.

Faludi, S. (1991). *Backlash: The Undeclared War against Women*. New York: Anchor Books.

Fast, J. E., and J. A. Frederick. (1996). "Working Arrangements and Time Stress." *Canadian Social Trends* 43:14–19.

Fishman, P. A. (1978). "Interaction: The Work Women Do." *Social Problems* 25 (4):397–406.

Hall, E. M. (1994). "Double Exposure: The Combined Impact of the Home and Work Environments on Psychosomatic Strain in Swedish Women and Men." In *Women's Health, Politics and Power*, ed. E. Fee and N. Krieger, 117–140. New York: Baywood.

Hood, J. C. (1986). "The Provider Role: Its Meaning and Measurement." *Journal of Marriage and the Family* 48 (May):349–59.

Hunter, A. G., and J. E. Davis. (1992). "Constructing Gender: An Exploration of Afro-American Men's Conceptualization of Manhood." *Gender and Society* 6 (3):464–79.

Jackson, C. (1996). "Measuring and Valuing Households' Unpaid Work." *Canadian Social Trends* 42:25–29.

Jacobsen, J. P., and L. M. Levin. (1995). "Effects of Intermittent Labor Force Attachment on Women's Earnings." *Monthly Labor Review* 118 (9):14–19.

Jensen, J. (1996). "Part-Time Employment and Women: A Range of Strategies." In *Rethinking Restructuring: Gender and Change in Canada*, ed. I. Bakker, 92–108. Toronto: University of Toronto Press.

Karambayya, R., and A. H. Reilly. (1992). "Dual Earner Couples: Attitudes and Actions in Restructuring Work for Family." *Journal of Organizational Behavior* 13:585–601.

Krahn, H. J., and G. S. Lowe. (1988). *Work, Industry and Canadian Society.* Scarborough, Ontario: Nelson Canada.

Leach, B. (1996). "Behind Closed Doors: Homework Policy and Lost Possibilities for Change." In *Rethinking Restructuring: Gender and Change in Canada*, ed. I. Bakker, 203–16. Toronto: University of Toronto Press.

Lero, D. S., and K. L. Johnson. (1994). *Canadian Statistics on Work and Family.* Ottawa: Canadian Advisory Council on the Status of Women.

Livingstone, D. W., and E. Asner. (1996). "Feet in Both Camps: Household Classes, Divisions of Labour, and Group Consciousness." In *Recast Dreams: Class and Gender Consciousness in Steeltown*, ed. D. W. Livingstone and J. M. Mangan, 72–99. Toronto: Garamond Press.

Marshall, K. (1993). "Employed Parents and the Division of Housework." *Perspectives on Labour and Income* 5 (3):23–30.

Messing, K. (1997). "Women's Occupational Health: A Critical Review and Discussion of Current Issues." *Women and Health* 25 (4):39–68.

Papanek, H. (1972). "Men, Women, and Work: Reflections on the Two-Person Career." *American Journal of Sociology* 78 (4):852–72.

Phillips, P., and E. Phillips. (1993). *Women and Work: Inequality in the Canadian Labour Market.* Toronto: James Lorimer.

Potuchek, J. L. (1992). "Employed Wives' Orientation to Breadwinning: A Gender Theory Analysis." *Journal of Marriage and the Family* 54 (Aug.):548–58.

Rinehart, J., C. Huxley, and D. Robertson. (1994). "Worker Commitment and Labour Management Relations under Lean Production at CAMI." *Relations Industrielles* 49 (4):750–773.

Robertson, D., J. Rinehart, C. Huxley, and the CAW Research Group on CAMI. (1992). "Team Concept and Kaizen: Japanese Production Management in a Unionized Canadian Auto Plant." *Studies in Political Economy* 39 (autumn): 77–107.

Seymour, J. (1992). " 'No Time to Call My Own': Women's Time as a Household Resource." *Women's Studies International Forum* 15 (2):187–92.

Shelton, B. A., and J. Firestone. (1989). "Household Labor Time and the Gender Gap in Earnings." *Gender and Society* 3 (1):105–12.

Smith, J. (1984). "The Paradox of Women's Poverty: Wage-Earning Women and Economic Transformation." *Signs* 10 (2):291–310.

Stone, L. (1994). *Dimensions of Job-Family Tension.* Ottawa: Statistics Canada, Family and Community Support Systems Division.

Sunter, D., and R. Morissette. (1994). "The Hours People Work." *Perspective on Labour and Income* 6 (3):8–13.

U.S. Bureau of the Census. (1996). *Statistical Abstract of the United States: 1996.* 116th ed. Washington, D.C.: U.S. Bureau of the Census.

U.S. Department of Labor, Bureau of Labor Statistics. (1997). *Employment and Earnings* 44 (4). Washington, D.C.: U.S. Department of Labor.

Walters, V., et al. (1995). "Paid and Unpaid Work Roles of Male and Female

Nurses." In *Invisible: Issues in Women's Occupational Health*, ed. K. Messing et al., 125–49. Charlottetown, P.E.I.: Gynergy Books.

Weiss, R. S. (1987). "Men and Their Wives' Work." In *Spouse, Parent, Worker: On Gender and Multiple Roles*, ed. F. J. Crosby, 109–21. New Haven, Conn.: Yale University Press.

For Further Reading

Abu-Lughod, L. *Writing Women's Worlds: Bedouin Stories*. Berkeley: University of California Press, 1993.

Behar, R. *Translated Woman: Crossing the Border with Esperanza's Story*. Boston: Beacon Press, 1993.

Beneria, L., and S. Feldman, eds. *Unequal Burden: Economic Crises, Persistent Poverty and Women's Work*. Boulder, Colo.: Westview Press, 1992.

Bertaux, D., and P. Thompson. *Between Generations: Family Models, Myths, and Memories*. New York: Oxford University Press, 1992.

Bhabha, H. "The World and the Home." *Social Text* 31/32, 10.2–3 (1992): 141–53.

Blumberg, R. L., C. A. Rakowski, I. Tinker, and M. Monteon, eds. *EnGENDERing Wealth and Well-Being*. Boulder, Colo.: Westview Press, 1995.

Bradbury, B., ed. *Canadian Family History*. Toronto: Copp Clark Pitman Ltd., 1992.

Brettell, C., and C. Sargent, eds. *Gender in Cross-Cultural Perspective*. Englewood Cliffs, N.J.: Prentice-Hall, 1993.

Carter, C. "Nuclear Family Fall-Out: Postmodern Family Culture and the Media." In *Theorizing Culture*, ed. B. Adam and S. Allan, 186–200. New York: New York University Press, 1995.

Cheal, D. *Family and the State of Theory*. Toronto: University of Toronto Press, 1991.

Chow, R. *Writing Diaspora: Tactics of Intervention in Contemporary Cultural Studies*. Bloomington: Indiana University Press, 1993.

Coontz, S. *The Way We Never Were: American Families and the Nostalgia Trap*. New York: Basic Books, 1992.

Davidoff, L., and C. Hall. *Family Fortunes: Men and Women of the English Middle Class, 1780–1850.* London: Routledge, 1992.

Delaney, C., and S. Yanagisako, eds. *Naturalizing Power.* New York: Routledge, 1995.

Di Leonardo, M., ed. *Gender at the Crossroads of Knowledge: Feminist Anthropology in the Postmodern Era.* Berkeley: University of California Press, 1991.

Escobar, A. *Encountering Development: The Making and Unmaking of the Third World.* Princeton, N.J.: Princeton University Press, 1995.

Fox, B., ed. *Family Patterns, Gender Relations.* Toronto: Oxford University Press, 1993.

Ghorayshi, P., and C. Belanger, eds. *Women, Work and Gender Relations in Developing Countries.* Westport, Conn.: Greenwood Press, 1996.

Ginsburg, F., and R. Rapp, eds. *Conceiving the New World Order: The Global Politics of Reproduction.* Berkeley: University of California Press, 1995.

Glen, E. N., G. Chang, and L. R. Forcey, eds. *Mothering: Ideology, Experience, and Agency.* New York: Routledge, 1994.

Grimes, R. *Marrying and Burying: Rites of Passage in a Man's Life.* Boulder, Colo.: Westview Press, 1995.

Grosz, E. "Women, *Chora*, Dwelling." In *Postmodern Cities and Spaces*, ed. S. Watson and K. Gibson, 47–58. Oxford: Blackwell, 1995.

Hoodfar, H. *Between Marriage and the Market: Intimate Politics and Survival in Cairo.* Berkeley: University of California Press, 1996.

hooks, b. *Outlaw Culture: Resisting Representations.* New York: Routledge, 1994.

Judd, E. *Gender and Power in Rural North China.* Stanford: Stanford University Press, 1995.

Kaplan, E. A. *Motherhood and Representation: The Mother in Popular Culture and Melodrama.* London and New York: Routledge, 1992.

Kendall, L. *Getting Married in Korea: Of Gender, Morality, and Modernity.* Berkeley: University of California Press, 1996.

Kinsman, G. *The Regulation of Desire.* Montreal: Black Rose, 1996.

Knowles, C. *Family Boundaries: The Invention of Normality and Dangerousness.* Peterborough: Broadview Press, 1996.

Lancaster, R. *Life Is Hard: Machismo, Danger, and the Intimacy of Power in Nicaragua.* Berkeley: University of California Press, 1992.

Lewin, E. *Lesbian Mothers: Accounts of Gender in American Culture.* Ithaca, N.Y.: Cornell University Press, 1993.

Martin, E. *Flexible Bodies: Tracking Immunity in American Culture—From the Days of Polio to the Age of AIDS.* Boston: Beacon Press, 1994.

Michel, S., and S. Koven, eds. *Mothers of a New World: Maternalist Politics and the Origins of the Welfare State.* New York: Routledge, 1993.

Probyn, E. *Outside Belongings.* New York: Routledge, 1996.

Ragone, H. *Surrogate Motherhood: Conception in the Heart.* Boulder, Colo.: Westview Press, 1994.

Robertson, A. F. "Time and the Modern Family: Reproduction in the Making of History." In *NowHere: Space, Time and Modernity*, ed. R. Friedland and D. Boden, 95–126. Berkeley: University of California Press, 1994.

Roderick, I. "Household Sanitation and the Flow of Domestic Space." *Space and Culture* 1 (1997): 105–32.

Sarup, M. "Home and Identity." In *Travellers' Tales: Narratives of Home and Displacement*, ed. G. Robertson et. al., 93–104. London: Routledge, 1994.

Scheper-Hughes, N. *Death without Weeping: The Violence of Everyday Life in Brazil.* Berkeley: University of California Press, 1992.

Seccombe, W. *Weathering the Storm: Working-Class Families from the Industrial Revolution to the Fertility Decline.* London: Verso, 1993.

Smart, C., ed. *Regulating Womanhood: Historical Essays on Marriage, Motherhood and Sexuality.* London: Routledge, 1992.

Stacey, J. *Brave New Families: Stories of Domestic Upheaval in Late Twentieth Century America.* New York: Basic Books, 1990.

———. *In the Name of the Family: Rethinking Family Values in the Postmodern Age.* Boston: Beacon Press, 1996.

Stallybrass, P., and A. White. *The Politics and Poetics of Transgression.* Ithaca, N.Y.: Cornell University Press, 1986.

Stewart, K. *A Space on the Side of the Road: Cultural Poetics in an "Other" America.* Princeton, N.J.: Princeton University Press, 1996.

Stichter, S., and Jane Parpart, eds. *Women, Employment and the Family in the International Division of Labour.* London: Macmillan, 1990.

Toulmin, C. *Cattle, Women and Wells: Managing Household Survival in the Sahel.* Oxford: Clarendon Press, 1992.

Townsend, J. G. *Voices from the Rainforest.* London: Routledge, 1995.

Ursel, J. *Private Lives, Public Policy: 100 Years of State Intervention in the Family.* Toronto: Women's Press, 1992.

Weeks, J. *Invented Moralities: Sexual Values in an Age of Uncertainty.* New York: Columbia University Press, 1995.

Index

About the Editors and Contributors

JUDITH M. ABWUNZA is an assistant professor in the Department of Sociology and Anthropology and the coordinator of Women's Studies at Wilfrid Laurier University in Ontario, Canada. She is the author of *Women's Voices, Women's Power: Dialogues of Resistance from East Africa* (Broadview Press, 1997) and "Mulugulu Avakali: City Women in Nairobi," *Journal of Contemporary African Studies* (1996). Her current research concentrates on the conditions and survival strategies of the urban poor, particularly women, in Nairobi, Kenya.

BARRY D. ADAM is a professor in the Department of Sociology and Anthropology at the University of Windsor in Ontario, Canada, and the author of *The Survival of Domination* (Elsevier, 1978), *The Rise of a Gay and Lesbian Movement* (Twayne, 1995), and *Experiencing HIV* (with Alan Sears, Columbia University Press, 1996). He has written extensively on AIDS and sexuality issues and is currently researching safer decision making among gay men. Website: http://www.cs.uwindsor.ca/users/a/adam/

SALLY COLE is an associate professor in the Department of Sociology and Anthropology at Concordia University in Montreal, Canada. She is the author of *Women of the Praia: Work and Lives in a Portuguese Coastal Community* (Princeton University Press, 1991) and editor of *Ethnographic Feminisms: Essays in Anthropology* (with Lynne Phillips, Carleton University Press, 1995). She has also introduced the reedition of Ruth Landes'

The City of Women (University of New Mexico Press, 1995). Her current research deals with issues of gender and development in Brazil.

ANTHONY DAVIS is a professor in the Department of Sociology and Anthropology at St. Francis Xavier University in Nova Scotia, Canada, and professor II in the Department of Local Planning and Community Studies at the University of Tromso in Norway. He is the author of *Dire Straits, the Dilemmas of a Fishery: The Case of Digby Neck and the Islands* (ISER Books, 1991) and a recent editor of a special issue of *Society & Natural Resources*. His articles appear in *Canadian Review of Sociology and Anthropology, Human Organization, Maritime Anthropological Studies, Journal of Canadian Studies, Marine Policy*, and *Canadian Public Policy*. He engages in fisheries-centered social research with a view to generate comparative studies on local culture, social history, and facets of human agency.

ANNE FORREST is the chair of the Women's Studies program and an associate professor in the Faculty of Business Administration at the University of Windsor where she teaches labor-management relations. She has published feminist critiques of industrial relations theory and collective bargaining legislation in *Relations Industrielles*. At present, she is researching the problems of women employed in nontraditional jobs.

PARVIN GHORAYSHI is a professor in the Department of Sociology at the University of Winnipeg in Manitoba, Canada. Her research interests include feminist theories and gender relations in developing countries, with a focus on the Middle East. She is the author of *Women and Work in Developing Countries* (Greenwood Press, 1994) and co-editor of *Women, Work, and Gender Relations in Developing Countries: A Global Perspective* (Greenwood Press, 1996). Her most recent articles appear in *Canadian Journal of Development Studies* and *Women and Politics*. She is presently engaged in a research project on rural women in Iran.

ALAN HALL is an assistant professor in the Department of Sociology and Anthropology at the University of Windsor. He has recently authored articles on mining (*Critical Sociology* and *Canadian Journal of Sociology*) and agriculture (*Canadian Review of Sociology* and *Anthropology* and *Rurales*). His current research interests include environmental issues in agriculture, occupational health, and corporate crime.

MAX HEDLEY is an associate professor in the Department of Sociology and Anthropology at the University of Windsor. He is the author of numerous articles on farming communities in Canada and New Zealand and continues to research aboriginal issues through his ties to the research unit at the Walpole Island Reserve in Ontario. He is currently working on a comparative study of fishing, farming, and trapping in Canada.

SUZAN ILCAN is an associate professor in the Department of Sociology and Anthropology at the University of Windsor. She has recently edited *Postmodernism and the Ethical Subject* with Barbara Gabriel (Carleton University Press, in press) and authored essays on gender, household, and cultural politics in *Space and Culture, Ethnology, International Migration Review*, and *Culture*. She is currently doing research for a book on gender, space, and the politics of movement.

DANIEL MACINNES is a professor in the Department of Sociology and Anthropology at St. Francis Xavier University in Nova Scotia, Canada. He is co-editor of *Social Research and Public Policy Formation in the Fisheries: Norwegian and Canadian Experiences* (Dalhousie University, 1991). His most recent articles appear in *International Journal of the Sociology of Language* and *Maritime Anthropological Studies*. His current interests include maritime social history, public policy and fisheries management, and Gaelic culture and language.

KATHY M'CLOSKEY is a research associate at Southwest Center, University of Arizona. She received her Ph.D. from York University in 1996. Her dissertation, "Myths, Markets and Metaphors: Navajo Weaving as Commodity and Communicative Form," is currently under revision and is slated for publication by the University of New Mexico Press. She recently curated "First Nations/Fine Weavers" for the Burlington Art Center in collaboration with the Arizona Commission of the Arts.

B. LYNNE MILGRAM is a postdoctoral fellow at the University of Toronto and an adjunct curator for Asian Textiles at the Museum for Textiles in Toronto. Her dissertation (York University, 1997) examines the commercialization of household crafts in the upland Philippines and its effects on women and their work. She has published articles on women and crafts in Southeast Asia, most recently "Women and the Diversification of Crafts in the Upland Philippines," in *Southeast Asia and Globalization: New Domains of Analysis* (Université Laval, 1997). Her current research on women's craft cooperatives in the northern Philippines addresses issues of gender and development and tourist art production.

LYNNE PHILLIPS is an associate professor in the Department of Sociology and Anthropology at the University of Windsor. She has edited *Ethnographic Feminisms: Essays in Anthropology* (with Sally Cole, Carleton University Press, 1995) and *The Third Wave of Modernization in Latin*

America: Cultural Perspectives on Neoliberalism (Scholarly Resources Press, 1998). Her current interests include gender and health issues and the impact of free trade on rural families in Latin America.

ALAN SEARS is an associate professor in the Department of Sociology and Anthropology at the University of Windsor. He writes about the changing welfare state and AIDS/HIV. His research on the welfare state examines the historical development of public health and immigration controls as forms of moral regulation (published in *Studies in Political Economy, Critical Sociology*, and the *Journal of Historical Sociology*). He has worked with Barry Adam on two ethnographic AIDS research projects, leading to the co-authored book *Experiencing HIV* (Columbia University Press, 1996). He is currently working on a book examining contemporary welfare cuts in relation to regimes of lean production.

PATRICIA TOMIC is an associate professor in the Department of Anthropology and Sociology at the Okanagan University College in British Columbia, Canada. She received her Licencia from the Universidad de Chile and her Ph.D. from OISE/University of Toronto. As a Chilean-Canadian she works on both Canadian and Chilean issues in the areas of gender, language, and racism.

RICARDO TRUMPER is an associate professor in the Department of Anthropology and Sociology at the Okanagan University College in British Columbia, Canada. He received his Ph.D. in social and political thought from York University, Canada. He has recently published articles on issues dealing with Latin America and neoliberalism in *Race and Class* and *Alternatives*. His current research focuses on neoliberalism, health, and the city.

ISBN 0-89789-518-5

90000>

EAN

9 780897 895187

HARDCOVER BAR CODE